RAND NATIONAL DEFENSE RESEARCH INSTITUTE

T0289472

Realigning the Stars

A Methodology for Reviewing Active Component General and Flag Officer Requirements

RAND National Defense Research Institute

Prepared for the Office of the Secretary of Defense
Approved for public release; distribution unlimited

For more information on this publication, visit www.rand.org/t/RR2384

Library of Congress Cataloging-in-Publication Data is available for this publication.
ISBN: 978-1-9774-0070-3

Published by the RAND Corporation, Santa Monica, Calif.

© Copyright 2018 RAND Corporation

RAND® is a registered trademark.

Support RAND
Make a tax-deductible charitable contribution at
www.rand.org/giving/contribute

www.rand.org

Realigning the Stars Study Team

Principal Investigator
Lisa M. Harrington

Structure and Organization Analysis
Igor Mikolic-Torreira, team lead
Kimberly Jackson
Lisa Davis
Matthew Sargent

Position-by-Position Analysis
Paul Mayberry, team lead
Sean Mann
Joslyn Fleming

Position Pyramid Health Analysis
Katharina Ley Best, team lead
Peter Schirmer
Alexander D. Rothenberg
Ricardo Sanchez
Christina Panis
Russell Hanson

Forced-Choice Exercise
David R. Frelinger, team lead
Igor Mikolic-Torreira
Bart E. Bennett
Jenny Oberholtzer
Sebastian Joon Bae

Command Chain Application
Bart E. Bennett, team lead
Mitch Tuller
Ben Goirigolzarri
Hilary A. Smith

Legal and Historical Research
Geoffrey McGovern
Connor P. Jackson
Steven Deane-Shinbrot

Project Communications
Barbara A. Bicksler

Foreword

The size, reach, and complexity of the U.S. Department of Defense (DoD) demands an executive corps with the skill, expertise, and temperament appropriate to the challenges that a world power faces.[1] With personnel in more than 180 countries to carry out its responsibilities, the department commands a budget that rivals the gross domestic product of Sweden—and with its service contractors, it employs an equivalent labor force. Its leaders are responsible for military capabilities that include Special Operations, classic conventional units (Army maneuver battalions, air superiority squadrons, etc.), and nuclear missiles, and for business functions that range from basic research to a worldwide school system for the children of servicemembers. In the last generation, DoD's missions have included disaster relief, the insertion of military units halfway around the world on a week's notice, and the takedown of nation-states.

In order to lead a department that is this large and this complex (on a command and control basis, no less) and that is one of society's most respected institutions, how large an executive corps is needed? DoD is an institution on which Americans depend to protect their society from attack and to help advance their interests internationally. It's an institution to which they turn for support in domestic emergencies and one whose virtues are widely celebrated as worthy of broader emulation. What career experience should prepare members of such a corps for their leadership responsibilities?

Today, that executive corps—the general and flag officers and the Senior Executive Service—numbers just over one individual per thousand federal personnel (interestingly, one of the lowest ratios among Cabinet agencies). The majority of its members and all the uniformed leaders come from within the department's ranks. That's understandable, given the developmental paths that the department favors, which are intended to build expertise in the diversity of DoD operations. Most executives bring two decades or more of experience to their senior responsibilities. A closed personnel system, of course, requires sufficient billets to develop the experience needed within its own confines. Other possibilities could be considered, and the U.S. Congress

---

[1] These ideas are elaborated at greater length in David S. C. Chu, *Reflections on Executive Leadership for the Department of Defense*, IDA document P-8943, May 2018.

v

has started to encourage lateral entry, at least for middle management in technical disciplines.

Each Secretary of Defense will have distinct perspectives on selecting and shaping the executive corps. One key issue is the corps' size, although the Secretary's latitude may be limited by statutory and regulatory constraints on this matter. Those constraints reflect the reality that the size of an executive corps is an especially contentious subject in DoD, as one of several issues involving "tooth to tail" balance. Most recently, Congress has challenged the size and shape of the general and flag officer force, mandating reductions for most of the services and in the joint pool, and considering additional cuts in the future.

Ultimately, what's optimal is a matter of judgment. But judgment is presumably improved if it is informed by tools that allow one to weigh the pros and cons of available options. The tools developed and implemented in this volume could be used not only to help the department respond to the immediate query to review current requirements for general and flag officers, but also to inform decisions about the flexibility any Secretary needs to sustain the success of the defense enterprise—an enterprise on which the American public so frequently relies and in which it reposes such great trust.

David S. C. Chu
President, Institute for Defense Analyses and former
Under Secretary of Defense for Personnel & Readiness

Preface

Statutory requirements exist to ensure that military departments have the appropriate authorized number of general and flag officers (G/FOs) on active duty. But how many G/FOs are required to meet military leadership requirements in the Department of Defense (DoD) has long been a point of debate. In the National Defense Authorization Act (NDAA) for fiscal year 2017, Congress took initial steps to reduce the number of G/FOs. In addition, Congress mandated that the department conduct "a comprehensive and deliberate global manpower study of requirements for general and flag officers." The Office of the Under Secretary of Defense for Personnel and Readiness (USD [P&R]) and the Joint Staff, Manpower and Personnel Directorate (J1) asked the RAND National Defense Research Institute to assist in responding to this mandate and conduct an independent study of G/FO requirements. The study's principal objective was to develop a methodology to assess active component G/FO requirements and authorizations. This report contains the results of RAND's analysis, with particular emphasis on details of the methodology developed to assess G/FO requirements.

In conducting this study, RAND worked closely with the DoD General/Flag Officer Working Group, established in December 2016 by the USD (P&R), to address the provisions in the fiscal year 2017 NDAA pertaining to general and flag officers.[2] The working group was chaired by the Deputy Assistant Secretary of Defense for Military Personnel Policy and the director for Manpower and Personnel, J1, Joint Staff.[3] The working group was charged with facilitating the active component G/FO requirements analysis as well as preparing and executing implementation of the NDAA provisions. This includes identifying required general and flag officer reductions and developing the department's implementation plan to be submitted to Congress in conjunction with the fiscal year 2019 budget. The working group was comprised of representatives from:[4]

---

[2] Under Secretary of Defense for Personnel and Readiness, General/Flag Officer Requirements Study, memorandum, December 6, 2016.

[3] Under Secretary of Defense for Personnel and Readiness, Expanded General/Flag Officer Working Group, memorandum, January 6, 2016.

[4] Office of the Secretary of Defense General and Flag Officer Management, Terms of Reference, November 21, 2016.

- Office of the Secretary of Defense General and Flag Officer Management
- Cost Assessment and Program Evaluation
- Washington Headquarters Services
- Joint Staff
- Military departments
- Service Manpower and Reserve Affairs offices
- Service/Joint Staff General and Flag Officer Management offices.

The working group's terms of reference called for RAND to provide analytical support to the working group and, specifically, to provide a global review of G/FO requirements. The General and Flag Officer Management office, within the Office of the Secretary of Defense, provided the conduit to the other members of the working group and facilitated RAND's access to G/FO management information and data required for the analysis.

This research was sponsored by the Deputy Assistant Secretary of Defense for Military Personnel Policy and the Joint Staff, Director for Manpower and Personnel, J1, and conducted within the Forces and Resources Policy Center of the RAND National Defense Research Institute, a federally funded research and development center sponsored by the Office of the Secretary of Defense, the Joint Staff, the Unified Combatant Commands, the Navy, the Marine Corps, the defense agencies, and the defense Intelligence Community.

For more information on the RAND Forces and Resources Policy Center, see www.rand.org/nsrd/ndri/centers/frp or contact the director (contact information is provided on the webpage).

Contents

Figures

Tables

Summary

In line with its oversight role, Congress regularly conducts periodic reviews of the laws that govern the management and provision of general and flag officers (G/FOs). Generally, legislators utilize the annual National Defense Authorization Act (NDAA) as the vehicle to exercise their authority over Department of Defense (DoD) personnel matters. Indeed, the FY 2017 NDAA reduces G/FO authorizations by 110, with implementation to be completed by December 2022. The NDAA further directs the Secretary of Defense to undertake a study with goals of evaluating the justification for each G/FO requirement, identifying a further 10 percent reduction in G/FO authorizations, and planning for these cuts.

To support DoD's analysis in response to this mandate, the Office of the Under Secretary of Defense for Personnel and Readiness (OUSD [P&R]) and the Joint Staff, Manpower and Personnel Directorate (J1) asked the RAND National Defense Research Institute to conduct an independent study of G/FO requirements. The goals of this effort were three-fold:

- Develop a methodology to assess active component G/FO requirements and authorizations.
- Use the methodology to identify opportunities to eliminate, downgrade, or convert (to civilian) G/FO positions.
- Assess the adequacy of existing statutes and policies to provide G/FOs to meet requirements and recommend changes, if needed.

Study Approach

The study's principal objective was to develop a methodology to assess active component G/FO requirements and authorizations. RAND's analytical approach was influenced by various sources of information. We consulted literature on organizational theory and personnel management, previous studies of G/FO requirements and management and critiques of those studies, subject matter experts, and relevant statutes

Figure S.1
Overarching Methodology

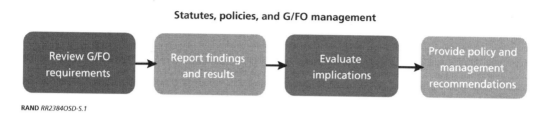

Statutes, policies, and G/FO management

Review G/FO requirements → Report findings and results → Evaluate implications → Provide policy and management recommendations

RAND *RR2384OSD-S.1*

and policies. These various sources together informed the criteria and guidelines used in our analysis.

RAND developed an analytic methodology that is rigorous, adjustable, transparent, and repeatable. The overarching methodology contains four broad elements, as illustrated in Figure S.1. First, we conducted an in-depth review of G/FO requirements using four complementary and interrelated approaches. We then developed a rule set to integrate findings across the four analytic approaches to arrive at a set of consolidated results. Using these results as an example of potential changes in G/FO requirements, our team used several RAND-developed tools to evaluate implications. Based on the totality of our work, we identified policy and management recommendations that would facilitate the success of future reviews.

As the basis for our assessment, we used requirements data collected from the military services and the joint community by the Office of the Secretary of Defense (OSD) General and Flag Officer Management, as of March 2017. The data received from OSD contained 1,113 G/FO requirements. In addition, the analysis was conducted within the context of existing statutes, departmental policies, and services practices governing G/FO management, but these constraints did not limit the rigor with which we evaluated each current requirement.

Review of G/FO Requirements

The four approaches used to evaluate G/FO requirements, the central element of our work and of this report, are: (1) structure and organization, (2) position-by-position, (3) forced-choice exercise, and (4) position pyramid health.

Structure and Organization Analysis

We conducted a systematic assessment of the functions performed by G/FOs within and across organizations. To analyze G/FO requirements from an organizational perspective, we combined insights from organizational literature with additional foundational principles specific to military organizational structure to arrive at organization-level and position-level guidelines.

The organization-level guidelines are:

- Keep G/FOs in the upper levels of the organization.
- Decrease the use of G/FO deputies and, particularly, assistants to deputies, deputies to assistants, assistants to assistants, etc.
- Reduce circumstances where one G/FO reports to another G/FO of the same grade.
- Avoid "breaks" in G/FO hierarchy (e.g., O-7 reporting to an O-9).
- Avoid duplicative responsibilities in the same immediate organization.
- Increase the span of control of G/FOs.
- G/FOs should have direct reports.
- Maintain parity across equivalent types of internal organizations.
- The use of G/FOs must support the direct mission of the organization.

These are the position-level guidelines:

- Military essentiality of the position (i.e., could this position be filled by a senior civilian?)
- Span of control or responsibilities inconsistent with peers (e.g., much smaller span than equivalent positions without mitigating additional duties)
- Rank and number of immediate subordinates
- Rank of immediate superiors
- Parity with other like organizations, such as across services or combatant commands
- Precedents in filling the position with more junior and/or civilian persons.

We used these guidelines to examine a position both within the context of its own organization and across similar organizations (e.g., other combatant commands or other intelligence organizations). This assessment focused on organizations most affected by language in the FY 2017 NDAA (such as joint organizations), those containing significant numbers of G/FOs, specialty non-line communities, and other organizations of particular interest to the DoD G/FO Working Group or Congress. We reviewed 16 groups of positions including the Joint Staff, combatant commands, defense agencies and DoD field activities, special staffs, and service major headquarters and commands. In total, these groups covered about 95 percent of the 1,113 positions in the data set.

Position-by-Position Analysis

In the position-by-position analysis, we evaluated all 1,113 G/FO requirements against a defined set of criteria. The criteria were derived based on job content and context and service and Joint Staff perspectives, and was heavily informed by methodologies used in prior G/FO studies—most directly from a recent RAND study of reserve component G/FO requirements. The following 11 factors were used to evaluate each position:

Mandatory requirement:
1.   Does the position fulfill a mandatory requirement as defined in statute?
Military essentiality:
2.   Does the position exercise command of a military unit?
3.   Does the position reside in an organization with an operational military focus?
4.   Does the position lead a significant military formation?
Magnitude of responsibilities:
5.   Does the position manage a significant amount of personnel?
6.   Does the position manage a significant amount of money?
Senior-level interaction:
7.   Does the position frequently interact with senior government officials?
8.   Does the position frequently interact with senior political officials, state and local authorities, foreign government and foreign military leaders, nongovernmental organization senior leadership, and the press at the national level?
Subordinates:
9.   Does the position have a general/flag officer subordinate?
Span of decisionmaking:
10.   Does the position require independent span of decisionmaking?
Area of responsibility:
11.   Does this position oversee an extensive physical or virtual operating area?

Based on the recommendation of the DoD G/FO Working Group, RAND added two more factors:

1.   Is the position a deputy of an organization?
2.   Is the position currently not filled by a general/flag officer?

Prior studies that reviewed G/FO positions all were based on a similar underlying principle: if a position has enough factors associated with a general or flag officer, then the requirement is justified. In our more conservative methodology, we identified positions that do not meet any of the key factors associated with a general or flag officer.

Forced-Choice Exercise

RAND hosted an exercise to explore DoD's G/FO requirements and the implications of potential reductions in G/FO authorizations. The overall aim of the exercise was to identify priorities for how four- and three-star G/FOs should be used by forcing participants to choose which G/FO requirements to fill when faced with constraints. The game served as a way to understand the preferences and cultural norms of those familiar with current DoD organization and G/FO management practices—

understanding that these norms have evolved over time and are different today than in previous eras.

Five four-person teams participated in the exercise. The teams were composed of senior-level participants—both military and civilian—from the services, OSD, the Joint Staff, and other subject matter experts. These representatives included both active-duty and retired G/FOs up to the three-star level. The teams were structured so that ranks of participants were roughly equal within a team to preclude a single higher-ranking player dictating team play. RAND experts in gaming methodology structured the game around two moves.

- *Move One: Four-Star G/FOs.* Teams responded to a theoretical NDAA mandate to reduce the total number of active-duty officers in the grade of general or admiral from 38 to 20. The teams decided which four-star requirements to fill and what to do with unfilled positions (e.g., downgrade to a lower grade, convert to a civilian position, dual-hat positions, consolidate organizations under a single position, or eliminate the position).
- *Move Two: Three-Star General and Flag Officers.* Teams responded to a theoretical NDAA mandate to reduce the number of active-duty officers in the grade of lieutenant general or vice admiral by 33 percent, from 167 to 110. The NDAA also directed the Secretary of Defense to assess the consequences of limiting service component commanders to O-9 and recommend whether this is advisable. Because of the number of positions at the three-star grade, three-star positions were grouped; added to these groups were the positions downgraded to three-star during Move One.

De facto guidelines and factors for making these decisions emerged from team discussions and included: strategic importance of a position, service parity, the principle that command relationships should drive G/FO rank decisions, and the role of the position in military operations.

Position Pyramid Health

This analytic approach focused on position pyramid health. Position pyramids have a strong effect on career paths in the military and on developing G/FOs for future leadership positions. Examining these pyramids provides insights into how well the system meets the needs of the organization in these areas.

We categorized the 1,113 positions into 12 functional pyramids, which we evaluated using a set of metrics designed to quantify the degree to which a potential reduction in requirements alters the shape of the G/FO pyramid. The metrics used to assess the overall size and shape of a G/FO pyramid are:

- Pyramid size quantifies the overall size (in number of positions) of the pyramid at each grade and is measured in number of promotions. This metric helps identify especially small or large communities or grades within communities.

- Vertical movement is measured in terms of selectivity, which captures the relationship between personnel counts across grades to assess bench strength and promotion opportunity.
- Lateral movement is measured using a joint to in-service ratio at each grade and rank, providing insight into the number of joint opportunities available, the reliance on joint paths for development, and the possible challenges of managing joint versus in-service inventories.

Because Congress directed a global manpower study of requirements and the DoD G/FO Working Group required a method for reviewing each G/FO requirement, we were challenged to identify a way to not only associate the metrics with individual jobs but to collapse the three into one, which we accomplished by combining the geometric mean of the three metrics described previously. We selected a 5 percent decline as the cut-off point at which pyramid health would worsen if a position in that pyramid were eliminated.

Evaluating the Findings

Each of the four approaches yielded findings important for validating requirements and implementing a reduction in the number of G/FOs. From the structure and organization review of requirements, we observed considerable variation in how similar positions in different organizations were filled, along with internal inconsistencies within single organizations. From the position-by-position analysis we observed that a number of G/FO positions did not meet any of the key criteria for a G/FO requirement. From the forced-choice analysis, we observed that senior decisionmakers could reach agreement on certain positions eligible for elimination or downgrading. Finally, from the position pyramid analysis we observed that for approximately two-thirds of the positions, eliminating that position would not degrade pyramid health. The question, then, is how do we integrate the findings from each approach into an overall determination for whether a position does or does not meet the criteria for a G/FO requirement?

We developed a systematic way of integrating the findings of the structure and organization, position-by-position, and forced-choice exercise analysis—a rule set that takes into account the possible findings and the contexts and strengths of each of the approaches. A position is assigned an integrated result according to the following:

- Agreement between two or more findings
- One conclusive finding not contradicted by another finding, as long as the position is reviewed by at least two approaches
- One conclusive finding that a position meets the criteria for a G/FO requirement, even if it is only reviewed by one approach

- A structure and organization approach finding of "subject to policy decision"
- A result of "conflicting findings" for positions in which findings from more than one approach disagree or that are reviewed by only one approach and found to not meet the criteria for a G/FO requirement.

With these results in hand, we looked at the findings of the position pyramid analysis for those positions that might require action (downgrade to O-6, convert, or eliminate)—thereby highlighting for further consideration positions that might worsen pyramid health should these actions be taken.

Using this rule set, 615 positions meet the criteria for a G/FO requirement and 132 do not meet the criteria for a G/FO requirement in our consolidated results (of the 1,113 requirements reviewed). We have inconclusive results for the remaining 366 positions, either because of conflicting findings or because a set of positions was deemed subject to policy decision. Of the 132 positions that did not meet the criteria for a G/FO requirement, 35 positions were in position pyramids where the elimination of the position on its own would worsen the health of the overall position pyramid.

The department should consider further investigation of the 132 positions that did not meet the combined criteria for a G/FO requirement, asking more seriously why these positions need to be filled by a G/FO, whether alternatives might be used to fill the requirements (such as a senior civilian or lower grade military officer), or whether the requirement might be eliminated. There may be sound justification for why some of these positions should be filled by a G/FO, but that rationale was not evident in the requirements data or research conducted by our team. The 366 positions for which we ended up with inconclusive results are another area for departmental investigation.

The management of G/FO requirements across an enterprise the size and diversity of the Department of Defense is a complex and dynamic undertaking. Since our study began, there have assuredly been changes in military strategy, service priorities, organizational structures, and G/FO job characteristics. However, the combined results highlight a group of positions that are not well defended as G/FO requirements. The analysis that led to these results also illustrates how to apply the RAND-developed methodology that we believe DoD should employ.

Once the department identifies a group of positions for elimination, it is prudent to evaluate the implications of the proposed decision. For example, how would eliminating a group of positions affect career paths and experiences of officers, especially joint experiences that officers may need for career development? There is also value in evaluating communities of G/FOs and the implications of reductions that are targeted to particular groups of officers. In addition, the need will arise to evaluate emerging requirements for G/FOs that result from organizational change or other motivations. RAND has developed several tools that can be used to support such analyses.

Recommendations

The findings and results in this report can assist DoD in making choices among G/FO requirements in response to congressional directives. However, the primary purpose of this study was to develop a rigorous and systematic approach for making such choices. In that vein, our recommendations center on steps the department should take to ensure G/FO requirements meet current needs and are well justified in the future. The recommendations are divided into two groups, policy and management.

Policy Recommendations

- *Establish a philosophy for using all available workforce talent to fill DoD leadership requirements—active and reserve component general and flag officers, senior civilians, and officers at the grade of O-6 or below (Under Secretary of Defense for Personnel and Readiness [USD (P&R)] and service secretaries).* The services and joint organizations have responded to ever-pressing constraints on the total number of G/FOs by "trimming around the edges." DoD needs to take a holistic approach that draws on talent from all parts of the workforce when filling leadership positions.
- *Issue overarching policy guidance related to G/FO leadership roles and requirements (Secretary of Defense).* DoD lacks formal policy guidance regarding what constitutes a G/FO requirement and how these requirements should be prioritized in the face of limited G/FO resources. Guidance such as this would help defuse outside criticism, establish a basis for future reviews, and serve as guidance for developing effective, well-justified G/FO requirements.
- *Establish a standing central body for vetting G/FO requirements in accordance with Secretary of Defense strategic guidelines and with up-to-date and on-the-shelf data (USD [P&R], lead).* A standing body with knowledgeable representatives from the services and joint community is key to an effective review process. It will encourage discussion and engagement among the members, help reduce service-centric perspectives, and ensure the department speaks with one voice about the priorities for uniformed senior executives.

Management Recommendations

- *Conduct targeted reviews of G/FO positions to determine the need for G/FO requirements and provide guidance to clarify apparent inconsistencies in the use of G/FOs within each group today (OUSD [P&R], Joint Staff, and service secretaries).* We recommend the following targeted reviews: G/FO positions within OSD, G/FOs assigned as defense attachés, contingency G/FO positions, G/FOs in joint task forces, G/FOs in combatant commands, G/FOs in numbered air forces, and G/FOs in "deputy," "vice," and "assistant" positions.

- *To facilitate management and review of G/FO requirements, maintain updated, well-defined position descriptions; assign standardized job titles and position identifiers; and compile and maintain a repository of organization charts with standardized nomenclature for defining organizational relationships (the military services and Joint Staff).* Maintaining standardized and updated organizational and position information will enable better management and justification of positions held by general and flag officers.

- *Adopt a systematic approach to identifying leadership needs for organizational changes (creating or dissolving) in response to emerging requirements so they are well understood before changes are adopted (USD [P&R] and Joint Staff, co-lead).* Deliberations within the department on which positions require G/FO leadership should be systematic and transparent. The tools developed in RAND's review of G/FO requirements can be used to evaluate leadership requirements when organizational change is called for.

- *Evaluate whether to seek lower joint pool floors and the elimination of joint pool ceilings to ensure the right balance between service control in joint positions and flexibility in managing G/FOs—in particular, the balance between flexibility in developing G/FOs and ensuring qualified G/FOs are available to serve in joint positions (OUSD [P&R]).* The new joint pool specifications for each service established in the FY 2017 NDAA limit flexibility in managing the joint pool and may constrain service options for assigning and developing G/FOs to fill joint positions. A revision to the recent change in statute may be needed.

DoD needs a more analytic foundation with which to justify its G/FO requirements. RAND has offered such a method that the department could adopt. By undertaking periodic, systematic reviews of G/FO requirements, the department is less likely to be issued congressional cuts beyond those mandated for 2022 that are potentially detrimental. Our results suggest that, at this time and with the requirements information provided, there are positions that should not be filled by G/FOs and that it is possible to achieve the 110 reduction mandated by Congress while retaining sufficient senior uniformed leadership. However, in the future, with a smaller G/FO population and the potential of emerging requirements, it will be much more difficult to identify reductions in the G/FO corps. Continuing to respond to pressures to reduce the number of G/FOs serving in leadership positions in the department by "counting stars" rather than systematically evaluating and establishing requirements that are well justified will be unsustainable.

Acknowledgments

This study benefitted from the contributions of many individuals in the Department of Defense and within the RAND Corporation. We appreciate the guidance and direction provided by our sponsors, Lernes J. Hebert, Principal Director for Military Personnel Policy in the Office of the Under Secretary of Defense for Personnel and Readiness; and Brigadier General Kyle J. Kremer, Director for Manpower and Personnel, the Joint Staff (J1). William Atkinson, Director, Senior Officer Policy and Special Assistant for Senior Officer Matters; Lieutenant Colonel Carolyn Ammons, OSD General and Flag Officer Management; and Lieutenant Colonel Thomas Manion, Joint Staff General and Flag Officer Matters assisted us in ways too numerous to list, but particularly as conduits to the DoD G/FO Working Group, which greatly facilitated our work.

The participants of the DoD G/FO Working Group, especially the staffs of the service and Joint Staff general and flag officer management offices, were generous with their time at many points during the study, from providing background information on general and flag officer management to answering many questions regarding requirements data to reviewing findings and results. Their assistance was invaluable. Of note, we appreciate the continued involvement from the leadership of the G/FO management offices: Colonel Lisa Griffin, Colonel T. J. Edwards, Brett Genoble, Brigadier General David Kumashiro, and Lieutenant Colonel Robyn Mestemacher. We also thank the staff of the Department of Defense Deputy Chief Management Officer for the data and resources they provided.

We thank RAND colleagues Sandra Evans for her research support, Leah Hershey and Barbara Hennessey for their administrative assistance, and Yvonne Crane for her creative efforts in designing the game materials in support of the forced-choice exercise. Harry Thie, our internal reviewer, offered wise advice and counsel throughout the study drawing from his vast experience in military manpower and personnel policy. John Winkler, Director of the Forces and Resources Policy Center, also provided advice during the course of our work.

We are grateful for the many hours spent with our senior advisory group—David S. C. Chu, President IDA; Christine Fox, former Acting Deputy Secretary of Defense; General (Retired) William M. Fraser III, USAF; and G. Kim Wincup, former service assistant Secretary and Chairman of the Reserve Forces Policy Board. Since the early days of the project, this group provided strategic guidance that helped chart our course and asked difficult questions that challenged our assumptions and refined our findings and results.

We also thank the reviewers of this report, David S. C. Chu, Andrew Hoehn, and Harry Thie. Each provided a thoughtful review that resulted in numerous improvements to the manuscript.

CHAPTER ONE

Introduction

Since Congress began directing the number of general and flag officers (G/FOs) authorized to the Department of Defense (DoD) in 1947, the size and composition of the general and flag officer corps has been the subject of substantial congressional interest. As end strength, force structure, and operational requirements have fluctuated, so too have efforts to balance G/FO requirements with force size, growing personnel costs, and overall budget constraints. These efforts have resulted in many hearings and studies on G/FO requirements in DoD over the past several decades and have highlighted concerns in Congress about the number of G/FO authorizations and the proportion of G/FOs relative to the total force.

Congress often argues that higher numbers of G/FOs reduce efficiency, increase personnel costs, and add to bureaucratic lags in decisionmaking, while the department is concerned that current authorizations do not satisfy demands that result from its wide-ranging responsibilities. DoD has provided several justifications to Congress for its increased ratio of G/FOs relative to the total force, which include increased joint requirements, escalating coalition operations, the force's current organizational structure, and changes in technology.[1]

In line with its oversight role, Congress regularly conducts periodic reviews of the laws that govern the management and provision of G/FOs. Generally, legislators utilize the annual National Defense Authorization Act (NDAA) as the vehicle to exert their authority over DoD personnel matters. Indeed, the FY 2017 NDAA directs a reduction in G/FO authorized strength of 110 by December 2022. The NDAA further directs the Secretary of Defense to undertake a study with goals of evaluating the justification for each G/FO requirement, identifying a further 10 percent reduction in G/FO authorizations, and planning for these cuts. Specifically, the FY 2017 NDAA mandates:

> the Secretary of Defense shall conduct a comprehensive and deliberate global manpower study of requirements for general and flag officers with the goal of identifying—

---

[1] Lawrence Kapp, *General and Flag Officers in the U.S. Armed Forces: Background and Considerations for Congress*, Washington, D.C.: Congressional Research Service, February 18, 2016, pp. 7–9.

(A) the requirement justification for each general or flag officer position in terms of overall force structure, scope of responsibility, command and control requirements, and force readiness and execution;

(B) an additional 10 percent reduction in the aggregate number of authorized general officer and flag officer positions after the reductions required by subsection (a); and

(C) an appropriate redistribution of all general officer and flag officer positions within the reductions so identified.[2]

To support DoD's analysis in response to this mandate, the Office of the Under Secretary of Defense for Personnel and Readiness (OUSD [P&R]) and the Joint Staff, Manpower and Personnel Directorate (J1) asked the RAND National Defense Research Institute to conduct an independent study of G/FO requirements. The goals of this effort were three-fold:

- Develop a methodology to assess active component G/FO requirements and authorizations.
- Use the methodology to identify opportunities to eliminate, downgrade, or convert (to civilian) G/FO positions.
- Assess the adequacy of existing statutes and policies to provide G/FOs to meet requirements and recommend changes, if needed.

The study's principal objective was to develop a methodology to assess active component G/FO requirements and authorizations. Our intent was to create an evaluation framework that is rigorous, adjustable, transparent, and repeatable. We developed a methodology that can be used to evaluate G/FO positions across the services and the department—to evaluate current G/FO positions, reevaluate positions that are not a G/FO requirement but should be, or determine future leadership requirements.

Although our analytic results are based on a single dataset provided by OSD, the methodology was specifically designed to be employed in the future, in whole or in part, by other users, such as the service G/FO management offices. The findings of our study are based on specified guidelines and criteria, which can be revised to capture different assumptions, potentially leading to different outcomes. Before describing our approach to this study, we provide an overview of G/FO requirements and summarize criticisms of previous studies, which influenced the methodology adopted in our research.

---

[2]   National Defense Authorization Act for Fiscal Year 2017, Sec. 501(c)(1).

General and Flag Officer Requirements

As the military's senior-most officers, G/FOs are responsible for a wide range of duties across hundreds of organizations in the United States and abroad. The Navy refers to these officers as flag officers, while the rest of the services use the term general officers. G/FOs are composed of grades O-7 (brigadier general or rear admiral lower half), O-8 (major general or rear admiral upper half), O-9 (lieutenant general or vice admiral), and O-10 (general or admiral), and serve in either service-coded positions or joint positions.

Entering the G/FO ranks is more difficult than simply becoming an O-6 and then earning one more promotion. There is a significant break between the field grade officer grade of O-6 and the G/FO grade of O-7 in terms of career progression and selectivity. At each of the steps prior to O-6, between 50 and 100 percent of candidates are selected for promotion to the next higher grade.[3] The promotion rate from O-6 to O-7, however, falls to less than 5 percent.[4] As an example of this extreme selectivity, the military services collectively had 11,362 O-6 officers, but only 404 O-7s, as of March 2017.[5] Once promoted to O-7, promotion rates to higher grades bounce back to above 20 percent at each step.

Whether a position requires a G/FO to execute its responsibilities depends on a range of factors, some of which are more important than others, depending on the position. While no definitive list of criteria exists to designate G/FO positions, within DoD or the individual services, much has been written on the topic. Drawing from this literature and discussions with individuals in DoD, general considerations include:

- Statutory requirements, or the laws that dictate whether a position must be filled at a certain grade or is required by statute to perform particular duties.
- Military essentiality, which concerns the level or echelon of military establishment at which the duty is performed, whether the position is a warfighting role, whether the position is command-oriented, and to what degree the position is characterized by independence of operation requiring senior military judgment.
- Magnitude of responsibilities, or the significance of duties to oversee mission, personnel, budgets, property, equipment, and more. This can also include positions that have the authority to obligate the United States to commitments or international agreements, or control foreign resources. Further, the effect of the position on national or U.S. military prestige may also be a factor.[6]

---

[3]   Department of Defense (DoD) Instruction 1320.13, "Commissioned Officer Promotion Reports," July 22, 2009.

[4]   Military Leadership Diversity Commission, "Issue Paper #45: Recent Officer Promotion Rates by Race, Ethnicity, and Gender," June 2010, p. 4.

[5]   Defense Manpower Data Center reports for March 31, 2017.

[6]   Clifford L. Stanley and William E. Gortney, "General and Flag Officer Requirements," testimony at hearing before the Subcommittee on Personnel of the Senate Armed Services Committee, September 14, 2011.

- Level of experience, or the combination of duties, education, and personal development that are obtained over the course of an officer's career and contribute to military and functional competencies of a general or flag officer.
- Level of engagement, or the grade of lateral counterparts (military and civilian, across services or other comparable organizations) with whom the individual in that position interacts. This can also include interaction with Congress, the media, and international entities at a level that requires a uniformed senior executive.
- Parity with similar organizations, or the grade of a position in comparable organizations.
- Reporting relationships, which are the grades and responsibilities of subordinates who report to the position, and the grades and responsibilities of superiors to whom the position reports.
- Span of decisionmaking, or the responsibility the individual has for making consequential decisions that may shape future actions and impact national-level policy.
- Area of responsibility, which is the size and complexity of a region for which a position retains responsibility. The region can also be virtual in nature.

These considerations are featured prominently in the criteria and guidelines used in RAND's methodology to evaluate G/FO requirements, which is discussed in more detail in subsequent chapters of this report.

A small number of G/FO positions, such as service chiefs, the Chairman of the Joint Chiefs of Staff, and combatant commanders, are established by statute (see Appendix C). All other G/FO requirements are established and managed by DoD. The United States Senate reviews and confirms all G/FO promotions at all grades as well as all assignments to O-9 and O-10 G/FO positions.[7]

The task of managing G/FO requirements and assigning G/FOs to fill these requirements falls to the service-specific G/FO management offices and the Joint Staff General/Flag Officer Matters office. These G/FO management offices use various methods to manage these senior officer positions within statutory limitations, balancing requirements and inventory against authorized strength. Most often, these offices will attempt to preserve flexibility in managing these positions by leaving vacant a small number of positions. This buffer between authorized positions and filled positions is carefully managed and, due to personnel shifts, changes frequently.

This analysis of general and flag officer requirements necessitates careful distinction of related terms that are sometimes used interchangeably among the military

---

[7] Per 10 U.S.C. § 601, the President may designate certain positions deemed to be of "importance and responsibility" to grades of O-9 and O-10. Further, while the Senate is also responsible for confirming all field grade officer promotions, G/FO confirmations are subject to greater reporting requirements and scrutiny. DoD Instruction 1320.04, "Military Officer Actions Requiring Presidential, Secretary of Defense, or Under Secretary of Defense for Personnel and Readiness Approval or Senate Confirmation," January 3, 2014.

personnel management community and external participants. We highlight and define them here as they are used in this report.

- The term *requirement* denotes those positions that have been designated for a G/FO of a specific rank (whether the requirement has been filled or not).
- An *authorization* is a position that is designated to be filled with a G/FO, either by the services or the Chairman of the Joint Chiefs of Staff (CJCS).
- *G/FO inventory* is the total number of personnel eligible to fill G/FO authorized positions.
- *Authorized strength* is the total number of G/FOs that Congress has authorized across the services and the joint pool, in active and reserve components, and includes both basic authorized strength and any additional authorizations and exemptions.
- *Allocation* refers to the way G/FO authorizations are issued across the services and the joint pool.
- *Distribution* is how G/FO authorizations are spread across grades (O-7 through O-10).

It is important to emphasize that these terms should not be used interchangeably. While requirements and authorizations refer to numbers of positions available, G/FO inventory is the total number of officers that could fill those positions, and authorized strength is the number of officers that Congress has authorized to fill G/FO positions. These numbers are rarely equal, which creates challenges in managing G/FO manpower. In general, the number of requirements exceeds the number of authorizations because requirements are not subject to authorized strength limits: a requirement can be designated as such whether it can be filled or not. Authorizations, on the other hand, can be filled only based on total authorized strength, so those numbers tend to track more closely.

Previous Studies on G/FO Requirements

RAND's analysis was informed by a number of prior studies of G/FO requirements. These studies were generally mandated by Congress as part of or in preparation for statutory changes to the G/FO authorization framework. DoD and the services have also independently undertaken reviews of G/FO requirements as part of their own G/FO reorganization efforts or to inform congressional decisionmaking.

Most of these prior studies began by collecting data on the existing set of G/FO requirements identified by DoD and the services at the time of the study. They then applied a formal job evaluation methodology that scored or categorized each requirement across a particular set of dimensions or factors. Positions meeting a minimum threshold or other set of criteria for each factor were determined to be of sufficient importance to be filled by a G/FO. The factor-based assessments would often be combined, generally using a weighting scheme, into an overall score or officer grade determination for each position.

DoD took a different approach in its most recent review of active component G/FO requirements conducted in 2010 and 2011, which aimed to identify at least 50 positions for elimination.[8] This effort similarly began with a review of all existing G/FO requirements. Yet rather than applying the job evaluation approach to individual positions as in previous studies, the DoD study group, instead, sought to compare sets of similar positions across services, functions, and organizations. The business rules that guided the study group's analysis did not automatically invalidate any G/FO requirements, but rather flagged potentially questionable positions that needed further examination. DoD's comparative approach in this review was particularly useful in identifying redundancies and potential options for restructuring.

Criticisms of Prior Studies

Criticism of prior studies has tended to focus on the degree to which they have been subjective, incomplete, or inconsistent. First, determining which factors to use in evaluating G/FO requirements and how to distinguish between G/FO and non-G/FO positions using these factors necessarily involves subjective judgment. While this is inherent to job evaluation methods and does not invalidate their results, the United States Government Accountability Office (GAO) has criticized previous studies for not explicitly discussing the subjective judgments and assumptions that underlie their methodology.[9] Subjectivity also affects data collection and analysis, particularly in the absence of clear guidelines and mechanisms to double check survey responses and analysts' interpretations. GAO has also been critical of study results being subject to "unexplained adjustments" by high-level DoD leaders such as service secretaries.[10]

Second, past studies have often been criticized as being incomplete. Some studies only sought to determine whether a position was of sufficient importance to be filled by a G/FO rather than a field grade officer, and did not consider other valid questions, such as whether a position might be filled, instead, by a high-level civilian.[11] G/FO studies based on job evaluation methods also generally take the existing organizational structure as a given, limiting their ability to consider whether a particular G/FO requirement might be eliminated, combined, or changed as part of a restructur-

---

[8]   This effort was carried out by the General and Flag Officer Efficiencies Study Group as part of Defense Secretary Robert Gates' Track Four Efficiency Initiatives. See Stanley and Gortney, 2011.

[9]   U.S. General Accounting Office (GAO), *Military Personnel: General and Flag Officer Requirements Are Unclear Based on DOD's 2003 Report to Congress*, GAO-04-488, April 2004, p. 14.

[10] Mark E. Gebicke, "General and Flag Officers: DoD's Draft Study Needs Adjustments," testimony before the Subcommittee on Military Personnel of the House Committee on National Security, April 8, 1997, p. 5.

[11] Gebicke, 1997, p. 8; GAO, 2004, pp. 23–24.

ing effort.[12] They are similarly limited in addressing potential new or emerging G/FO requirements since they are based on a particular snapshot in time.[13]

Third, criticism has also sometimes focused on whether studies were consistent in their treatment of G/FOs across the services. In 1996 and 1997, each military service carried out its own separate review of G/FO requirements using different methodologies, making it difficult to compare results across the services.[14]

Of note, accounting errors have also challenged some previous studies, given the difficulty of maintaining an accurate inventory of G/FO requirements throughout the study process. GAO identified 35 G/FO positions that were double-counted in DoD's 1997 review.[15] Multi-hatted G/FO requirements, in which one G/FO fills multiple related positions, can also be a source of accounting errors and inconsistencies as well.[16]

The criticisms levied against past G/FO studies informed the development of RAND's methodology. In particular, our study team developed an analytic methodology, described in the following section and in more detail in subsequent chapters, that brought together different perspectives in evaluating G/FO requirements.

Study Approach and Organization of the Report

Numerous sources influenced the design of our analytic methodology, and they are discussed in further detail throughout this report as they pertain to particular topics. Overall, we consulted:

- Literature on organizational theory and personnel management to gain an appreciation of how organizations structure their senior leadership, taking into account philosophies toward echelonment, unity of command, unity of direction, division of labor, order, and span of control.
- Previous G/FO requirements and management studies and critiques of those studies to understand options, strengths, and shortfalls in those efforts.
- Subject matter experts, including representatives of the Joint Staff, service G/FO management offices, DoD G/FO Working Group members, current and former G/FOs, current and former DoD civilian officials, and RAND experts in G/FO management and manpower policy.

---

[12] John Glenn, "General and Flag Officer Requirements," opening statement at the hearing of the Senate Armed Services Committee Subcommittee on Manpower and Personnel, Washington, D.C., August 10, 1988; GAO, 2004, pp. 13–14.

[13] GAO, 2004, p. 13.

[14] Gebicke, 1997, pp. 4–5.

[15] Gebicke, 1997.

[16] GAO, 2004, pp. 16–17.

- Relevant statutes and policies to include G/FO numerical limits to service and joint community, G/FO grade distributions, and specific position requirements (Chapter Two and Appendix C).

The overarching methodology contains four broad elements, illustrated in Figure 1.1: (1) review G/FO requirements, (2) report findings and results, (3) evaluate implications, and (4) provide policy and management recommendations.[17]

We systematically reviewed G/FO requirements, the central element of our work and of this report, using four complementary and interrelated approaches, as follows:

- *Structure and organization.* We conducted a systematic assessment of how G/FOs are staffed within organizations using a defined set of guidelines. This assessment focused on comparing organizational structures across DoD and highlighted positions that were outliers or inconsistent with other similar organizations, similar to DoD's own Track Four Efficiencies study (Chapter Three and Appendix D).
- *Position-by-position.* We evaluated all G/FO requirements against a set of specific criteria. Broadly speaking, the criteria defined job content and context for positions requiring a G/FO. Positions had to meet at least one criterion to be considered a G/FO requirement (Chapter Four).
- *Forced-choice exercise.* In this exercise, participants from the services, the Office of the Secretary of Defense (OSD), the Joint Staff, and other subject matter experts explored DoD's G/FO requirements and the implications of potential reductions in G/FO authorizations (Chapter Five).
- *Position pyramid health.* In our fourth approach, we developed metrics to give insight into the overall health of a career field based on promotions, selectivity, and lateral movement between joint and in-service (Chapter Six and Appendix E).

Figure 1.1
Overarching Methodology

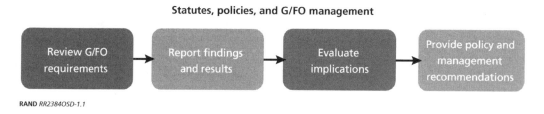

RAND *RR2384OSD-1.1*

---

[17] The research approach was reviewed and approved by RAND's Human Subjects Protection Committee.

We then developed a rule set to integrate findings from the individual analyses (Chapter Seven) and evaluated implications of potential changes to the requirements that are filled with a G/FO using RAND's Military Career Model (Chapter Eight).

As the basis for our assessment, RAND used requirements data collected from the military services and the joint community by the OSD General and Flag Officer Management office as of March 2017. RAND developed the data collection protocol used by OSD so the data collected would cover the totality of information required to conduct the RAND review. (Appendix A contains details on the data collection protocol and data preparation.)

The data received from OSD contained 1,113 G/FO requirements. Table 1.1 shows how these requirements are distributed by grade and service, with joint positions accounting for well over one-quarter of the requirements submitted. Tables 1.2 through 1.4 provide other defining characteristics of the requirements. Table 1.2 highlights the functional areas in which each position falls. Military operations, which includes unit training roles such as predeployment preparations and exercises, constitutes almost one-third of all positions. In Table 1.3, each position is categorized according to the type of position. Commanders make up the highest concentration of these positions. Table 1.4 arrays these positions by organization type.

To facilitate our analysis, RAND developed a Command Chain Application—a computerized, graphical depiction of G/FO positions organized in a hierarchical chain of command. We developed this tool to provide a way to organize, manage, and visualize the relationships between general and flag officer positions within the military chain of command. We used modules within the tool to categorize positions according to type (such as combatant command, professions, staff, and others), which supported our structure and organization and position-by-position approaches. We also used the application for assessing the downstream effects of potential policy decisions to eliminate or downgrade a position or groups of positions—such as downgrading all medical or Judge Advocate General (JAG) positions or limiting the number of four-star positions within each service—and for evaluating future requirements (Chapter Nine). (Appendix B describes the Command Chain Application in greater detail.) Our analysis concludes with management and policy insights drawn from the totality of our research (Chapter Ten).

Table 1.1
G/FO Requirements by Grade and Service

	Army	Air Force	Navy	Marine Corps	Joint	Total in Grade
O-10	6	9	6	2	15	38
O-9	36	30	25	13	45	149
O-8	104	83	47	39	116	389
O-7	144	114	93	34	152	537
Service total	290	236	171	88	328	1,113

Table 1.2
G/FO Requirements by Functional Area

Functional Area	Number
Military operations	391
Materiel and logistics	113
Special staff (legal, medical, chaplain)	105
Research, development, and acquisition	92
Force management, development, education and training	91
Strategic plans and policy	66
Intelligence	52
Manpower and personnel	41
Capabilities development and integration[a]	38
Command, control, communications, computers, and intelligence	30
Program management and financial management	25
Engineer	18
Other	51

[a] Capabilities development and integration is the training, sustainment, mobilization, and procurement of warfighting systems.

Table 1.3
G/FO Requirements by Type of Position

Type of Position	Number
Commander	389
Director	296
Deputy or vice commander	158
Deputy director	104
General/flag staff	101
Program Executive Officer (PEO)/Deputy PEO	30
Chief of staff	26
Other	9

Table 1.4
G/FO Requirements by Type of Organization

Type of Organization	Number
Direct reporting unit/shore based bureaus/acquisition activity/ supporting establishment/field operating agencies	219
Operating forces	174
Service chief staff headquarters	152
Combatant command	137
Major commands/service commands/type commands	110
Defense, joint, or service agency	78
Service component command	74
Theater	49
Joint Staff	44
Service secretariat	42
Office of the Secretary of Defense	18
National	12
Other	4

CHAPTER TWO

Statutory Requirements and Legislative Management of General and Flag Officers

In the FY 2017 NDAA, Congress directed a reduction in the number of G/FO authorizations from 962 to 852 (an 11 percent reduction) to be implemented by December 2022. To establish a baseline for understanding how these changes could affect the department, we conducted an analysis of relevant sections of Title 10 and more recent legislative guidance that apply to G/FO positions. In this section, we will:

- Analyze G/FO authorizations, allocations, and grade distributions as they existed prior to the FY 2017 NDAA's changes.
- Discuss context and history of the joint pool.
- Review the legislative changes to G/FO authorizations, allocations, and grade distributions in the FY 2017 NDAA, including year-over-year changes, and the reductions required by 2022.

General and Flag Officer Authorizations and Distributions

Congress establishes and controls the number of G/FOs working at DoD by setting:

- The overall authorized strength, or the maximum number of G/FOs that DoD could potentially employ.
- The allocation of those authorizations across the services; for example, how many go to the Army, the Navy, the Air Force, or the Marine Corps, and the pool of officers serving in joint duty positions.
- The distribution of those officers in officer grades O-7 through O-10.

Congress's mechanism for authorizing, allocating, and distributing G/FOs is Title 10 of the United States Code, §§ 525–526.[1] Section 525 concerns the distribu-

---

[1] A section-by-section analysis of relevant Title 10 authorizations relating to G/FO authorizations and G/FO positions is included in Appendix C.

tion of commissioned officers on active duty in various G/FO grades, while section 526 concerns the limitations to the number of G/FOs on active duty, including authorizations for joint duty requirements. Per 10 U.S.C. § 527, the President of the United States can suspend these caps in case of war or national emergency.

Service-Specific Authorizations

Prior to the FY 2017 NDAA, Congress had approved 652 G/FO authorizations to the services for nonjoint duty positions. The FY 2017 NDAA then added one Marine Corps authorization, resulting in the distribution of authorizations across the services depicted in Table 2.1.[2] Of note, Congress does not specify a minimum number of authorizations that have to be filled by G/FOs for each of the services the way it does for the joint pool.

Beyond the authorizations allocated by service, Congress has established the distribution of G/FOs in each service at certain officer grades. For example, 10 U.S.C. § 525(a)(1) assigns grade distributions for the active-duty Army such that the Army may have, at most, seven generals (grade O-10), 46 combined generals and lieutenant generals (O-10s plus O-9s), and 90 major generals (O-8). Since section 526 sets the overall general officer allocation to the Army at 231, the remaining 95 G/FO authorizations would represent the minimum number of brigadier generals (grade O-7) available to the Army.

Two additional sections of Title 10 relate to service-specific G/FO numbers, generally. Sections 3210 and 8210, which respectively apply to the Army and the Air Force, establish a ratio for the number of general officers and the number of commissioned active-duty officers. By law, for both services, there is a 75/10,000 ratio.

Table 2.1
Authorizations and Allocations of G/FOs in March 2017

Service	Number of G/FO Authorizations (Service Positions Only)	Number of G/FOs[a] (Service and Joint Positions)
Army	231	300
Navy	162	207
Air Force	198	284
Marine Corps	62	86
Total	653	877

[a] Defense Manpower Data Center reports for March 31, 2017.

---

[2]   The number of G/FOs in the right hand column of Table 2.1 and allocations of G/FOs in subsequent charts in this chapter represent the number of G/FOs serving in positions as of the time this report was published. These numbers are dynamic as positions are vacated and filled.

Table 2.2
Distribution of G/FO Authorizations by Grades

	Army	Navy	Air Force	Marine Corps
Total service authorization	231	162	198	62
Grade O-10 maximum	7	6	9	2
Combined grade O-9 and O-10 maximum	46	33	44	17
Grade O-8 maximum	90	50	73	22
Grade O-7 minimum[a]	95	79	81	23

[a] The O-7 minimum authorization is not in statute but is calculated as the difference between the total service authorization and the sum of the maximum O-8 through O-10 grades for each service.

Table 2.2 shows the breakdown of total authorizations, allocations, and distributions by service per 10 U.S.C. § 526(a). As depicted in the table, Congress has established statutory guidelines for the total number of authorizations for each service and has, additionally, specified rules for the distribution of those officers in grades O-8 through O-10.

The Joint Pool

Congress has also established a set number of authorizations for G/FOs with joint duty assignments called the "joint pool." The joint pool is a set of G/FO positions that are exempt from the service-specific limitations on the number of G/FOs.[3] While each individual position within the pool can be filled by a G/FO from any service, some positions are habitually aligned with one or two of the services. The joint pool includes positions in the Joint Staff, OSD, defense agencies and DoD field activities, and combatant commands. Because these positions represent a special category to be managed, we provide a brief background on them.

Prior to the creation of the joint pool, the increasing size of the G/FO ranks relative to the military as a whole was attributed to growth of joint G/FO requirements.[4] Goldwater-Nichols had elevated the importance of joint G/FO positions and led to a significant expansion in their number over the following years.[5] The services filled these positions from their own authorized number of G/FOs, at times having to eliminate internal G/FO positions to stay within statutory limits.[6]

---

[3] 10 U.S.C. § 526 (a) establishes service-specific limitations on G/FO authorizations.

[4] Priscilla Offenhauer, "General and Flag Officer Authorizations for the Active and Reserve Components: A Comparative and Historical Analysis," Federal Research Division, Library of Congress, December 2007, p. 36.

[5] Kapp, 2016, p. 7.

[6] Offenhauer, 2007, p. 36.

Congress established the joint pool in the FY 2009 NDAA. The nearest prede-cessor to the joint pool was the Chairman's 12, which Congress authorized in the FY 1993 NDAA.[7] The Chairman's 12 was a set of up to 12 joint G/FO positions that the CJCS could designate as exempt from the service-specific limitations on G/FO num-bers. The FY 2009 NDAA replaced the Chairman's 12 with a pool of 324 joint G/FO positions and gave the Secretary of Defense authority to designate these positions.[8] The Secretary of Defense, in turn, delegated authority over 294 of the 324 original joint pool positions to the CJCS.[9]

The initial set of joint pool positions was determined by the Joint Staff in coor-dination with the combatant commands and defense agencies. Each service was then allocated a set number of the 294 positions. This allocation—the Joint Pool Service Fair Share—exceeded the statutory minimums but followed their same proportional distribution, as described later in this section.[10] The 30 remaining authorizations that were not delegated to the CJCS were termed the Joint Pool Buffer. This buffer is man-aged by the OUSD P&R and reserved for temporary and emerging G/FO position requirements.[11]

The FY 2012 NDAA later shrank the pool slightly, to its current maximum of 310 positions.[12] The FY 2017 NDAA maintains this authorized number through the end of 2022, at which point it directs a reduction in the number of G/FO positions in the joint pool to 232.

The creation of the joint pool in the FY 2009 NDAA was also paired with a significant increase in the statutory limits on the total number of G/FOs. The loss of 230 service-specific G/FO authorizations was made up for by the gain of 312 joint G/FO authorizations in 10 U.S.C. § 526(b), for a net increase of 82 positions overall.[13] This increase was reflected in subsequent changes to the total number of G/FOs on active duty, which rose from 920 at the end of FY 2008 to 981 at the end of FY 2010.[14]

Since the FY 2012 NDAA, Congress has authorized 310 positions for the joint pool but has not specified the allocation of those authorizations across the services; that

---

[7]   Public Law 102-484, "National Defense Authorization Act for Fiscal Year 1993," October 23, 1992, Sec. 403.

[8]   Public Law 110-417, "Duncan Hunter National Defense Authorization Act for Fiscal Year 2009," October 14, 2008, Sec. 506.

[9]   By Chairman of the Joint Chiefs of Staff Instruction (CJCSI) policy, these 294 positions were referred to as the "Joint Pool." CJCSI 1331.01D, "Manpower and Personnel Actions Involving General and Flag Officers," August 1, 2010, p. A-A-1.

[10]   For more on the management rules used by the services to track whether they are meeting these requirements, see CJCSI 1331.01D, pp. A-A-1–A-A-4.

[11]   CJCSI 1331.01D, pp. A-A-1, A-A-3.

[12]   Public Law 112-81, "National Defense Authorization Act for Fiscal Year 2012, December 31, 2011, Sec. 502.

[13]   Public Law 110-417, 2008, Sec. 503, 506; 10 U.S.C. § 526(a), 2006.

[14]   Defense Manpower Data Center reports for September 30, 2010 and September 30, 2008.

allocation was ostensibly left to the Secretary of Defense. However, Congress required a minimum number of officers serving in joint duty positions from each of the services, as follows: 85 from the Army, 61 from the Navy, 73 from the Air Force, and 21 from the Marine Corps, for a total of 240 positions. These minimums set a lower bound on the number of G/FOs from each service represented in the joint pool. The distribution of these minimums across the services has stayed fairly constant over time and reflects the overall number of nonexempt G/FOs authorized for each service. The Army has consistently been allocated 34 percent to 36 percent of all G/FO authorizations, both overall (since at least 1997) and in the joint pool (since its creation in 2009). In the same way, the Navy's allocation has been 24 percent to 26 percent, the Air Force's 30 percent to 32 percent, and the Marine Corps' 8 percent to 10 percent.

By both establishing an aggregate authorization for joint pool officers and allocating a minimum number of G/FO joint pool officers from each of the services, Congress has allocated 77.4 percent of the available authorizations across the services. The remaining 23 percent of authorizations may be allocated by the Secretary of Defense from any of the services.

In the last several years, mandated reductions to the number of G/FOs have often targeted the joint pool. In 2011, Secretary of Defense Robert Gates' Track Four Efficiency Initiative marked 102 G/FO positions for elimination. Of these, 58 were joint pool positions, which were to be placed in the joint pool buffer rather than kept within the joint pool for reallocation to other requirements.[15] As mentioned previously, the FY 2012 NDAA reduced the statutory ceiling for the joint pool from 324 to 310 positions. For its part, of the 110 mandated reductions in the FY 2017 NDAA, 78 are to come from the joint pool.

Total Authorized G/FO Numbers

The FY 2016 NDAA authorized a total of 962 G/FO positions, consisting of 652 for the services and 310 for the joint pool, as depicted in Table 2.3.

FY 2017 NDAA Requirements

In the FY 2017 NDAA, Congress directed a reduction in the number of G/FO authorizations by December 31, 2022, from 962 (652 service and 310 joint pool authorizations) to 852 (an 11 percent reduction). The law allocates these reductions across the services and specifies that the reductions must be implemented not later than December 31, 2022.[16] These changes are codified in 10 U.S.C. § 526a, which replaces the

---

[15] U.S. Secretary of Defense, "Track Four Efficiency Initiatives Decisions," memorandum, March 14, 2011, pp. 22–30.

[16] Public Law 114-328, National Defense Authorization Act for Fiscal Year 2017, December 23, 2016, Sec. 501(a)(1).

Table 2.3
Total Authorization and Allocations of G/FOs in 2016 from § 526

	Number of G/FO Authorizations	Minimum Number of G/FOs
Service		
Army	231	—
Navy	162	—
Air Force	198	—
Marine Corps	61	—
SUBTOTAL	**652**	—
Joint Duty		
Army	—	85
Navy	—	61
Air Force	—	73
Marine Corps	—	21
SUBTOTAL	**310**	**240** **(77.4% of authorizations)**

current statute governing authorized G/FO strength (10 U.S.C. § 526[a]). Table 2.4 depicts the future allocation as well as the change from the current allocation of G/FO authorizations. As the table shows, each service except the Marine Corps received a reduced number of G/FO authorizations.

The reductions in G/FO authorizations allocated to the services sums to a net loss of 32 authorizations. A disproportionate amount of the reductions directed in the FY 2017 NDAA are assigned to the joint pool, which is reduced by 78 authorizations from the current level of 310 to 232. However, as temporary relief from the reductions in the face of ongoing overseas contingency operations (OCO), Congress authorized 30 G/FO positions "as an additional maximum temporary allocation to the joint pool."[17]

In addition to reductions in the authorizations for the joint pool, Congress fully allocated the joint pool authorizations across the services for the first time. In the past, Congress has allocated a minimum number of G/FOs from each service that must serve in the joint pool, and this practice is continued. However, these minimums that previously accounted for 77 percent of the available authorizations will account for nearly 92 percent of the available joint pool G/FOs that are statutorily allocated in 2022 (with

---

[17]   Public Law 114-328, National Defense Authorization Act for Fiscal Year 2017, December 23, 2016, Sec. 501(a)(3).

Table 2.4
G/FO Authorizations and Allocation in 2022

Service	New Number of G/FO Authorizations[a]	Change From Prior Authorization[a]
Army	220	−11
Navy	151	−11
Air Force	187	−11
Marine Corps	62	+1
Subtotal	620	−32

[a] Prior authorization was codified in 10 U.S.C. § 526(a).

Table 2.5
Authorizations and Allocation for Joint Pool G/FOs in 2022

Joint Duty	New Number of G/FO Authorizations	New Minimum Number of G/FOs
Army	82[a]	75 (−10)
Navy	60[a]	53 (−8)
Air Force	69[a]	68 (−5)
Marine Corps	21[a]	17 (−4)
Subtotal	232[b] (−78)	213 (−27) (91.8%)

[a] First time this allocation is established by law.

[b] Total does not include 30 OCO authorizations.

NOTE: The number in parentheses is the reduction from the previous statutory levels.

the remainder available for allocation by the Secretary of Defense). Table 2.5 depicts the authorizations and allocations for the joint pool in 2022.[18] The number in parentheses is the reduction from the previous statutory levels.

Previously, 10 U.S.C. § 526 specified grade maximums within the joint pool. The new statute 10 U.S.C. § 526a does not. In addition, the previous statute (U.S. Code § 526[b][5]) allowed the Chairman of the Joint Chiefs of Staff to designate up to 15 general and flag officer positions in the unified and specified command and up to three general or flag officer positions on the Joint Staff as positions to be held by reserve component officers in a grade below O-9. These positions are referred to as Chairman's Reserve Positions (CRP). While serving in these positions, reserve component officers

[18] 10 U.S.C. § 526a.

are not counted against the limitations on the number of general or flag officers for each armed service in § 526(a). The new statute 10 U.S. Code § 526a does not include this provision and effectively does away with CRP positions.

Additionally, Congress changed the distribution of general officers in the Marine Corps, adding two authorizations for officers in a grade above major general and subtracting one authorization for an officer in a grade of major general.[19] Likewise, the Marine Corps' overall § 526 authorization allocation was immediately increased from 61 to 62.[20] The other services' distributions and allocations remained the same as 2016 levels until 2022 or future congressional action.

With this overview of the NDAA 2017 changes in service and joint G/FO authorizations as background, we turn to RAND's evaluation of current G/FO requirements in the next chapters.

---

[19] Public Law 114-328, National Defense Authorization Act for Fiscal Year 2017, December 23, 2016, Sec. 503(a).

[20] Public Law 114-328, National Defense Authorization Act for Fiscal Year 2017, December 23, 2016, Sec. 503(b).

CHAPTER THREE

Structure and Organization Analysis

The structure and organizational analysis consisted of a systematic assessment of how G/FOs are staffed within organizations using a defined set of guidelines developed by RAND. This assessment focused on examining organizational structures within DoD, reviewing internal hierarchical structures within an organization, and comparing organizational structures across DoD. The goal was to highlight G/FO positions that were not consistent with an organization's goals, missions, and internal hierarchical structures, and/or that were inconsistent with other similar organizations across DoD, based on the principles guiding the assessment.

This assessment did not include an exhaustive look across all positions within DoD organizations but, instead, focused on organizations most affected by language in the FY 2017 NDAA (such as joint organizations), those containing significant numbers of G/FOs, specialty non-line communities, and other organizations of particular interest to the DoD G/FO Working Group or the Congress.

The 16 groups reviewed by RAND are:

- The Joint Staff
- Combatant commands (including subordinate unified commands and joint task forces)
- Positions in international organizations (e.g., North Atlantic Treaty Organization [NATO])
- Positions associated with contingency operations
- Positions in the Office of the Secretary of Defense and the State Department
- Defense agencies and DoD field activities (DAFA)
- Intelligence positions within the services, combatant commands, and agencies
- Judge Advocates General
- Medical positions (e.g., U.S. Army Medical Command [MEDCOM]), command surgeons, veterinary corps)
- Chaplain positions
- PEOs involved in acquisition and procurement and the so-called "Gansler 5" positions
- Education-related positions (e.g., military academies, senior service colleges)

- Army major headquarters and commands, together with their major subordinate commands
- Navy major headquarters and commands, together with their major subordinate commands
- Marine Corps major headquarters and commands, together with their major subordinate commands
- Air Force major headquarters and commands, together with their major subordinate commands.

These groups were selected based on major components of DoD organizational structure (e.g., Joint Staff, defense agencies and DoD field activities); specialty, non-line communities that span the services (e.g., chaplains, surgeons general); and positions with functional job areas that might not belong to a particular command structure (e.g., education-related positions). In some cases, specific positions were members of two or three candidate categories (e.g., Judge Advocates General and major service commands).

The groups in total comprise about 95 percent of the 1,113 positions in our data set. The structure and organization approach evaluated well-defined groups of positions—either because they were the focus of prior queries or clear logical groups. The positions not reviewed in this assessment did not fall into any of the 16 groups and, therefore, did not have any common characteristics that we could use as a basis for organizational or position comparisons.

To conduct this assessment, we derived a set of organizational principles; applied these principles to the G/FO positions within each group; applied additional principles depending on the characteristics of the particular group; and, based on the application of those principles, drew conclusions for each group.

Our assessments examined a position both within the context of its own organization and also across similar organizations within a particular group (e.g., other combatant commands or other intelligence organizations). The internal look within an organization served to identify possible discrepancies in how a G/FO position fit within the role and mission of that organization; the look across similar organizations served to identify discrepancies as compared to peer positions as well as potential opportunities to perform similar functions using G/FOs of lower grades and/or civilians (or in a few cases, the need to upgrade positions).

The findings from this approach answer the following question: Does the position meet the structure and organization criteria for a G/FO requirement? Because this approach involved detailed comparison of individual positions both within and across organizations, we were able to arrive at nuanced findings for each requirement as follows:

- Meets criteria for a G/FO requirement at current or higher grade
- Meets criteria for a G/FO requirement, neutral on grade

- Meets criteria for a G/FO requirement at a lower grade (downgrade)
- Does not meet criteria for a G/FO requirement (eliminate, reduce to O-6, or convert to civilian)
- Conflicting findings
- Neutral
- Subject to policy decision
- Not reviewed.

The finding of "subject to policy decision" indicates that we defer to department leadership to review the group of positions and/or to consider the value of G/FOs in that organization writ large.

The remainder of this chapter presents the fundamental organizational principles used in this analysis and the relationship of these principles to the organization research literature and to the unique requirements of DoD and other military organizations. We then provide a summary of our findings. Appendix D contains detailed analysis for each group reviewed.

General Principles for This Review

As a basis for analyzing positions within a structural context, we reviewed literature on echelonment structure and span of control. We also reviewed organizational principles used in past reviews of DoD G/FO positions as well as reviews of DoD organizational structures. Based on these foundational principles, we defined a set of guidelines and used them to systematically analyze how G/FOs are staffed within organizations.

Foundational Principles: Echelonment and Span of Control

Although the missions and degree of risk taken by military organizations differ from commercial entities, Bernard Rostker et al. argue that "essential management structures are strikingly similar" and "civilian notions of information processing and decision-making have close counterparts in the military's concept of command and control."[1]

Classical management theory provides a prescriptive view about how organizations should function to achieve maximum productivity.[2] From this perspective, an organization should be hierarchical, have unity of command (subordinates receive orders from one supervisor), unity of direction (tasks that are similar should be organized under the purview of one supervisor), division of labor (specialized roles), order

---

[1] Unpublished research on military organizations and echelonment by Bernard Rostker, M. Hix, and L. Scott, RAND Corporation.

[2] Marjolijn S. Dijksterhuis, Frans A. J. Van den Bosch, and Henk W. Volberda, "Where Do New Organizational Forms Come From? Management Logics as a Source of Coevolution," *Organization Science*, Vol. 10, No. 5, 1999, pp. 569–582.

(each organizational member has an assigned role and set of tasks), and traditionally defined span of control (the number of subordinates a supervisor can effectively manage).[3] These industrial-age principles are still relevant today, particularly in industries that emphasize efficiency and consistency, such as manufacturing and retail.[4] These standards also align well with command and control principles in terms of chain of command, staffing, and levels of authority.[5]

With regard to G/FO roles and guidelines, the concepts of span of control and hierarchy are particularly relevant. Span of control is a central element to echelonment structure and management practices. However, in business literature, span of control, in most cases, focuses very narrowly on how many immediate direct reports a manager has—effectively "span of supervision"—as opposed to the broader meaning of span of control on which the military usually focuses.

Span of control, in the sense most relevant to the military, is determined primarily by the scope of role, the complexity of assigned tasks and/or missions, the breadth and depth of information the individual must process and comprehend, the range of interaction and coordination demands (up and down the chain of command, as well as laterally), and the numbers and types of forces and resources commanded.[6] Thus, the narrower concept of span of supervision is generally a minor factor when considering span of control in a military sense.

Turning to hierarchy, in a military context, the number of levels in a hierarchy can be determined based on "the nature of the job and the need for effective span of control; the scale of the organization; vertical task differentiation and the need to maintain focus; and, the need to achieve efficiency through the effective management of pooled resources."[7] Business literature addresses the elimination of echelons, or layers, in an organization by assessing complementary skills and getting rid of positions that overlap or are no longer creating value for an organization. Examples include cutting intermediary positions if there is overlap of responsibilities or assessing the degree to which formal roles map onto the work being conducted, to make sure that roles and responsibilities are appropriately designated.

---

[3]   Eric B. Dent and Pamela Bozeman, "Discovering the Foundational Philosophies, Practices, and Influences of Modern Management Theory," *Journal of Management History*, Vol. 20, No. 2, 2014, pp. 145–163; Henri Fayol, 1949, as cited in: Katherine Miller, Chapter 2: Classical Approaches, in K. Miller (ed.), *Organizational Communication: Approaches and Processes*, 7th ed., Stamford, Conn.: Cengage Learning, 2015, pp. 17–35.

[4]   Dijksterhuis et al., 1999; Mildred Golden Pryor and Sonia Taneja, "Henri Fayol, Practitioner and Theoretician–Revered and Reviled," *Journal of Management History*, Vol. 16, No. 4, 2010, pp. 489–503.

[5]   Joint Publication 1, Doctrine for the Armed Forces of the United States, Washington, D.C., Joint Chiefs of Staff, March 25, 2013.

[6]   Unpublished research by Rostker et al.

[7]   Unpublished research by Rostker et al.

Considerations about the factors that inform echelonment and span of control can help military organizations determine the most effective leadership and management structure.

In discussing the concept we refer to here as span of supervision, business literature identifies some rules of thumb that can be helpful even in a military setting. In general, span of supervision tends to be narrower at the top of an organization and wider lower down in the hierarchy because there are greater coordination demands at the top.[8] The broad rule is that top managers should supervise a maximum of six people.[9] For lower-level managers, 20 to 30 subordinates are considered permissible.[10] However, these rules do not take into account organizational context or the broader considerations of span of control in a military sense. Also, there can be inconsistencies in how span of supervision is operationalized across organizations and at different points in time within an organization's lifecycle.[11]

The business literature also highlights that span of supervision varies depending on the design of an organization, whether the environment is consistent and predictable or more complex and highly variable, whether the organization itself (or the large organizational structure of which it is a part) is divisional and matrixed,[12] and the level of interactions and coordination required with external organizations.[13]

While the factors identified in business literature apply specifically to span of supervision, we believe these factors are also relevant considerations for how span of control in the broader military sense will vary: a broad span of control in an environment that is highly variable and complex will result in a more demanding position than the same span of control in an environment that is consistent and predictable. This, then, may influence considerations for whether a G/FO, lower ranking officer, or civilian should fill the position.[14]

---

[8] W. H. Starbuck, "Organizational Growth and Development," in W. H. Starbuck, ed., *Organizational Growth and Development*, Harmondsworth, U.K.: Penguin Books, 1971.

[9] Daniel A. Wren and Arthur G. Bedeian, *The Evolution of Management Thought*, 6th ed., John Wiley & Sons, 2009.

[10] Miller, 2015.

[11] Henry Mintzberg, 1979, as cited in Kenneth J. Meier and John Bohte, "Span of Control and Public Organizations: Implementing Luther Gulick's Research Design," *Public Administration Review*, Vol. 63, No. 1, 2003, pp. 61–70.

[12] Lara Schmidt et al., *Cyber Practices: What Can the U.S. Air Force Learn from the Commercial Sector?* Santa Monica, Calif.: RAND Corporation, 2015.

[13] Gary L. Neilson and Julie Wulf, "How Many Direct Reports?" *Harvard Business Review*, Vol. 90, No. 4., 2012.

[14] Unpublished research on general officers versus senior civilians in leadership positions by Michael Schiefer, Al Robbert, and Steve Drenzner, RAND Corporation.

Guidelines for Assessing G/FO Requirements

Similar to other organizations, DoD has limited resources and needs to judiciously use its senior leaders within its structure. To effectively analyze whether positions meet the criteria for a G/FO requirement, we combined insights from the organizational literature with additional foundational principles specific to military organizational structure to develop a set of organization-level and position-level guidelines. These broad principles are similar to those the Army developed for its 2015 review of Headquarters, Department of the Army.[15]

The organization-level guidelines are:

- Place G/FO positions in the upper levels of the organization.
- Decrease the use of G/FO deputies and, particularly, assistants to deputies, deputies to assistants, assistants to assistants, etc.[16]
- Reduce same-grade reporting.
- Avoid "breaks" in G/FO hierarchy (e.g., O-7 reporting to an O-9).
- Avoid duplicative responsibilities in the same immediate organization.
- Increase the span of control of G/FOs.
- G/FOs should have direct reports.
- Maintain parity across equivalent types of internal organizations.
- The use of G/FOs must support the direct mission of the organization.

These are the position-level guidelines:

- Military essentiality of the position: Could this position be filled by a senior civilian?
- Span of control or responsibilities that are inconsistent with peers (e.g., much smaller span than equivalent positions without mitigating additional duties)
- Rank and number of immediate subordinates
- Rank of immediate superiors
- Parity with other like organizations, such as across services or combatant commands
- Precedents in filling the position with more junior and/or civilian persons.

---

[15] Thomas Spoehr et al., "Reducing the Size of Headquarters, Department of the Army—An After-Action Review," *Military Review*, January–February 2017, Army University Press.

[16] We, in principle, considered "vice" and "deputy" positions equivalently, relying on the job description to understand and/or distinguish their roles. The data showed that the title (deputy or vice) was not a significant factor in distinguishing roles; what mattered was the nature of the organization overall and where the position was within the organization. A deputy or vice to a combatant commander is very different from a deputy or vice to the combatant command J3, or to the A/G/N/S3 on the service headquarters or major command staff. The latter positions (regardless of whether they were called deputy or vice) in most cases resemble a chief of staff within that staff directorate or section or a highly empowered executive assistant.

These guidelines informed our review but were not applied blindly. For example, the Military Assistant to the Secretary Defense does not have direct reports of any significance, nor is it appropriate for this position to have direct reports of any consequence; nevertheless, this position is appropriate for a G/FO given the broad activities this position carries out on behalf of the Secretary and the diverse set of senior individuals with whom he or she must interact.

Applying the Guidelines

Once the guidelines were established, we analyzed the 16 groups of positions defined previously, comparing the positions within each group as well as across services, commands, or other relevant factions. (Appendix D contains a detailed description of how this analysis was conducted.) To assess whether the grade of each position within a group was justified, we applied the guidelines listed previously across all candidate categories. In cases where these guidelines did not reflect the specific circumstances of a category, we developed category-specific guidelines that captured particular characteristics, responsibilities, and requirements relevant to the group.

Because we conducted independent reviews for each of the candidate categories, many positions were reviewed more than once through a different lens. For example, the U.S. Central Command (CENTCOM) J2 was reviewed both as part of the combatant command group and also as part of the intelligence group. It was possible (and, indeed, occasionally happened) that the two reviews would produce differing findings. Furthermore, different members of the team reviewed different groups. To ensure consistency and resolve potential conflicts, the final step in the structure and organization approach was to collectively review the findings across categories as a team and reconcile differences or inconsistencies identified.

Summary of Structure and Organization Findings

The findings of the structure and organization approach are shown in Tables 3.1 and 3.2, which summarize the findings first by service and then by grade. As mentioned, the possible outcomes of this approach are: meets criteria for a G/FO requirement at current or higher grade; meets criteria for a G/FO requirement, neutral on grade; meets criteria for a G/FO requirement at a lower grade (downgrade); does not meet criteria for a G/FO requirement (eliminate, reduce to O-6, or convert to civilian), subject to policy decision, neutral, or not reviewed.

Except for two, the findings are self-explanatory. "Conflicting findings" indicate that a position was examined in more than one group (e.g., the Vice-Commander of the Air University position was looked at both as an education-related position and also as part of the review of Air Force major headquarters, as a subordinate of Air Education and Training Command), and these different looks produced conflicting findings.

Table 3.1
Findings of Structure and Organization Approach by Service

Service	Meets Criteria for a G/FO at Current or Higher Grade	Meets Criteria for a G/FO, Neutral on Grade	Meets Criteria for a G/FO at a Lower Grade	Does Not Meet Criteria for a G/FO	Conflicting Findings	Neutral	Subject to Policy Decision	Not Reviewed	Total
Army	161 56%	2 1%	46 16%	51 18%	5 2%	0	0	25 9%	290
Air Force	128 54%	5 2%	26 11%	53 22%	2 1%	0	8 3%	14 6%	236
Navy	109 64%	0	17 10%	27 16%	3 2%	0	0	15 9%	171
Marine Corps	44 50%	10 11%	16 18%	10 11%	7 8%	1 1%	0	0	88
Joint	131 40%	42 13%	11 3%	39 12%	2 1%	23 7%	75 23%	5 2%	328
Total	573 51%	59 5%	116 10%	180 16%	19 2%	24 2%	83 7%	59 5%	1,113

NOTE: Percentages represent percent of row totals and may not add up to 100 percent due to rounding.

Table 3.2
Findings of Structure and Organization Approach by Grade

Grade	Meets Criteria for a G/FO at Current or Higher Grade	Meets Criteria for a G/FO, Neutral on Grade	Meets Criteria for a G/FO at a Lower Grade	Does Not Meet Criteria for a G/FO	Conflicting Findings	Neutral	Subject to Policy Decision	Not Reviewed	Total
O-10	28 74%	1 3%	8 21%	0	0	0	1 3%	0	38
O-9	91 61%	13 9%	29 19%	4 3%	0	1 1%	4 3%	7 5%	149
O-8	186 48%	21 5%	79 20%	25 6%	18 5%	7 2%	30 8%	23 6%	389
O-7	268 50%	24 4%	0	151 28%	1 0%	16 3%	48 9%	29 5%	537
Total	573 51%	59 5%	116 10%	180 16%	19 2%	24 2%	83 7%	59 5%	1,113

NOTE: Percentages represent percent of row totals and may not add up to 100 percent due to rounding.

Of the 19 conflicting findings, 17 are conflicts between "does not meet criteria for a G/FO requirement (eliminate, reduce to O-6, or convert to civilian" and "meets criteria for a G/FO at a lower grade (downgrade)"; the remaining two conflicts are between "meets criteria for a G/FO requirement" and "does not meet criteria for a G/FO requirement (eliminate)."

The other finding that is not self-explanatory are the 83 positions "subject to policy decision." This finding indicates that the determination of whether a G/FO position should be retained or eliminated hinges on a fundamental policy decision. The specific policy decisions are:

- *Appropriate role of G/FO positions within OSD.* Although the positions would benefit from the experience, perspectives, and liaison of G/FOs, they could effectively be filled by appropriately qualified senior civilians. Does that benefit justify the opportunity cost of using a G/FO for these positions? Is it appropriate to put G/FOs in leadership positions in OSD, the organization responsible for oversight of the military? Neither the pros nor the cons are entirely compelling. We recommend the Department of Defense conduct a review to provide overarching guidance on the appropriate uses of G/FO positions within OSD.
- *Appropriate role of G/FO positions in civilian organizations outside of the Department of Defense (such as the State Department).* Again, while senior civilians can fill these positions effectively, G/FOs bring distinct advantages. It is a policy decision as to whether the advantages outweigh the opportunity costs of using a G/FO to fill such positions.
- *Allocation and assignment of G/FOs to defense attaché positions.* Determining which attaché positions merit a G/FO as opposed to an officer of lower grade is beyond the scope of this study. The logic behind the current set of G/FO attachés was not evident from the data, and we recommend OSD review the attaché G/FO positions.
- *Phasing out OCO positions as contingencies wind down.* A significant number of G/FO positions are closely coupled to contingency operations. We expect these positions would be eliminated over time as operations scale down, but the timing and sequencing of such eliminations will be driven by events and policies.
- *Use of G/FOs in joint task forces and joint functional combatant commands.* In some cases such commands have G/FO positions and in other cases do not. It was not evident from the data what factors distinguish these, and there are sufficient differences between them to make comparisons across organizations unreliable. We recommend DoD review these organizations and establish guidelines for when G/FOs are and are not appropriate.

Table 3.3 summarizes the distribution of the "subject to policy decision" findings. As the table shows, 65 percent of the positions are OCO-associated G/FO positions.

Table 3.3
Positions with Finding of Subject to Policy Decision

Type of Policy Decision	Number of Positions
Appropriate role of G/FO positions within the Office of the Secretary of Defense	9
Appropriate role of G/FO positions in civilian organizations outside the Department of Defense	2
Allocation and assignment of G/FOs to defense attaché positions	10
Phasing out OCO positions as contingencies wind down	54
Use of G/FOs in joint task forces and joint functional combatant commands	8
Total	83

When the findings are examined on a group-by-group basis, some interesting patterns and insights arose. A few are worth highlighting:

- Defense Agencies and Field Activities are often a target for G/FO reductions.[17] However, this group comprises only 25 G/FO positions, and of these we found that 17 positions (68 percent) meet the criteria for a G/FO requirement due to their significant global responsibilities and the need for close integration of their organizations' operations with military operations.
- In reviewing legal positions, we found arguments to reduce the grades of the Judge Advocates General and the Deputy Judge Advocates General (DJAG) unpersuasive in view of the rationale articulated by the Congress leading up to the 2008 NDAA that set the current grades of these positions.
- The 2017 NDAA guidance regarding the Defense Health Agency (DHA) and medical activities of the military departments has significant impact on the G/FO positions that manage delivery of medical care through medical treatment facilities and ensure effective operation of DHA as a combat support agency. In view of this language, we found that while senior leadership positions should be retained, a significant number of positions responsible for the management of medical facilities, centers, and regions could be converted to civilian leadership or reduced in grade to non-G/FO positions.
- Within the military departments, we found several major headquarters in which large-scale reductions in grades of position are consistent with responsibilities of those positions and grades of positions in other similar organizations. The findings lead to a net reduction in the number of G/FO positions as O-7 positions are downgraded to O-6.

---

[17] From meetings with subject matter experts and G/FO management offices, November–January 2017.

- Within military departments, we also identified groups of G/FO positions that were inconsistent in grade with their peers in the same service. The best example of this is the wing commanders in the Air Force, which vary between O-7 and O-6 even across wings of similar size and aircraft type.

These as well as other group-specific findings are described in greater detail in Appendix D.

CHAPTER FOUR

Position-by-Position Analysis

RAND conducted a position-by-position analysis of all G/FO requirements against a defined set of criteria using the database provided by OSD (as of March 2017). Requirements included positions that are existing (those that are filled, dual or multi-hatted, gapped temporarily, or filled by lesser grades or civilians), unfilled (those that did not meet service or Joint Staff prioritization within authorization limits), and emerging (those that represent new priorities or areas of emphasis). The criteria used to analyze G/FO requirements were derived based on job content and context, service, and Joint Staff perspectives; it was heavily informed by methodologies used in prior G/FO studies. The aim of the analysis was to identify positions that did or did not meet criteria for a G/FO requirement. It was not intended as a rank ordering of positions, justification of G/FO grade distributions, or a turnkey method to assess requirements.

Developing the Analytic Approach: Review of Prior Studies

Of the four analytical approaches in RAND's methodology, the position-by-position analysis most closely resembled prior studies of G/FO requirements. The filtering approach described in this chapter is adapted most directly from a recent RAND study of reserve component G/FO requirements.[1] The criteria used in this filtering approach were adapted from the set of G/FO attributes common to nearly all prior G/FO review efforts; however, supplemental attributes were added to capture expanded dimensions of G/FO requirements that were confirmed by the DoD G/FO Working Group.

The studies RAND reviewed in developing the position-by-position analytical approach are listed in chronological order:

- *Report of General and Flag Officer Requirements*, Secretary of Defense, April 1978

---

[1] Lisa M. Harrington et al., *Reserve Component General and Flag Officers: A Review of Requirements and Authorizations*, Santa Monica, Calif.: RAND Corporation, RR1156-OSD, 2016.

- *Zero-Based Analysis of General Officer Billet Requirements*, Kapos Associates Inc., 1988
- *Study of General/Flag Officer Requirements and Distributions in the Department of Defense*, Hay Group, 1988
- *Military Officers: Assessment of the 1988 Defense Officer Requirements Study*, GAO, April 1988
- *Analysis of U.S. Marine Corps General Officer Billet Requirements*, Kapos Associates Inc. July 31, 1996
- "General and Flag Officers: DoD's Draft Study Needs Adjustments," GAO, April 8, 1997
- *Review of Active Duty General and Flag Officer Authorizations*, DoD (based on assessment by Logistics Management Institute), March 2003
- *Military Personnel: General and Flag Officer Requirements Are Unclear Based on DoD's 2003 Report to Congress*, GAO, April 2004
- *General/Flag Officer Review*, Logistics Management Institute, June 2005
- *General and Flag Officer Efficiencies Study Group*, DoD, 2010
- "General and Flag Officer Requirements," hearing before the Subcommittee on Personnel of the Committee on Armed Services, United States Senate, September 14, 2011
- *Reserve Component General and Flag Officers: A Review of Requirements and Authorizations*, RAND Corporation, 2016.

These studies collected data at the individual position level for all G/FO requirements and then applied a formal methodology to determine whether each position, in fact, merited G/FO status. This "job evaluation" approach is similar to approaches used in the private sector that attempt to rank positions based on their worth to an organization.[2] The Hay Group, which carried out the 1988 G/FO review, was, in fact, a primary developer of this job evaluation methodology.[3] This method most commonly involves collecting data on individual positions and then applying a set of chosen criteria to judge the relative worth of jobs using various scoring and weighting schemes. The overall score assigned to a position based on this scheme is then used to sort positions by relative value, which, along with the use of cutoff thresholds, can provide the basis for determining the rank or pay grade of each position.

The criteria used in most prior G/FO studies can be traced back to a set of 16 factors established by DoD to help determine what type of job responsibilities should be fulfilled by military officers. These factors were established over 50 years ago and have

---

[2] Unpublished research on job evaluation methods by Rudolph H. Ehrenberg Jr., Scott Naftel, and Harry J. Thie, RAND Corporation.

[3] Hay Group, *Study of General/Flag Officer Requirements and Distributions in the Department of Defense*, Washington, D.C., 1988, pp. 3–12.

been variously attributed either to the Department of Defense Ad Hoc Committee to Study and Revise the Officer Personnel Act of 1947 (also known as the Bolte committee, after its chairman General Charles L. Bolte) or to DoD's Officer Personnel Study Group and the 1968 Report on General and Flag Officer Requirements.[4] These 16 factors were grouped into three categories.[5]

The first was the nature of the position, which includes the type of position, special qualifications, and engagement with high-level officials, as well as the grade of supervisors, subordinates, and peers. The second category centered on the magnitude of the position's responsibilities, measured in terms of mission, geographic area, decisionmaking authority, or the number of personnel and equipment managed. The third category was the significance of actions and decisions to national security, prestige of the nation, and effectiveness of the national defense establishment.

As recently as 2011, Under Secretary of Defense for Personnel and Readiness Clifford Stanley testified before Congress that DoD still uses a slightly modified version of these same factors in determining whether a position should be filled by a G/FO.[6] Studies by DoD in 1968, 1972, and 1978, by Kapos Associates in 1988 and 1996, by LMI in 2003 and 2005, and by RAND in 2016 also used evaluation frameworks based on these factors.[7] A 1988 study of G/FO requirements conducted by the Hay group used a different framework that, nevertheless, took into account many of these same factors, such as number of personnel managed and impact of decisionmaking.[8]

The position-by-position analysis described in this chapter used data on all these factors for 1,113 G/FO requirements. (The data were collected by the OSD G/FO Management Office using a RAND-developed data protocol described in Appendix A.) We, then, used select criteria to determine whether a position was or was not a valid G/FO requirement. This approach was also used in RAND's 2016 study of reserve

---

[4] The 16 factors are: (1) characteristic of function, (2) grade and position, (3) supervision over the position, (4) official relations with U.S. and foreign governmental officials, and with the public, (5) reflection of national emphasis and determination, (6) special qualifications required by the position, (7) missions of the organization and special requirements of the position, (8) number, type, and value of resources managed and employed, (9) geographical area of responsibility, (10) authority to make decisions and commit resources, (11) development of policy, (12) national commitment to international agreements, (13) auxiliary authorities and responsibilities inherent to the position, (14) impact on national security or other national interests, (15) importance to present and future effectiveness and efficiency of the national defense establishment, (16) effect on the prestige of the nation or the armed forces. See GAO, *Military Personnel: General and Flag Officer Requirements Are Unclear Based on DOD's 2003 Report to Congress*, April 2004, pp. 14–15; Secretary of Defense, *Report of General and Flag Officer Requirements*, Washington, D.C., April 1978, pp. 23–28, Appendices E and I.

[5] Kapos Associates, *Analysis of U.S. Marine Corps General Officer Billet Requirements*, Final Report–Basic Phase, Arlington, Va., KAI 152.96F, July 31, 1996a, pp. 24–26.

[6] Stanley and Gortney, 2011, p. 62.

[7] Secretary of Defense, *Report of General and Flag Officer Requirements*, pp. 23–28, Appendices E and I; Kapos Associates, 1996a, pp. 24–29; GAO, 2004, pp. 14–15; Harrington et al., 2016, pp. 31–32.

[8] Hay Group, 1988, pp. 17–19.

component G/FOs.[9] Unlike many previous studies, RAND's analysis did not rank order positions using a criteria-based weighting scheme and chose, instead, to designate positions based on whether they met any one of the G/FO criteria, as described in the second half of this chapter.

Analysis of Current General and Flag Officer Positions

Prior studies that reviewed general and flag officer positions all were based on a similar underlying principle: if a position has enough factors associated with a general or flag officer, then the requirement is justified. In our more conservative methodology, we identify positions that do not meet any of the key factors associated with a general or flag officer. RAND selected factors for use in its position-by-position evaluation based on priorities outlined by DoD. In his comments to Congress in 2011, Clifford Stanley, then Under Secretary of Defense for Personnel and Readiness, outlined the services' approach to validating general officer requirements:

> They assess any statutory requirements; the nature of the position's duties and magnitude of its responsibilities; the span of control and scope of resources managed; and the significance of actions and decisions required by the position along with the importance of the position's mission accomplishment to national security and other national interests.[10]

Using this as a blueprint for evaluation, RAND further defined these characteristics and developed a filtering approach that assessed each position against a defined set of criteria according to the data provided by OSD. If a position met one or more of the criteria it warrants being filled by a general or flag officer. The filters were applied sequentially, which affects the relative number of positions filtered by each factor but does not change the final number of positions assessed to be G/FO requirements. The rest of this section discusses each factor, in turn, and the number of requirements identified.

In our evaluation, we identified 11 factors (emphasized in bold font) organized under the following questions that characterize G/FO requirements:

Does the position fulfill a mandatory requirement as defined in statute?
The first filtering criteria determined if the position was explicitly authorized in the U.S. Code and was, therefore, a **mandatory requirement**. The majority of these positions included service chiefs and vice chiefs as well as combatant commanders.[11] These

---

[9] For further discussion of this method and its application to reserve G/FOs, see Harrington et al., 2016.

[10] Stanley and Gortney, 2011, pp. 62–63.

[11] The specific statutory positions filtered for included: 10 USC §152, §154, §164, §604, §3033, §3034, §3084, §5033, §5035, §5043, §5044, §8033, §8034, §10502, 50 USC 2406.

positions have specific functions or duties defined by Congress that require a G/FO in the position. In our position-by-position evaluation, these positions meet the requirement for a G/FO based solely on this single factor. Other approaches in the RAND methodology did not assume statutory authorization was sufficient justification for requiring a G/FO. Twenty-nine positions, almost all at the grade of O-10, met the criteria for a G/FO requirement due to this factor.

Does the position require filling by an officer due to its military essentiality?

Many of the prior G/FO studies emphasized that military essentiality was a defining characteristic of why a position requires a general or flag officer. However, this factor supports that a position be filled by an officer but not necessarily a general or flag officer. The two questions that assisted in characterizing a position as militarily essential were questions about the nature of the position, in this case if the position was characterized as "commander," and the characteristics of the organization—whether the organization was categorized as "operating forces" or "theater." These two criteria establish that the position either **exercises command of a military unit** or the position **resides in an organization with an operational military focus.**

After additional consideration and feedback from the services and Joint Staff, text analysis of the data was also performed to determine if the position was **in charge of significant military formations.**[12] This additional factor would take into consideration the essence of generalship by reflecting the significance of leading considerable military formations, of military responsibilities in the employment of force, of military duties in being held accountable for mission effectiveness and readiness, and of military powers to pronounce judgment on discipline and punishments.

This factor had the single largest impact on the filtering process, with 376 positions assessed as meeting the criteria for G/FO requirements due to their characterization as commanders and another 75 positions assessed as G/FO requirements due to the positions being categorized as military operations or theater. An additional 78 positions met criteria for a G/FO requirement because the position was in charge of significant military formations.

Does the position have a significant magnitude of responsibilities?

Another factor used by many previous G/FO studies to justify a position as requiring a general or flag officer was whether the position had significant responsibilities. In this case, the RAND team defined this to mean: Does the individual in the position **manage a significant number of personnel?** Or does the individual **manage a significant amount of money?** The thresholds for these quantitative metrics were set to be relatively stringent and, thus, conservative; only the positions in charge of the greatest magnitude of resources were assessed to be G/FO requirements on this basis

---

[12] Text analysis was run on the position's direct reporting units for the following words: Army/Corps, Brigade/MEB/AAMDC, COCOM, Division, Fleet, Group, MAJCOM, MEF, NAF/Equivalent, Operation, Service Component, SFC, Staff, Subunified, Training Command, TSC/ESC/Log Group, TYCOM, Wing/AEW/MAW.

alone. The threshold for "significant number of personnel" was if the number of authorized personnel managed (including commissioned officers, warrant officers, enlisted personnel, and civilians) totaled 15,000 or more. Only around 16 percent of all G/FO positions managed more than this number of personnel.

RAND's determination of whether a significant amount of monetary resources was managed was based on the annual total obligation authority reported for each position. In some cases, however, the submitted data portrayed deputy commanders and deputy program directors as managing the same level of monetary resources as the full commanders and directors of their organizations. Due to the tendency for this particular metric to be inflated at times in the data, RAND applied a quite stringent threshold of $15 billion in the filtering process. Only around 8 percent of all G/FO positions managed more than this level of monetary resources. (The issue of deputy or vice commanders and directors will be handled with another criterion.)

Seventy-seven total positions were assessed as G/FO requirements due to the magnitude of their responsibilities—29 due to the magnitude of personnel managed and 48 due to the magnitude of monetary resources managed.

Does the position interact at a senior level with other organizations?

A common justification for why a position requires a general or flag officer is that the position often interacts on a frequent basis with other senior level positions and, therefore, the position requires parity with those other positions. The protocol included questions that asked that the role of a position be evaluated at the national and international level by determining (1) **the frequency of interaction with senior government officials,** or (2) **the frequency of interaction with senior political officials, state and local authorities, foreign government and foreign military leaders, nongovernmental organization senior leadership, and the press at the national level.** If the position was deemed as interacting with any of these types of officials as part of their primary duties (defined as greater than or equal to 50 percent of their monthly responsibilities) then it was determined that the position met the criteria for a general or flag officer requirement.

These criteria also filtered out a relatively large number of positions as G/FO requirements. One hundred seventy-seven positions were assessed as G/FO requirements on the basis of their engagement with senior U.S. government officials and another 39 positions were assessed as G/FO requirements on the basis of their extensive engagement with other senior authorities and organizations.

Does the position have a general/flag officer subordinate?

The **grade of principal subordinates managed** by the position was another factor used to determine whether a position warranted a general or flag officer. If the position managed an O-8 or higher, then the position met the criteria for being filled by a general or flag officer as it most likely requires a senior managing official. However, it is possible that these positions could adequately be filled with a high-level civilian placed in the managerial position—a determination we did not make in this approach. But the factor at least points to the need for a more-senior manager to fill the position.

Only 16 positions were determined to meet the criteria for G/FO requirements on the basis of this factor alone.

Does the position require independent span of decisionmaking?

Prior G/FO studies have shown that **significant independent decisionmaking** is a critical element in the evaluation of military general officership. This factor was formed from a free-response question in the protocol specifically asking for areas of decision-making authority and independence. Not all respondents completed this question.

While responses were somewhat subjective in nature, RAND developed a scheme to categorize the responses into one of three progressive categories based loosely on Bloom's taxonomy of intellectual behaviors.[13] From least to most complex, the three categories addressing span of decisionmaking were characterized by the following representative actions, behaviors, or descriptions:

- Understand, comprehend, experience, learn, implement, assimilate, apply, catalog, formulate, affect, interpret, commit, explain, describe
- Analyze, balance, efficient, effectiveness, tradeoff, generalize, create alternatives, allocate resources, determine
- High order critical thinking, integration, evaluation, diversity of perspective, expansive, agility, innovation, decide.

RAND reviewed all submissions and coded the free-form responses into one of these three categories. Only positions that fell into the third category, characterized by high-order critical thinking, were filtered out as G/FO requirements. While some positions met this criterion because it was one of the final filters applied, no additional positions met the criteria for a G/FO requirement based solely on this criterion.

Does this position oversee an extensive physical or virtual operating area?

Similarly, **responsibility for significant geographical areas** has been found in prior studies to be related to generalship. Given the complexity and expanse of today's battle space, RAND extended this variable to also include virtual areas of responsibility (such as space and cyber). Free-form responses to this question were wide-ranging and had to be recoded into a more meaningful scale. Judgments were made to categorize responses into one of the following four categories:

- None or minimal: oversight or involvement but not direct responsibility of geographical or virtual space

---

[13] Lorin W. Anderson and David R. Krathwohl, et al., eds., *A Taxonomy for Learning, Teaching, and Assessing: A Revision of Bloom's Taxonomy of Educational Objectives*, Boston, Mass.: Allyn & Bacon (Pearson Education Group), 2001.

- Limited physical or virtual areas: classrooms, buildings, offices, some small amount of air, sea, land, or virtual area
- Training areas or installations: physical or virtual
- Extensive physical or virtual operating areas of responsibility.

Analysis of responsibility for extensive operating areas showed that many positions met this filter. Most of these, however, also met other criteria, such as military essentiality, which were applied earlier in the process. Fourteen positions were identified as G/FO requirements based solely on the extent of their areas of operational responsibility.

Additional Factors

Once these 11 factors were established, RAND worked with the DoD G/FO Working Group to determine if additional criteria should be considered based on RAND's preliminary findings. As noted earlier, the DoD working group requested the position-by-position approach also include the construct of "leads significant military formation" in the specification of military essentiality factor. Based on the services and Joint Staff experiences and recommendations, RAND added two more factors to review a position. These two inclusion factors were:

- Does a general/flag officer not currently fill the position?
- Is the position a deputy of an organization (to include deputies, vices, and chiefs of staff not in significant military formations)?[14]

If a position was not filled by a general or flag officer (as of March 2017, when the data were collected) it was flagged as "does not meet criteria for a G/FO requirement" given that this factor generally reflects a relatively lower level of service priority for the particular position. Sixty-four positions assessed as G/FO requirements during the initial filtering process were recategorized as not being G/FO requirements on the basis of this factor.

Deputies of organizations that were not deemed as militarily significant formations (such as Army corps, Air Force wings, and other organizations in charge of military operations) were also assessed as not being G/FO requirements. For this factor, it was determined there may be redundancies in the position or these might be positions to consider for conversion to civilian positions. Ninety positions were affected by this filter.

---

[14] The filtering process for G/FO requirements used titles as provided by the services and Joint Staff. There was no service or Joint Staff policies or instructions that guided the consistent application of the titles of "deputy," "vice," and "chief of staff." Therefore, we treated all such positions as equivalent. However, for such positions that were part of a "significant military formation" (defined earlier), we did consider deputy, vice, or chief of staff as sufficient to be a G/FO requirement.

Once positions were filtered through each of the factors, RAND examined the findings to ensure there were no anomalous outcomes. Similarly, we reviewed all positions that met criteria for a G/FO to determine if the positions were properly filtered. Particular attention was given to those positions that only met one or two criteria for a general or flag officer.

Figure 4.1 depicts the results of the filtering process and the number of requirements affected at each step. We began, as noted, with 1,113 positions. In filtering positions for "mandatory requirements," the first factor listed in the figure, 29 positions met this criterion and so were set aside. This left 1,084 positions, which were filtered through the next criteria, "nature of position: commander." Here, 376 positions met the criteria. The filtering process continued in a similar fashion through the remaining criteria, at which point 232 positions remained that did not meet any of the 11 criteria. Then the 881 positions that did meet one or more of the 11 criteria were tested against the two additional criteria, "filled by non-G/FO," which resulted in 64 positions not

Figure 4.1
Findings from Position-by-Position Filtering Process

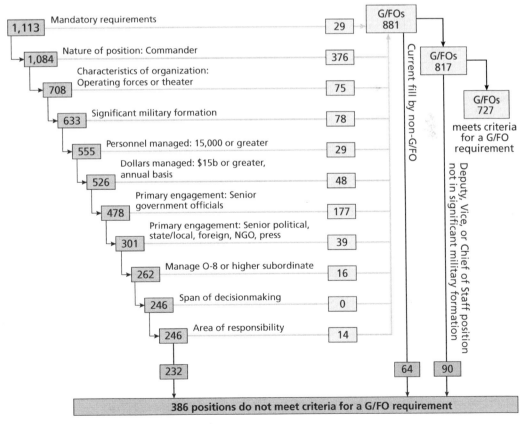

meeting the criteria, and "deputy, vice, or chief of staff positions not in a significant military formation," which resulted in 90 positions that did not meet the criteria. In the end, 727 positions met the criteria for a G/FO requirement and 386 (232 + 64 + 90) did not.

The findings from this approach answer the following question: Does the position meet the position-by-position criteria for a G/FO requirement? The findings are reported for each requirement as:

- Yes, meets criteria for a G/FO requirement.
- No, does not meet criteria for a G/FO requirement.

One limitation of this approach is that the filters were applied singularly and a position either met or did not meet the criteria. While this was helpful in determining whether a position merited a general or flag officer, it was not designed to indicate the officer grade or the distribution of those grades, O-7 to O-10, that was best suited for the position. In future studies, a combination of filtering factors could help identify that level of granularity. RAND did review each position to determine how many factors it met, but, ultimately, did not make any additional judgments about a position on this basis. It could be argued that some factors might be more indicative of requiring a G/FO than others; this is another area that could be investigated in future studies.

Summary of Position-by-Position Findings

A total of 727 positions (65 percent) were assessed in the position-by-position evaluation as meeting the criteria for G/FO requirements. Conversely, 386 positions (35 percent) were assessed as not G/FO requirements. Although the filtering method was applied independent of service, the results in Table 4.1 show slightly larger numbers of Air Force and Army G/FO positions did not meet the criteria for a G/FO requirement. Of all categories, joint positions were most likely to not meet the criteria for a

Table 4.1
Position-by-Position Findings by Service or Joint

Service/Joint	Meets Criteria for G/FO Requirement	Does Not Meet Criteria for G/FO Requirement
Air Force	64%	36%
Army	68%	32%
Marine Corps	73%	27%
Navy	79%	21%
Joint	57%	43%

Table 4.2
Position-by-Position Findings by Grade

Grade	Meets Criteria for G/FO Requirement	Does Not Meet Criteria for G/FO Requirement
O-10	100%	0%
O-9	88%	12%
O-8	67%	33%
O-7	57%	43%

G/FO requirement. This was, perhaps, expected to some degree, given that Congress identified the joint pool as the source of the largest number of mandatory cuts in the 2017 NDAA.

The distribution of results by grade, in Table 4.2, shows a strong relationship between the proportion of positions not determined to be G/FO requirements and authorized grades. While all of the O-10 requirements were assessed to be G/FO requirements, only 57 percent of O-7 positions were. This conforms to expectations, in that the filtering process was applied consistently regardless of grade. Moreover, many of the criteria are most likely to be met by the positions that the services have determined should be filled by the most experienced G/FOs rather than by more-junior level O-7s or O-8s.

The results were markedly different across different types of positions, as shown in Table 4.3. Almost all commander positions were assessed to be G/FO requirements,

Table 4.3
Position-by-Position Findings by Type of Position

Type of Position	Meets Criteria for G/FO Requirement	Does Not Meet Criteria for G/FO Requirement
Commander	96%	4%
Deputy or Vice Commander	63%	37%
Director	56%	44%
Deputy Director	5%	95%
General/Flag Staff	64%	36%
Chief of Staff	4%	96%
Program Executive Officer (PEO)/ Deputy PEO	73%	27%
Other	56%	44%

with the sole exception being the 4 percent of commander positions that were not currently filled by a G/FO. Conversely, nearly all Chiefs of Staff and Deputy Director positions were not assessed as G/FO requirements given that the DoD G/FO Working Group wanted to make this factor an explicit filtering element to allow the service and Joint Staff the opportunity to specifically review such positions for potential redundancy.

Results also varied by functional area of the position and type of organization, as shown in Tables 4.4 and 4.5, respectively. More than half of positions in the Intelligence, Manpower and Personnel, Program Management/Financial Management, Strategic Plans and Policy, and Special Staff categories were not assessed as G/FO requirements. Conversely, the great majority of military operations positions (80 percent) were assessed as G/FO requirements. Positions at the Joint Staff and in national-level organizations were less frequently assessed as G/FO requirements in the filtering process, while positions associated with operating forces were frequently assessed as G/FO requirements.

Table 4.4
Position-by-Position Findings by Functional Area

Functional Area	Meets Criteria for G/FO Requirement	Does Not Meet Criteria for G/FO Requirement
Acquisition/Research and development	68%	32%
Command, control, communications, computers and intelligence (C4I)	63%	37%
Capabilities development/Integration	55%	45%
Engineer	67%	33%
Force management, development, education and training	73%	27%
Intelligence	46%	54%
Manpower and personnel	44%	56%
Materiel and logistics	72%	28%
Military operations	80%	20%
Other	67%	33%
Program management/Financial management	48%	52%
Special staff (legal, medical, public affairs, chaplain, congressional affairs)	50%	50%
Strategic plans and policy	33%	67%

Table 4.5
Position-by-Position Findings by Type of Organization

Type of Organization	Meets Criteria for G/FO Requirement	Does Not Meet Criteria for G/FO Requirement
Combatant command	59%	41%
Defense, joint, or service agency	54%	46%
Direct reporting unit/ Shore-based bureaus/ Acquisition activity/Supporting establishment/Field operating agencies	72%	28%
Joint Staff	34%	66%
Major commands/Service commands/Type commands	63%	37%
National	33%	67%
Operating forces	84%	16%
Office of the Secretary of Defense	56%	44%
Service chief staff headquarters	51%	49%
Service component command	78%	22%
Service secretariat	67%	33%
Theater	88%	12%
Other	75%	25%

CHAPTER FIVE

Forced-Choice Exercise

As part of our effort to review DoD's G/FO requirements, we asked senior-level military and civilian representatives to participate in a forced-choice exercise hosted by RAND in August 2017. The aim of the half-day exercise was to identify priorities for how four- and three-star G/FOs should be used and to identify areas of consensus and tension. Key themes participants were asked to consider included:

- How to evaluate grade and position tradeoffs between line and non-line functions.
- The roles for G/FOs in OSD, defense agencies, and DoD field activities.
- Guidelines for when grade parity is preferred in international environments.
- Whether legislation should be drafted to specify grade caps for service component commands.
- The most essential service and joint leadership positions.

Forcing Choices and Learning from Games

Igor S. Mayer explains simulation games as both experimental and experiential. They are:

> *rule-based, interactive* environments, where players *learn* by *taking actions* and by *experiencing* their *effects* through *feedback mechanisms* that are deliberately built into and around the game. Gaming is based on the assumption that the *individual* and *social learning* that emerges *in* the game can be *transferred* to the world *outside* the game [italics in original].[1]

We chose a game format to learn about senior-level priorities for G/FO positions for several reasons. First, a game tends to produce more participant engagement than a survey, interview, or workshop. This type of engagement creates a greater possibility of observing types of interactions that would be difficult or unlikely to be reproduced by

---

[1] Igor S. Meyer, "The Gaming of Policy and the Politics of Gaming: A Review," *Simulation & Gaming*, Vol. 40, No. 6, 2009.

other analysis, such as rebuttals, cross-team coordination, and decisions impacted by another participant's concerns. As economist and RAND alumnus Thomas Schelling observed about the benefits of gaming, "One thing a person cannot do, no matter how rigorous his analysis or heroic his imagination, is to draw up a list of things that would never occur to him."[2]

Second, a game environment can help experts break out of behavioral and cognitive norms. Research suggests that substantial expertise can result in cognitive rigidity and adherence to traditional analytic frames.[3] By framing policy issues through different models, gaming can spur participants' creativity as they analyze information and make decisions outside of the normal parameters of their everyday roles. Eliciting participants' preferences and strategies via a different type of cognitive engagement can lead to valuable insights that more traditional analysis might not. To this point, Peter Perla and ED McGrady note:

> We believe that wargaming's power and success (as well as its danger) derive from its ability to enable individual participants to transform themselves by making them more open to internalizing their experiences in a game—for good or ill. The particulars of individual wargames are important to their relative success, yet there is an undercurrent of something less tangible than facts or models that affects fundamentally the ability of a wargame to transform its participants.[4]

An additional ancillary benefit of gaming is that the participants are exposed to a level of collaboration and interaction they might not otherwise experience and may come away with greater understanding and buy-in of the game topic. In our game's case, several participants are key leaders who are responsible for analyzing G/FO requirements in DoD. In addition to the valuable information the game play and results provided for our analysis, we also saw the game as a useful tool to expose these military and civilian leaders to other perspectives and possibilities in G/FO management.[5]

The exercise was loosely based on the forced-choice method, a common tool used in gaming and in other research fields, such as social psychology and consumer behavior. In games, the forced-choice method is used to understand absolute preferences and require the respondent to make definitive and consequential decisions even if they would prefer to remain neutral or uncommitted. Generally the forced-choice method is employed in a survey, where the respondent must select from a small set of provided

---

[2]   Pardee RAND Graduate School Center for Gaming, "Context," webpage, undated.

[3]   Gregory Schraw, "Knowledge: Structures and Processes," in Patricia A. Alexander and Philip H. Winn, eds., *Handbook of Educational Psychology*, 2nd ed. (American Psychological Association, 2006), p. 259.

[4]   Peter Perla and ED McGrady, "Why Wargaming Works," *Naval War College Review*, Vol. 64, No. 3, Summer 2001, pp. 111–130.

[5]   For additional information on the utility of gaming in policy analysis, see, for example, Yuna Wong, *How Can Gaming Help Test Your Theory?* The RAND blog, RAND Corporation, 2016.

answers, and is designed so the respondent is not able to defer or remain neutral in his or her response. Research shows participants tend to choose "neutral" or "no choice" options when it is difficult to determine the best option among the alternatives.[6]

The forced-choice method offers several benefits in games such as the exercise we hosted. At its most fundamental level, forcing choices prevents participants from avoiding tough decisions. Further, the desire to avoid criticism and negative judgment by others has been shown to influence participants to choose "no decision" or "neutral" options that do not require explanation when those responses are available.[7] Given the sensitivity of our game's topic to the participants, we wanted to preclude the possibility that some players might opt out of a decision for these reasons.

The forced-choice method is not always beneficial, depending on the answers that game planners are seeking and the types of players involved. For example, some argue that the forced-choice method requires participants to choose among alternatives they genuinely might not know about (as opposed to feeling neutral about or not wanting to choose among other available alternatives).[8]

Our exercise relied on the fundamental principles of the forced-choice method—requiring an active choice and removing the possibility of "no decision"—to ensure that participants were compelled to make difficult choices and employ strategies beyond an equitable cut across all positions. However, our game departed from the traditional forced-choice model in that no survey was administered. While participants' choices were constrained, decisions were rendered by physically placing counters on a game board, and choices could also be changed or traded under the game rules.

Game Purpose and Structure

As mentioned, the goal of the game was to identify participants' priorities for how four- and three-star G/FOs should be used. We intended to use the game's constraints and small mixed-team structure to highlight areas of consensus and tensions; to identify mediation or mitigation actions for current G/FO requirements that are not met; and to explore perceived risks or consequences that result from decisions, such as readiness or operational implications. In essence, the game served as a way to understand the preferences and cultural norms of those familiar with current DoD organization

---

[6] Ravi Dhar and Itamar Simonson, "The Effect of Forced Choice on Choice," *Journal of Marketing Research*, Vol. 40, No. 2, May 2003, pp. 146–160.

[7] Itamar Simonson and Stephen M. Nowlis, "The Role of Explanations and Need for Uniqueness in Consumer Decision Making: Unconventional Choices Based on Reasons," *Journal of Consumer Research*, Vol. 27, Issue 1, June 1, 2000, pp. 49–68.

[8] Douglas Ducharme, *Survey Response Categories: Guide for Using Neutral or N/A Options,* United States Naval War College Wargaming Department, undated.

and G/FO management practices—understanding that these norms have evolved over time and are different today than in previous eras.

The exercise was structured in two moves: the first move considered only four-star positions and the second focused on groups of three-star positions. Thus, decisions made in the first move of the game created consequences for the second move of the game. In both moves, teams were provided with notional reductions in G/FO authorizations that were purposely stringent to force the teams to make difficult choices—but the reductions were, nonetheless, based on realistic scenarios. Further, so participants could explore the full range of priorities, we removed from game play statutory constraints that govern G/FO positions and ranks.

Five four-person teams were composed of senior-level participants—both military and civilian—from the services, OSD, the Joint Staff, and other subject matter experts.[9] These representatives included both active-duty and retired G/FOs up to the three-star level. We purposefully organized the group into small teams to facilitate more participant interaction and to observe how the teams' strategies and decisions differed and how they collectively arrived at decisions in the larger group.[10] The teams were structured so that ranks of participants were roughly equal within a team to preclude a single higher-ranking player from dictating team play.

The entirety of the exercise followed the Chatham House Rule to encourage openness. While note takers were assigned to observe internal team deliberations as well as the group discussion, participants were assured that no remarks would be attributed to either an individual or an organization.

The findings from this approach answer the following question: Was the position identified during the forced-choice exercise as a priority three- or four-star requirement (relative to other positions)? The findings were reported as:

- Meets criteria for a G/FO requirement at current grade
- Meets criteria for a G/FO requirement at a lower grade (downgrade)
- Does not meet criteria for a G/FO requirement (eliminate or convert to civilian)
- Conflicting findings
- Not reviewed.

---

[9] The participants in the forced-choice exercise were currently serving three-star G/FOs, retired three-star G/FOs, and current and former civilian senior executives. Collectively the group reflected diverse operational experience in command, operations organizations staffs, service staffs, service secretariats, the Joint Staff, combatant command staff, OSD staff, and reserve component headquarters. They also represented a wide range of functional expertise in strategy and doctrine, acquisition, manpower and personnel, aviation, intelligence, medical, infantry, supply, security, training and education, and resources and programming.

[10] We allow that different participants could arrive at different results. However, we feel we mitigated such variability by (1) having five teams working independently, (2) building teams with diverse participant background and expertise, and (3) providing plenary sessions for group discussion, interaction, and consensus building.

Move One: Four-Star General and Flag Officers

In the first move, teams were asked to respond to a theoretical NDAA mandate to reduce the total number of active-duty officers in the grade of general or admiral from 38 to 20. The game board depicted all current four-star requirements; dual-hatted assignments were acknowledged but appeared only once on the game board. The teams received chips to physically allocate among the four-star positions on the board they chose to retain as a four-star. For the remaining four-star requirements that were not filled, the teams were directed to choose from the following options:

- Downgrade to a lower grade.
- Convert to a civilian.
- Multi-hat an individual holding two or more positions.
- Consolidate organizations under a single position.
- Eliminate the position.

Teams were forced to determine a specific action to apply to each four-star position; "neutral" or "no decision" determinations were not allowed. If four of the five groups selected the same decision for a particular position, game moderators determined that position to be "locked," meaning the group as a whole had collectively decided which action should be taken in that position's case. For the unlocked positions, the teams were given the option to barter with other teams to trade votes so that a particular position could become locked. Teams discussed the reasons for their decisions, the risks incurred by the unfilled four-star positions, and tensions between service and joint four-star positions. Following the four-star move, a list of positions downgraded to three-star rank was created to use in move two, or the three-star scenario.

While each team worked separately during their initial four-star move, and none arrived at the exact same answers as any other, a number of commonalities were observed. Most teams adopted a similar overall approach to the problem and adhered to similar decisionmaking principles in each move, which resulted in initial sets of findings that looked quite alike. This made consensus easy to reach on many of the positions, with disagreement tending to center on a more limited set of positions that teams had already identified as borderline cases.

Player Approaches and Principles

The teams' approaches to the exercise emerged organically out of their internal discussions, and certain principles were evident in discussions. Four of the teams approached the exercise by rebuilding their set of G/FO positions from zero up to the allotted 20, beginning first with the requirements that the team immediately agreed must be retained before considering other positions. This "zero-based" or bottom-up approach may have been adopted due to the sheer magnitude of the constraints on authorizations required by the exercise or due to a sense that many current G/FO allocations are already skewed or unjustifiable. Just one of the teams took the opposite approach, beginning with the full existing set of 38 positions and picking out individual positions that might be downgraded or eliminated until they reached 20, though other teams, at times, briefly switched to this paring-down approach as the exercise progressed.

All the teams explicitly considered parity across services and made sure this principle was reflected in their decisions. This was especially true of the "larger services" of the Army, Air Force, and Navy, though parity for the smaller Marine Corps was also desired. Participants discussed and judged positions that were clearly shared by all services as a collective group rather than discussing each position individually. Even the heads of the services' various major commands that had no exact counterparts were still considered in relation to positions in other services as much as possible. Parity was not seen in terms of each service reducing their existing G/FO allocation by the same number or by the same proportion of cuts but, rather, in the total number of G/FOs allocated to each service at the end of the exercise. This approach to parity would have significant consequences for the Air Force, in particular, as it started with the highest number of existing G/FO authorizations and had the most to lose.

Team decisionmaking also followed the principle that command relationships should drive G/FO rank decisions. This led many participants to adopt a hierarchical approach to establishing four-star requirements. At the top of the hierarchy, in the "tier one of untouchable jobs," were the five positions at the very top of the military chains of command, namely the Chairman of the Joint Chiefs of Staff and then the chiefs of each of the four armed services. Below these positions came the combatant commands, the vice chiefs, and, finally, the services' major commands and geographic component commands.

In the combatant command and the major command tiers, the teams weighed positions in terms of their relative strategic importance as measured by the level of threat addressed by the organizations they led. Participants sought to allocate three-star G/FOs to less important commands, particularly in the case of the services' major commands. In the case of international G/FO commands, participants prioritized relative strategic importance over ensuring parity in grade with allied counterparts when deciding whether to downgrade a position.

The teams also considered combining organizations to consolidate G/FO requirements, particularly in cases where organizations' geographic or functional mission sets overlapped or complemented each other. In general, participants favored combining organizations over dual-hatting a single G/FO position to oversee two separate organizations. Where one of the two organizations to be combined was deemed less strategically important, it was slated for absorption by the other. Greater consideration was given to organizational changes that reversed decisions made in the past decade or two and simply represented a return to an earlier U.S. military command structure.

Participants did consider the potential for converting some G/FO positions to a senior level civilian position. These discussions centered primarily on the degree to which an organization pursued a primarily civilian or military mission, though the relative proportion of military to civilian subordinates was also considered. At least one team also saw potential continuity benefits arising from civilianization of positions that required highly specialized expertise, given the often-shorter tenure of G/FOs in any given job. In the end, most teams rejected civilianization as a viable option for the positions currently held by O-10s due to the military nature of their responsibilities.

Findings from the Four-Star Move

Table 5.1 contains the findings from the four-star game move. There was widespread agreement between most of the teams on a majority of positions. All five teams separately reached the same decision on 19 of the 38 positions, and four of the five teams found agreement on another nine decisions. At the outset of the plenary session these 28 positions were automatically "locked" into place, leaving another ten positions subject to further deliberation. The teams eventually reached consensus on four of these, though none was reached on the remaining six. These six comprised the four service vice chief positions, the Chief of the National Guard Bureau, and the dual-hatted Director of the NSA and Commander of U.S. Cyber Command (USCYBERCOM). While most, but not all, participants eventually agreed that the vice chiefs should probably be retained as four-star officers, no agreement was reached on the other two positions.

The results clearly reflected the high importance participants gave to service parity. Four out of five teams allocated the exact same number of G/FOs to each of the "larger services" of the Army, Air Force, and Navy, with the smaller Marine Corps receiving one or two fewer positions. The fifth team, which differed in providing the

Table 5.1
O-10 G/FO Positions Retained in the Forced-Choice Exercise, by Type and Service/Joint

Position Type	Joint	Air Force	Army	Marine Corps	Navy	Total
Chief	1 *(1)*	1 *(1)*	1 *(1)*	1 *(1)*	1 *(1)*	5 *(5)*
Vice	1 *(1)*	1 *(1)*	1 *(1)*	1 *(1)*	1 *(1)*	5 *(5)*
Major command		1 *(5)*	1 *(3)*		1 *(2)*	3 *(10)*
Service component		0 *(2)*	0 *(1)*		0 *(2)*	0 *(5)*
Combatant command	7 *(10)*					7 *(10)*
Other	0 *(3)*					0 *(3)*
Total	9 *(15)*	3 *(9)*	3 *(6)*	2 *(2)*	3 *(6)*	20 *(38)*

NOTE: Number of initial G/FO positions provided in italics.

Army one fewer authorization, was, however, quick to acquiesce to a final set of positions in which the Air Force, Army, and Navy all ended up with three O-10 positions and the Marine Corps with two. This represented a loss of three positions each for the Army and the Navy (from a starting point of six), no change for the Marine Corps, which kept both of its existing O-10s, and a loss of six of the Air Force's nine original positions. These results stood in stark contrast to those that would have resulted from an approach to parity that focused on equal cuts to each service, under which the Air Force would have retained a higher number of G/FOs than the other services.

The uppermost tier of positions, consisting of the Chairman of the Joint Chiefs of Staff and the chiefs of each service, were unanimously retained as O-10s. Most teams also placed the combatant commands, which in their chain of command answer directly to the Secretary of Defense, in or near this top tier. Three of the four functional combatant commands were unanimously retained as O-10s, as were two of the six geographic combatant commands. The group as a whole agreed to combine the other four geographic combatant commands into two, a combined Europe and Africa command and a combined Northern and Southern Command in the Americas. Within the constraints of the exercise, participants judged that Africa and South America were relatively less strategically important than other regions and could be combined with an adjacent higher priority region under a single four-star commander.

The group also considered separating the multi-hatted position that includes Commander, USCYBERCOM and the Director of the National Security Agency/Central Security Service (DNA/CSS). If these positions were separated and the director position was not civilianized, however, there would be a new G/FO requirement (likely an O-9 position). If it were civilianized, there remains an O-10 requirement for the commander of USCYBERCOM (given its elevation to a unified combatant command) that is mandated in law. In the end, there is no reduction in the overall number of G/FOs. During the exercise, no consensus on this position was reached. Only one team considered downgrading any combatant commander position, a finding that was outweighed by the other teams' decision to require that positions at this level remain designated as O-10.

While the teams all agreed that the Vice Chairman of the Joint Chiefs of Staff should remain a four star, this agreement did not extend to the vice chiefs of the armed services. Although each team followed the principle of service parity, in that they considered the vice chiefs as a group and made a blanket recommendation that covered all of them, the teams differed somewhat on whether to downgrade these positions to O-9 or retain them as O-10s. More than half the participants thought the vice chiefs, in carrying out the daily management of the services, required equivalent grade as the four-star service chief. Maintaining the O-10 grade for the vice chiefs was particularly necessary to effectively exercise authority over the service major commands, which are currently led by O-10s. Participants who recommended downgrading argued that the vice chiefs would have sufficient authority even as O-9s, as long as they were understood clearly to be acting on behalf of the O-10 service chief. This debate was largely settled in the group discussion in favor of retaining the vice chiefs at the grade of O-10.

The services' functionally focused major commands fell into the second tier of existing four-star requirements that had a high potential for downgrading, as they were all subordinate to the O-10 service chiefs. Four of the five teams proposed the larger three services should each retain a single O-10 major command with a force-providing function, in keeping with the services' primary Title 10 responsibilities to organize, train, and equip their forces. These were Army Forces Command, Navy Fleet Forces Command, and the Air Combat Command. The other seven service major commands were all slated for downgrading based on a majority of team decisions, despite some dissent.

The geographic service component commands also fell into this second tier, and all of them were unanimously recommended for downgrading. This was even true of the Air Force and Navy service component commanders in Europe that are also dual-hatted as the heads of NATO's Allied Air Command and Allied Joint Force Command. Participants did not see an overriding need for parity of grade with international counterparts, with several stating that a U.S. three-star officer could effectively serve in a position that an ally might choose, instead, to fill with a four-star officer.

Similarly, participants recommended the commanders of U.S. Forces Afghanistan and of U.S. Forces Korea (USFK) be retained as O-10 requirements only on a temporary basis, as warranted by changes in level of hostilities. While most teams suggested the current mission and threats in Afghanistan did not currently require an O-10 commander, they were split on whether the commander of USFK should be retained as an O-10 or downgraded to O-9.

Move Two: Three-Star General and Flag Officers

In the three-star move, teams were asked to respond to a theoretical NDAA mandate to reduce the number of active-duty officers in the grade of lieutenant general or vice admiral by 33 percent, from 165 to 110.[11] The NDAA also directed the Secretary of Defense to assess the consequences of limiting service component commanders to O-9 and recommend whether this is advisable. Due to the number of positions at the three-star grade, the game board depicted all currently existing three-star requirements in groups of positions established by RAND rather than as individual positions. The teams were provided handouts that listed the specific positions in each group; multi-

---

[11] A total of 165 O-9 requirements were considered in the forced-choice exercise. Thirty-six of these 165 were part of larger multi-hatted sets of requirements that have generally been filled by a single G/FO. These component requirements were considered separately whenever they fell into a separate group of positions used in the exercise. In the final results dataset, however, these O-9 component requirements were combined into a single multi-hatted requirement, as described in Appendix A, resulting in a total of 149 O-9 requirements.

hatted positions appeared only once. The positions that were downgraded to three-star rank during the four-star move were also included on the game board.

Teams were given chips that represented three-star authorizations, for a total of 110, to allocate among the 165 three-star requirements. Similar to the four-star move, teams were instructed to decide what to do with the uncovered (unfilled) positions. After deliberations, teams transferred their decisions to the main game board, met in plenary session to explain their decisions, and discussed areas of agreement and disagreement.

Teams were explicitly asked to consider positions in the set groups and largely followed this structure in their discussions, refraining from disputing the position categories. Teams appeared to struggle more with the greater number and variety of positions at the three-star level and were often less systematic in their decisionmaking than during the four-star move. Nevertheless, they employed many of the same principles used in the four-star move, and the five teams reached a similar level of agreement on most positions.

Player Approaches and Principles

In the three-star move, all the teams began with the initial 165 positions and sought to cut the list down to 110 by first identifying "low hanging fruit." None of the teams started with the positions they wanted to retain and built up from there. The teams also tended to discuss the position categories in the order they were presented on the game board rather than taking a tiered approach based on the military chain of command. They also made decisions about individual positions rather than categories of positions, similar to the four-star approach.

Service parity remained an important consideration. Participants made uniform decisions on positions that were clearly shared by all services as a collective group. However, the variety of positions and the clear differences in service structures at the three-star level often made this difficult. The principle that command relationships should be reflected in G/FO grade was also still followed when possible; but again, this principle was less easily applied to the three-star grade given the complexity of command structures involved. Decisions made in the four-star move were played out to have identifiable cascading effects down the command hierarchy, with three-star subordinates in commands that lost O-10 status facing elimination, combination, or downgrading.

Teams continued to consider relative strategic importance in their decisions, with particular priority to those positions that played the most direct role in military operations, such as unit commanders and the services' deputy chiefs of staff for operations. Teams sometimes prioritized positions in the National Capital Region, which was viewed as being well represented with G/FOs, less than those elsewhere, particularly compared to positions in the field. Participants also looked for the potential to combine related positions and absorb one organization into another or convert positions from military to civilian leadership, as in the four-star move.

Forced-Choice Exercise 57

Findings from the Three-Star Move

The findings from the three-star move are shown in Tables 5.2 and 5.3. All five teams chose to retain the exact same number of G/FOs in just six of the 26 groups of positions, namely each of the services' medical category and the downgraded O-10 positions for the service major commands and the joint combatant commands. Yet their answers clustered closely together in many other cases, signaling general agreement. For 12 categories, four of five teams sought to retain the same or similar numbers of

Table 5.2
O-9 G/FO Positions Retained in the Forced-Choice Exercise, by Type and Service

Position Type	Air Force	Army	Navy	Marine Corps	Total
Service Chief of Staff	3–8 *(10)*	4–7 *(11)*	3–7 *(8)*	5 *(6)*	15–27 *(35)*
Development and training	4 *(8)*	2–10 *(16)*	1–9 *(9)*	4 *(5)*	11–27 *(38)*
Operations	5–13 *(13)*	5–9 *(9)*	4 *(5)*	4 *(5)*	18–30 *(32)*
Medical	0 *(1)*	0 *(2)*	0 *(1)*		0 *(4)*
IG/JAG	0 *(2)*	0 *(2)*	0 *(2)*		0 *(6)*
Major commands (formerly O-10)	6 *(6)*	3 *(3)*	3 *(3)*		12 *(12)*
Total	18–31 *(40)*	14–29 *(43)*	11–23 *(28)*	13 *(16)*	56–96 *(127)*

NOTE: A single number is given when teams reached consensus, otherwise the range of results is shown. Number of initial G/FO positions provided in italics.

Table 5.3
O-9 Joint G/FO Positions Retained in the Forced-Choice Exercise, by Type

Position Type	Total
Combatant command	7–15 *(15)*
Defense agency and DoD field activity	1 *(8)*
Intelligence	1 *(4)*
Joint Staff	3–7 *(8)*
NATO/Alliance	6 *(9)*
Office of the Secretary of Defense	1 *(6)*
Combatant command (formerly O-10)	4 *(4)*
Total	23–35 *(54)*

NOTE: A single number is given when teams reached consensus; otherwise, the range of results is shown. Number of initial G/FO positions provided in italics.

G/FOs, with *similar* defined as deviating less than one from the group average. These near-agreement categories included the service inspector general and judge advocate general positions, all of the Marine Corps position groups, and the joint intelligence, defense agency, OSD, and alliance positions. Less agreement was reached on the numbers of G/FOs to retain in the Army, Navy, and Air Force categories of operations, development/training, and, especially, service chiefs.

The final allocations resulted in the services receiving somewhat different numbers of G/FOs, unlike in the four-star move. Service parity still played a part in the discussions of individual positions that had counterparts in other services; however, parity was reflected most clearly in the categories to which it was most easily applied, particularly medical and legal positions. Parity also came into the discussion around positions in the service chief category, particularly regarding the heads of the various staff sections as well as the development and training category. Participants found it more difficult to include cross-service parity in discussion of unit commanders in the operational categories given the significant differences in how each service structures their operational commands. Nevertheless, total allocations to the services converged somewhat in the teams' results, representing a greater degree of parity than in the starting set of current G/FO positions.

Operations positions were retained at the highest rate of any category of service position, though some teams downgraded several of these positions from the Army and Air Force. Development and training positions received steep cuts, primarily in the form of downgrading, though service academy positions were often slated for civilianization. The service chief category also saw a number of cuts, though teams were fairly unanimous in the need for retaining the most operationally focused positions, such as the heads of the operations, planning, and resourcing staff sections. The heads of the logistics and, especially, information staff sections were often downgraded, however.

On the joint side, OSD, the defense agencies, and intelligence categories were seen by some participants as prime candidates for both downgrading and conversion to civilian positions. Only the heads of the DHA and the Defense Intelligence Agency (DIA) were commonly retained as three-star G/FOs within these categories. Relatively little change was made to the combatant command categories, despite a few positions being downgraded or combined. All the combatant command positions downgraded in the four-star move were retained as O-9s during the three-star move, with the view being that reduction of one rank was more than enough, even in the case where a position was in charge of an organization, such as U.S. Africa Command, that had been absorbed by another. Major service commands that had been downgraded in the four-star move were similarly retained at the three-star level. Some cuts were made to positions within the NATO/Alliance category, but these positions were generally deemed to be of sufficient strategic importance for retention.

Summary of the Forced-Choice Exercise Findings

A total of 187 positions were used in the forced-choice exercise, including 38 O-10 and 149 O-9 positions. The overall results of the exercise are presented by service and grade in Tables 5.4 and 5.5. Nearly all the positions assessed during the exercise were retained as G/FO requirements, though the game's strict constraints resulted in half of these positions being retained at a lower G/FO grade than currently authorized.

During the exercise, participants identified seven positions that did not meet G/FO requirements. These joint positions represented just 4 percent of the total number of O-9 and O-10 positions:

- O-10 Commander, U.S. Africa Command: Eliminate position and combine with U.S. European Command
- O-10 Commander, U.S. Southern Command: Eliminate position and combine with U.S. Northern Command

Table 5.4
Exercise Results by Service/Joint

Service/Joint	Meets Criteria for a G/FO Requirement at Current Grade	Meets Criteria for a G/FO Requirement at Lower Grade (Downgrade)	Does Not Meet Criteria for a G/FO Requirement (Eliminate or Convert)	Conflicting Findings
Air Force	44%	54%	0%	3%
Army	43%	57%	0%	0%
Marine Corps	73%	27%	0%	0%
Navy	52%	48%	0%	0%
Joint	52%	32%	12%	5%
Total	50%	44%	4%	2%

Table 5.5
Exercise Results by Grade

Grade	Meets Criteria for a G/FO Requirement at Current Grade	Meets Criteria for a G/FO Requirement at Lower Grade (Downgrade)	Does Not Meet Criteria for a G/FO Requirement (Eliminate or Convert)	Conflicting Findings
O-10	55%	34%	5%	5%
O-9	48%	47%	3%	1%

- O-9 Director, Defense Security Cooperation Agency: Convert to senior civilian
- O-9 Director, Joint Improvised Threat Defeat Agency: Convert to senior civilian
- O-9 Director, Defense Logistics Agency: Convert to senior civilian
- O-9 Director, Joint Strike Fighter Program: Convert to senior civilian
- O-9 Director, Defense Information Systems Agency: Convert to senior civilian.

Another four positions received "Conflicting Findings," meaning that some teams assessed them as meeting G/FO requirements and other teams did not, with no agreement reached during the full group discussion. These four positions were:

- O-10 Chief, National Guard Bureau
- O-10 Director, National Security Agency
- O-9 Military Deputy to the Under Secretary of Defense for Personnel and Readiness
- O-9 Commander and President, Air University.

The most important insights arising from the exercise did not concern individual positions but, rather, the set of considerations participants felt should be included in decisionmaking. The team results suggest a much greater willingness to downgrade a G/FO position by a single grade than to eliminate a position entirely. While the participants often considered civilianizing a position, and the game placed no restriction on the number of positions that might be added to the requirements for senior civilians, this was seen as viable only for a very small minority of positions, given the need for uniformed senior leaders in militarily essential positions and limitations on the authorized number of civilian senior executives. Participants were willing to downgrade or even, in two cases, eliminate some G/FO positions that are specifically mandated by statute, identifying these as lower priorities for retention at current grade than other nonmandatory positions.

The importance of service parity was a clear theme, though there was also a general sense that the current balance of G/FO authorizations among the services does not represent ideal parity and that the number of joint G/FO positions might be too high. The positions most clearly responsible for military operations were prioritized for retention at current grade, along with the positions that most directly supported the services' fulfillment of their Title 10 responsibilities to man, train, and equip their forces. Participants also sought to ensure that G/FO grades reflected superior-subordinate relationships and, thus, reinforced the chain of command. Overall, participants sought to make decisions systematically and were largely able to do so in the O-10 portion of the exercise. However, they had more difficulty putting this into practice when faced with the more complex, varied, and larger set of O-9 G/FO requirements.

While the game was designed to generate robust insights into expert decision-making around G/FO requirements, some of the overall results were shaped by the way the game was executed. Most clearly, the large proportion of O-9 and O-10 positions that did not meet G/FO requirements at their current grade was a direct function of the size of reductions mandated in the game rules. The time limits placed on game play led to less systematic and deliberative approaches. The participants' lack of access to detailed written information on each position likely meant that some decisions were made based on erroneous assumptions, even though this was mitigated by the high level of collective expertise on G/FO positions residing in each team.

The exercise results are, nevertheless, a valid reflection of expert views from throughout the military services and defense establishment on G/FO requirements. Were the game to be run again, but with different individual participants, the overall results would likely be unchanged (even if findings for some individual positions would shift slightly in one or another direction). The division of participants into separate teams allowed the exercise to effectively run five separate times, each with a different set of participants. That each team independently adopted similar approaches and arrived at the same conclusion on a majority of positions suggests that these results are robust and not due simply to chance decisions on whom to invite and which participants to place on which teams.

CHAPTER SIX

Position Pyramid Health

Position pyramids have a strong effect on career paths within the military because the military system allows very limited entry above the lowest grade and requires that individuals be promoted regularly or else separate from the system, thus imposing movement upward through the pyramid. Examining the pyramid structure of military positions reveals much about how military careers are shaped. Such an examination also provides insights into how well the system meets the needs of the organizations where the positions exist.

The sponsor and the OSD G/FO Working Group asked RAND to develop an approach that considered whether a reduction in a G/FO position could restrict or prohibit the development of G/FOs for senior positions. DoD Directive 1100.4 (Guidance for Manpower Management) states as policy: "Sufficient manpower positions shall be designated as military to enable development of combat-related skills or to promote career development in military competencies."

The analysis discussed in this chapter, therefore, focuses on position pyramid health. A "healthy" position pyramid has benefits for both the organization employing the people and the people filling the positions. A healthy position pyramid should provide selectivity in choosing people to fill increasingly senior positions. Organizations tend to want to have more than one qualified candidate to choose from when vacancies occur—and in the military qualified candidates generally come only from within the service. Qualified candidates have the skills, abilities, and experience appropriate for a position. The wider the range of developmental experiences and assignments a pyramid affords, the more positions a person may be qualified for, and presumably this makes for more interesting and fulfilling careers from the individuals' perspective.

There is no hard-and-fast rule as to what is the minimum or ideal number of candidates. More is better but with important caveats. First, an organization should have a selection process that is fair to the candidates but also efficient, and this becomes more challenging as the candidate pool grows. Second, greater selectivity for an organization means less opportunity for an individual. Opportunity is generally a bigger concern for people pondering whether to join an organization, and for junior people considering whether to make a long-term commitment to an organization, than it is for very senior people with long careers behind them. Still, other things being equal, the military services would like to give even their G/FOs some opportunity for continued advancement. One of the challenges of managing a collection of G/FO positions is the trade-off between selectivity and opportunity.

Another challenge is the fact that the G/FO position pyramid is composed of many sub-pyramids. Some of these are basically self-contained while others are quite open, even across the services in the case of joint positions. The types of experiences people have and the skills they hone as a result of having specific positions within the pyramid affect selectivity and opportunity. In addition, how people move not just vertically within a sub-pyramid but also laterally between pyramids can create both opportunities and challenges for managing those people. G/FO management offices take great care to ensure there is a balance between promotion opportunity and selectivity, that necessary growth and joint experiences are available when needed, and that the overall size of a cohort in a particular skill area is in line with the anticipated future needs for senior leaders. A change to the size and shape of the individual service sub-pyramids, joint, and overall pyramids has implications for individuals and organizations.

This chapter addresses those implications. It introduces a tool that can be used to analyze changes to the size, shape, and composition of the pyramid that affect the factors addressed above, which collectively are indicators of pyramid health. In the following section, we explore the concept of pyramid health and detail the set of metrics used to assess it. The findings from this approach answer the following question: Would elimination of this position potentially worsen the health of the position pyramid?

Measuring Pyramid Health

Managing the large pool of G/FOs is a complex task that requires attention to detail and an understanding of the intricacies of job requirements and career development needs. G/FO management offices are experts in this area and take into account a vast number of complicated signals when making assignment decisions. While this level of detail is well beyond the scope of the analysis presented here, the metrics used in our analysis serve to give a general idea of the degree to which a potential reduction in requirements alters the shape of the G/FO pyramid. Taken in context with the motivations for and desired goals of a potential change, these metrics can provide a comparative "before-and-after" assessment that highlights possible differences in the way a future G/FO pyramid will function or need to be managed.

Sub-Pyramid Categories

To understand the impact of potential reductions, it is important to understand not only the number of job reductions but also something about the types of jobs identified for possible elimination, reduction to O-6, or conversion to a senior civilian position.

Every position requires a unique set of experiences and endows the officer filling it with a specific set of skills to take forward in his or her career. Not all jobs are fungible along an individual's career track. We do not explicitly model the prerequisites for every single position here but provide a framework of job categories called "sub-pyramids" to simulate some of these restrictions.

Most immediately, jobs can be classified according to the rank and service of the officers who fill them, as well as according to whether they are in-service or joint positions. Any assessment of pyramid health must take into account the shape of the pyramid within each individual service and specialty, accounting for any joint positions within that specialty that might be filled by that service. To better understand the impact of potential reductions on specific types of jobs, we introduce a set of sub-pyramids that loosely categorize jobs based on the types of officers that generally fill them. The set of sub-pyramids includes:

- Acquisition/Research and development
- Command, control, communications, computer, and intelligence
- Chaplain
- Engineer
- Intelligence
- Legal
- Manpower and personnel
- Materiel and logistics
- Medical
- Military operations
- Other special staff
- Program management/Financial management.

The sub-pyramids used in this analysis are based on functional areas provided to RAND as part of the requirements data received from the OSD G/FO Management Office. While functional areas apply to the job in question, the concern of pyramid health analysis focuses primarily on the types of officers available in the labor pool over time. These are clearly not the same, but understanding the number of jobs within a specific functional area for each grade and service gives some insight into the likely future ability to create the desired pyramid of labor experience and desired flow through the pyramid. In many cases, personnel will flow across sub-pyramids, allowing for increased flexibility in the system that is not captured by the sub-pyramids. However, sub-pyramids provide a useful, simplified way to quantify the effect of potential reductions on the size and shape of the pyramid of positions within specific functional categories. Additional fidelity to rules about cross-flows across communities and required experiences is added in the analysis using RAND's Military Career Model, discussed in Chapter Eight.

Pyramid Size and Shape Metrics

The metrics used to assess the overall size and shape of the G/FO pyramid measure three dimensions of pyramid health: pyramid size, vertical movement, and lateral movement through the system, as shown in Figure 6.1. These metrics do not capture the movement of individuals through the pyramids but, rather, focus on rates of flow through the system that would be required to sustain a pyramid of the desired shape.

Pyramid size quantifies the overall size (in number of positions) of the pyramid at each grade. Pyramid size is measured in number of promotions to the grade in question.[1] The number of promotions is calculated for promotion to grades O-7 to O-10 by dividing the number of individuals in that grade by the estimated average time-in-grade for that grade.[2] As a simple example, if there are 100 positions in a grade and average time in grade is four years, then in any given year one would expect about 25 (100/4) officers leaving the grade and the same number entering.[3] This metric helps identify especially small or large communities or grades within communities. Pyramid

Figure 6.1
Dimensions of Pyramid Health

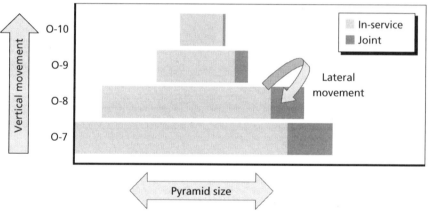

RAND *RR2384OSD-6.1*

---

[1]   For the purposes of our analysis we use the term *promotion* to mean promotion to the grades of O-7 and O-8 and *appointment* to the grades of O-9 and O-10. We also assume that promotions occur only from one grade below to the next higher grade (O-7 to O-8, O-8 to O-9, O-9 to O-10), acknowledging that actual promotions can, in some circumstances, skip one or more grades.

[2]   For modeling purposes, we assume time in grade of three years at O-7, three and a half years at O-8, four years at O-9, and five years at O-10. We do not use historical averages but, rather, idealized notional values, since the analysis we are performing is intended to model a future pyramid state, which does not necessarily mirror the past. Changing time in grade expectations to better support a new pyramid structure may be one technique for managing large changes to pyramid structure after eliminations.

[3]   This well-known relationship from queueing theory is known as Little's Law.

shape may be especially relevant for smaller communities, where changes to a small number of positions would have a larger overall effect.

Vertical movement is measured in terms of selectivity, which captures the relationship between personnel counts across grades to assess bench strength and promotion opportunity. This metric helps identify potential bottlenecks and areas with possible bench strength, opportunity, or selectivity issues. Selectivity measures the ratio between two grades. For example, selectivity from O-7 to O-8 is calculated as the number of officers promoted to O-7 per year (calculated as described above) divided by the number of people promoted to O-8 per year and measures the bench strength of the O-7 pool from which the O-8 pool can be selected. A related metric, the selectivity from O-8 to O-9, provides a measure of promotion opportunity to O-9 for those in the O-8 pool. Together, the selectivity from the lower grade and selectivity to the higher-grade metrics capture the overall shape of the pyramid.

Lateral movement is measured using a joint to in-service ratio at each grade and rank, providing insight into the number of joint opportunities available, the reliance on joint paths for development, and the possible challenges of managing joint versus in-service inventories. The joint to in-service ratio is calculated as the number of individuals leaving the joint pool annually at a certain grade divided by the in-service strength at that grade. The number of individuals leaving the joint pool annually is a function of the joint pool size at the current grade and the expected time in a joint job.[4] The joint to in-service ratio helps identify areas where development paths rely heavily (or not) on joint assignments and highlights areas where G/FO management offices may face challenges absorbing officers back into service positions following joint assignments.[5]

There are good reasons for these metrics to vary widely across services, specialties, and grades. However, extreme values for any of these metrics could highlight potential areas of concern given the size and shape of today's pyramids.[6] This analysis is not intended to provide a final assessment of the impact of eliminating or downgrading a particular job but simply to alert decisionmakers that further study of the pyramid size and shape may be warranted. Details of the metric calculations as well as some notes on values that could indicate areas for further investigation are provided in Table 6.1.

---

[4] As explained for the in-service time in grade, we assume an idealized notional time in job value of two years for joint jobs. Our computation again applies Little's Law.

[5] "Joint pool absorption" refers to the need to reabsorb officers leaving the joint pool back into in-service pyramids within specified authorization boundaries. G/FO management offices must plan ahead for the end of these officers' joint tenures to minimize in-service end-strength violations.

[6] Appendix E contains the values of these metrics for each service and joint pyramid.

Table 6.1
Pyramid Health Metrics

Metric	Metric Definition
Promotions (pyramid size)	Number in grade/time in grade. Generally, a smaller value could be indicative of negative pyramid health due to small pyramid size.
Selectivity (vertical movement)	Selectivity from grade X to grade Y: Number promoted annually to grade X divided by number promoted annually to grade Y. Generally, a smaller value could be indicative of negative pyramid health due to lack of selectivity. A larger value could indicate negative pyramid health due to lack of promotion opportunity.
Joint to in-service ratio (lateral movement	Number leaving joint pool annually in this grade divided by in-service grade strength. Generally, a larger number could be indicative of negative pyramid health due to a high reliance on joint jobs.

Pyramid Size and Shape

Using the pyramid calculator developed by RAND (and described in further detail in Appendix E), we were able to evaluate the size and shape of each functional pyramid. Each of the 1,113 G/FO positions in our database is associated with the three pyramid health metrics that apply to that position's service, grade, and functional sub-pyramid. For example, the Navy military operations sub-pyramid has 81 in-service positions once dual-hatted positions are taken into account. In addition, the Navy would be expected to have a proportional share of joint military operations positions. These numbers, by grade, are listed in Table 6.2 and provide the basis for our calculation of promotions, selectivity, and joint to in-service ratio. The Navy has 44 in-service military operations jobs at the grade of O-7, which represent 23 percent of all in-service O-7 military operations jobs (the Army has 75, the Air Force 54, and the Marine Corps 18). There are also 90 joint O-7 military operations jobs; 23 percent of that 90 is 20.7.[7] Thus the Navy's joint to in-service ratio for the military operations sub-pyramid is 0.47 at the grade of O-7.

With an average of 64.7 O-7 military operations positions to fill each year, the Navy would promote 21 or 22 officers in the military operations career fields to O-7 annually, if we assume an average time in grade of three years for O-7s. This is our second pyramid health number. Of course, promotions equal separations in a steady state, so 21 or 22 O-7s will leave each year, either through promotion or retirement. Assuming a slightly longer average time in grade for O-8 of 3.5 years would mean

---

[7]   Obviously, there's no such thing as seven-tenths of a job, but the way to interpret this number is that in a typical year the Navy would fill 21 O-7 joint jobs, only 20 O-7 joint jobs roughly every third year or so, and occasionally more than 21 or fewer than 20.

about 8 or 9 O-7s are promoted to O-8 in the military operations career fields each year. The ratio of 21 or 22 officers leaving O-7 to 8 or 9 officers entering O-8 each year is 2.5 (specifically, 21.6/8.6 = 2.5). This means the Navy has roughly five O-7s to choose from for every two O-8 vacancies. We have now calculated all three pyramid health metrics for the Navy's military operations pyramid at the grade of O-7.

We repeat these calculations for each service (including joint), functional sub-pyramid, and grade. The only difference in our calculations for joint positions is that the first two columns in Table 6.2 would include all in-service positions and all joint positions, respectively, for the functional subcategory in question. Table 6.3 shows how we calculate pyramid health numbers for joint positions in the military operations sub-pyramid.

It is important to note that promotion, selectivity, and joint to in-service metrics are associated with collections of positions—pyramids—not with any one individual

Table 6.2
Pyramid Health Calculations for Navy Military Operations Positions

Grade	In-Service	Joint Fair Share	Joint to In-Service	Total	Average TIG	Promotions per Year	Selectivity to Higher Grade
O-7	44	20.7	0.47	64.7	3	21.6	2.5
O-8	20	10.2	0.51	30.2	3.5	8.6	1.9
O-9	12	5.8	0.48	17.8	4	4.5	2.6
O-10	5	3.5	0.70	8.5	5	1.7	n/a

NOTE: The arrows in the table help the reader follow how the metrics are calculated.

Table 6.3
Pyramid Health Calculations for Joint Military Operations Positions

Grade	In-Service	Joint	Joint to In-Service	Total	Average TIG	Promotions per Year	Selectivity to Higher Grade
O-7	191	90	0.47	281	3	93.7	1.7
O-8	131	67	0.51	198	3.5	56.6	2.5
O-9	62	30	0.48	92	4	23.0	3.4
O-10	20	14	0.70	34	5	6.8	n/a

NOTE: The arrows in the table help the reader follow how the metrics are calculated.

position, as the results of the analysis of career field implications are reported in Chapter Eight. However, because Congress directed a global manpower study of requirements and the DoD G/FO Working Group required a method for reviewing each G/FO requirement, we were challenged to figure a way to not only associate the metrics with individual jobs but to collapse the three into one. This involved multiple steps. First, we had to determine what the metric would actually show, in a way that is consistent with the results of the other RAND approaches that focused on individual positions. Then we had to identify how to calculate the metric. Ultimately, we were able to combine the metrics to answer the question, "Would eliminating this position potentially worsen the health of the position pyramid?"

The first step to answering this question is to convert the joint to in-service ratio so that "bigger is better" from the perspective of the services. This entails calculating the inverse of the joint to in-service ratio (in other words, the in-service to joint ratio), the logic being that having a higher ratio of in-service to joint positions means the services have more control over the development and assignment of their officers and have fewer challenges managing their inventory within end strength constraints.

Now that all three metrics move in the same direction in terms of favorability from the perspective of the services, we take the geometric mean[8] of the three metrics for each service, functional sub-pyramid, and grade. Continuing with the Navy O-7 military operations example, the geometric mean of promotions, selectivity, and in-service to joint ratio is 4.85:

$$\sqrt[3]{\left(21.6 \times 2.5 \times \frac{1}{0.47}\right)}$$

Next, we eliminate a single Navy O-7 military operations position (in-service, not joint) and recalculate the three health metrics and their geometric mean. In other words, we recalculate the metric as though the Navy only had 43 in-service O-7 military operations positions instead of 44. The new measures are 21.1, 2.4, and 0.47, and their geometric mean is 4.78.

With the pre- and post-elimination numbers of 4.85 and 4.78, we can say that eliminating a single Navy O-7 military operations position reduced pyramid health, from the perspective of the Navy, by 1.58 percent (1 − 4.78/4.85).[9] We then repeat the

---

[8] The geometric mean is calculated as the *n*th root of the product of *n* numbers. It is often used when finding a single figure of merit among items that have different numeric ranges. The geometric mean tends to dampen the effect of very high or low values.

[9] Note, however, that this is the percentage decline in eliminating the first Navy O-7 military operations position going from 44 to 43 such positions. Eliminating a second Navy O-7 military operations position (i.e., going from 43 to 42 such positions) would result in a slightly larger decline (specifically, 1.62 percent). Each additional position eliminated would, similarly, generate a different percentage decline.

process for each combination of service, functional sub-pyramid, and grade. As before, for joint positions we calculate the metric using the total positions across all services within each grade and functional sub-pyramid.

The final step in answering the question, "Would eliminating this position worsen pyramid health?" entails setting a threshold based on the size of the decline in the consolidated pyramid health. Figure 6.2 shows ranges of the amount of decline of the geometric mean from eliminating a single position and the number of positions that fall within each range. For example, the geometric mean declined by between 5 and 10 percent for 126 positions.

To set the threshold for "worsening health," we looked at the distribution of percentage declines across all positions, and we consulted with the G/FO management offices who indicated that changes of less than 5 percent would be considered "noise" and only changes greater than 5 percent were worth investigating. Based on the data in Figure 6.2 and the G/FO management office perspectives, we selected a 5 percent decline as the cut-off point at which pyramid health would worsen. One-third of all G/FO positions in our database (350/1,044) would worsen their respective pyramid health by more than 5 percent if each position was eliminated individually, as shown

Figure 6.2
Distribution of Decline in the Geometric Mean from Eliminating a Single Position

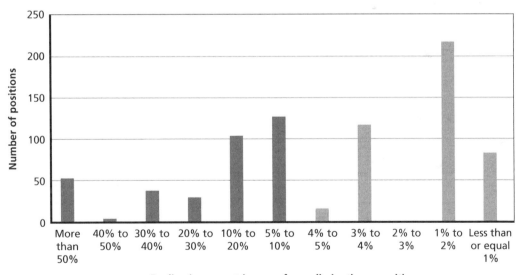

Decline in geometric mean from eliminating a position

NOTE: The chart represents a total of 779 positions. For the remaining 265 positions, the consolidated pyramid health metric did not decline at all or improved. 429 positions show decline in pyramid health of less than 5 percent (green bars). Forty-eight positions that are the only positions within their grade-service-category combination are included in the "More than 50%" category.

RAND RR2384OSD-6.2

by the blue bars in Figure 6.2.[10] If the finding for each position was reported as "yes," elimination of the position could potentially worsen position pyramid health; if "no," elimination of the position would not likely worsen pyramid health.

Summary of Position Pyramid Health Findings

We summarize the results of the pyramid health analysis in Figure 6.3. This figure shows whether the combined metric, calculated as the geometric mean of the three pyramid health metrics, would worsen by more than 5 percent if a single position were removed from a particular grade within each functional sub-pyramid. Areas where the

Figure 6.3
Would Removing a Position Worsen Pyramid Health?

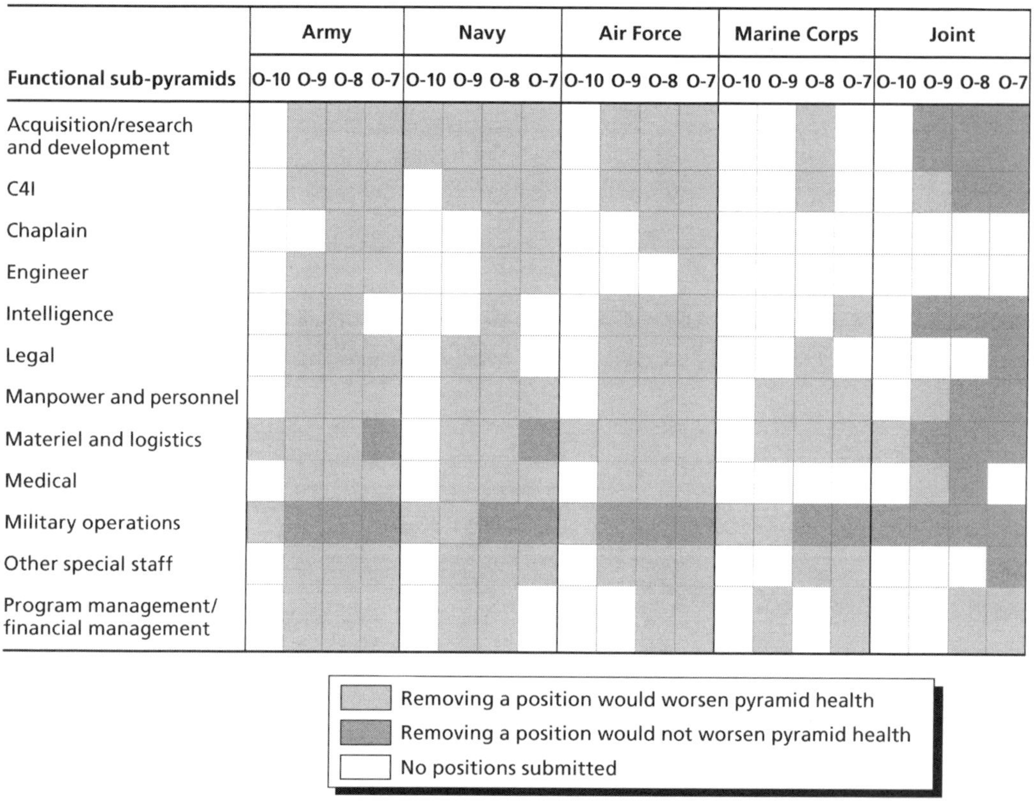

Removing a position would worsen pyramid health
Removing a position would not worsen pyramid health
No positions submitted

RAND RR2384OSD-6.3

---

[10] To give an idea of sensitivity around the 5 percent threshold choice, we note that 779/1,044 positions would not worsen their respective pyramid health at all if each position was eliminated individually. 224/1,044 positions would worsen by more than 10 percent.

combined metric would worsen by more than 5 percent are highlighted in yellow, while those areas where the metric worsens by less than 5 percent stays the same; improves are shown in green. At the 5 percent threshold, 114 of the 146 nonempty functional sub-pyramids indicate some concern (yellow). While this represents 78 percent of the nonempty sub-pyramids, it represents only 34 percent of all positions, again indicating that larger sub-pyramids are less likely to exhibit a large decline in pyramid health given removal of a single position. For reference, 129 (88 percent) of the nonempty functional sub-pyramids (containing 779 [75 percent] of the total positions) indicate any decline in the combined pyramid health metric at all.

Generally, larger functional sub-pyramids are much more likely to appear in green, since the impact of deletion of a single job is smaller. For example, for military operations, removing a single position does not significantly worsen the metrics (other than for O-10s, of which there are few). In most cases, functional sub-pyramids highlighted in yellow in Figure 6.3 show indications of potential negative pyramid health concerns in the individual pyramid health metrics. However, there are also instances where there may be no pyramid health concerns to begin with, but removing a position would worsen pyramid health. This includes selected grades of Army engineer, Navy and Air Force materiel and logistics, and joint program management/financial management positions.

CHAPTER SEVEN

Putting the Pieces Together: Evaluating the Findings

We now address the task of evaluating the findings from each of the approaches, as described in preceding chapters, to develop an overall determination for whether a position does or does not meet the criteria for a G/FO. These results can be used to inform DoD decisions about which requirements should or should not be filled with a G/FO in a constrained environment.

Developing a Construct for Combining the Findings

We investigated several ways to arrive at a combined result. One option was to look at the findings for each analytic approach individually and identify those positions that satisfy the criteria for a G/FO requirement for any one of the approaches. Using this option, 957 of the 1,113 total requirements satisfy the criteria for a G/FO for at least one of the three approaches: structure and organization, position-by-position, or the forced-choice exercise. Decisionmakers could decide that a single perspective on what constitutes a G/FO provides sufficient evidence to retain all these requirements and consider what actions to take for the remaining 156 positions for which the criteria was not satisfied for any of the approaches.

Equally valid is an option that examines requirements that do not meet the criteria for a G/FO for at least one of the approaches. There are 455 such positions. This group includes the 156 positions mentioned, as well as another 299 positions that received conflicting findings—that is, these positions conclusively satisfy the criteria for one approach while not satisfying the criteria for another.

Neither of these options for categorizing G/FO positions is especially useful for decisionmaking, however. They do not consider when the approaches provide complementary agreement, and they lack consideration of important nuances available in the findings of the individual approaches (e.g., neither considers whether the position meets the G/FO criteria but at a lower grade). Rather, these options allow a single perspective to wholly influence the overall result, eliminating the value of employing multiple analytic approaches.

A more useful construct is to combine the findings from the individual approaches. Table 7.1 shows the findings for O-7 and O-8 requirements from the structure and organization and the position-by-position approaches (positions at these grades were not reviewed during the forced-choice exercise). Of the 926 O-7 and O-8 requirements, 374 satisfied the criteria for a G/FO requirement for both approaches (shaded in green). Of these, 303 satisfied the criteria at the current grade. By combining the two findings there is significantly more evidence that these 374 positions should be considered valid requirements than provided by the single-approach option described previously.

In addition, 106 positions did not satisfy the criteria for a G/FO for either approach (shaded in red). Since these 106 positions failed to meet the criteria for a G/FO from two different perspectives, these positions should be investigated more fully to see if they should be considered for a reduction in grade to O-6, filled by a civilian, or possibly eliminated through reorganization or consolidation.

Making a decision based simply on these results, however, is not advisable. Some of these positions, for example, might be linchpins for a healthy functional pyramid, and we can get some indication of the degree to which this might be a concern by examining the findings of the position pyramid analysis. For the 106 O-7 and O-8 positions identified here, the health of the position pyramid would worsen with the removal of any one of 30 positions. These positions are primarily in the chaplain, legal, medical, and special staff position pyramids. For the remaining 76 positions, the metrics indicate that the position pyramid health would not be adversely affected by their removal. A decision might be made to eliminate a position or fill it with an O-6

Table 7.1
Findings for Structure and Organization and Position-by-Position Approaches, O-7 and O-8 Positions

		Does the Position Meet the Position-by-Position Criteria for a G/FO Requirement?		Total—Structure and Organization
		Yes	No	
Does the position meet the structure and organization criteria for a G/FO requirement?	Yes, at current or higher grade	303 ⎤	151	454
	Yes, neutral on grade	20 ⎬ 374	25	45
	Yes, at lower grade	51 ⎦	28	79
	No	70	106	176
	Inconclusive	82	38	120
	Not reviewed	41	11	52
Total—Position-by-Position		567	359	926

NOTE: Green = both approaches agree the position meets the criteria for a G/FO requirement; red = both approaches agree the position does not meet the criteria for a G/FO.

or senior civilian even if the position pyramid health might worsen, but that decision would be informed by the pyramid health approach, and G/FO management offices would be able to proactively take steps to mitigate the consequences.

Similarly, Table 7.2 shows how the findings for the structure and organization, position-by-position, and forced-choice approaches overlap for O-9 and O-10 positions. As shown in the table, 76 positions (shaded in green) met the structure and organization criteria at current or higher grade, and the forced-choice criteria at the current grade, and the position-by-position criteria (yes). Similarly, two positions (shaded in red) did not meet the structure and organization criteria and did not meet the position-by-position criteria but did meet the criteria of the forced-choice exercise participants at a lower grade. Here, 149 positions met the criteria for a G/FO requirement for all three approaches (the sum of the numbers shaded in green), while there were no positions that did not meet the criteria for a G/FO for all of the approaches. Three positions did not meet the criteria for the structure and organization approach and the position-by-

Table 7.2
Findings for Structure and Organization, Position-by-Position, and Forced-Choice Approaches, O-9 and O-10 Positions

		Was the position identified during the forced-choice exercise as a priority 3- or 4-star requirement (relative to other positions)?								Total—Structure and Organization
		Yes, at current grade		Yes, at lower grade		No		Inconclusive		
		Does the position meet the position-by-position criteria for a G/FO requirement?								
		Yes	No	Yes	No	Yes	No	Yes	No	
Does the position meet the structure and organization criteria for a G/FO requirement?	Yes, at current or higher grade	76	3	29	4	5		2		119
	Yes, neutral on grade	5		7	2					14
	Yes, at lower grade	3		29	2	2		1		37
	No		1	1	2					4
	Inconclusive			4	1				1	6
	Not reviewed	4	1	1	1					7
Total—Position-by-Position		88	5	71	12	7	0	3	1	187
Total—Forced-Choice Exercise		93		83		7		4		187

NOTE: Green = all three approaches agree the position meets the criteria for a G/FO requirement; red = two approaches agree the position does not meet the criteria for a G/FO.

position approach despite being retained during the forced-choice exercise (the sum of the numbers shaded in red). And the forced-choice exercise participants determined seven positions were not a priority three- or four-star requirement (no) that met both the structure and organization and position-by-position criteria. For the three positions that did not meet the criteria for a G/FO for at least two of the approaches, the position pyramid health measures do not significantly worsen if those positions were tapped for elimination.

Reviewing these combinations of findings can be confusing; moreover, it is unclear how to characterize overall results and what to do with inconclusive findings. Some systematic way of integrating the findings from each analytic approach is needed, taking into account strengths and weaknesses of each of the approaches so that no single approach determines the results. For example, the findings of the forced-choice exercise reflect current preferences and norms, which will likely evolve in the future. Similarly, the position-by-position analysis produces an all-or-nothing finding, and the structure and organization findings have a more subjective element. Integrating across the three approaches balances the weaknesses against the strengths.

We developed a rule set to integrate the findings of the structure and organization, position-by-position, and forced-choice exercise approaches considering the nuances of each approach in our methodology. A position is assigned an integrated result according to the following:

- Agreement between two or more findings
- One conclusive finding, not contradicted by another finding, as long as the position is reviewed by at least two approaches
- One conclusive finding that a position meets the criteria for a G/FO requirement, even if it is only reviewed by one approach
- A structure and organization approach finding of "subject to policy decision"
- A result of "conflicting findings" for positions in which findings from more than one approach disagree or that are reviewed by only one approach and found to not meet the criteria for a G/FO requirement.

The integrated rule set maps each possible combination of findings into a single integrated result. For O-10 and O-9 positions, there are 80 possible combinations of findings from the structure and organization (eight), positions-by-position (two), and forced-choice exercise (five) approaches. For O-8 and O-7 positions, there are 16 possible combinations of findings from the structure and organization (eight) and positions-by-position (two) approaches. For combinations that include conflicting findings, we considered the exact mix of findings in determining the integrated results.[1]

---

[1] When evaluating "conflicting findings" it is necessary to look at the actual findings in determining an integrated result. For example, six O-8 positions received conflicting findings from the structure and organization analysis that were split between "meets criteria for a G/FO at a lower grade" and "does not meet criteria for

With results from implementing this rule set in hand, we then looked at the findings of the position pyramid analysis for those positions that might require action (downgrade to O-6, convert, or eliminate), thereby highlighting for further review positions that might worsen pyramid health based on these actions.

Tables 7.3 through 7.6 show results of implementing this rule set. Of the 1,113 positions reviewed by RAND, 615 meet the criteria for a G/FO requirement and 132 do not meet the criteria for a G/FO requirement. The remaining 366 positions have inconclusive results, either because of conflicting findings or because a set of positions was deemed subject to policy decision. Of the 132 positions that did not meet the combined criteria for a G/FO requirement, 35 positions were in position pyramids where elimination of the position would worsen the overall health of the position pyramid.

The rows in Tables 7.3 and 7.4 show the different combinations of findings from the structure and organization, position-by-position, and forced-choice exercise that resulted in one or more O-10 and O-9 positions, respectively. The rows in Tables 7.5 and 7.6 show the different combinations of findings from the structure and organization and position-by-position analyses that resulted in one or more O-8 and O-7 positions, respectively. Each row shows the number of positions that correspond to the integrated result (based on the rule set) defined in each of the shaded columns on the right. For example, in the first row of Table 7.3, the structure and organization finding was that the position meets the criteria for a G/FO at the current or higher grade, the position-by-position finding was that the position meets the criteria for a G/FO, and the finding from the forced-choice exercise was that the position meets the criteria for a G/FO at the current or higher grade. For this combination of findings, the consolidated result is that 21 O-10 positions meet the criteria for a G/FO at a current or higher grade. Similarly, in Table 7.4, 55 O-9 positions meet the criteria for a G/FO at a current or higher grade. The remainder of this chapter further explores these results.

Using the Combined Results for Decisionmaking

At the time of our analysis, we were aware of 36 positions that the services were considering as part of the 110 positions mandated by Congress for reduction by 2022. Our combined result concluded that seven (19 percent) of those 36 positions satisfied the criteria for a G/FO, 20 did not satisfy the criteria, and nine of the positions had an inconclusive result. The service and joint organization leaders and G/FO management offices consider many factors when determining which requirements not to fill with a G/FO when reductions are mandated. Many, perhaps even most, of those factors are

---

a G/FO." In the position-by-position analysis these same positions received a finding of "meets criteria for a G/FO." Combining these findings led to an integrated result of "meets criteria for a G/FO at a lower grade." In practice, for our analysis of the 1,113 positions, this affected only nine positions.

Table 7.3
Overall Results for O-10 Positions

Structure and Organization Finding	Position-by-Position Finding	Forced-Choice Exercise Finding	Consolidated Result					
			Meets Criteria for a G/FO at Current or Higher Grade	Meets Criteria for a G/FO, Neutral on Grade	Meets Criteria for a G/FO at a Lower Grade	Does Not Meet Criteria for G/FO	Conflicting Findings	Subject to Policy Decision
Meets criteria for a G/FO at current or higher grade	Meets criteria for a G/FO	Meets criteria for a G/FO at current or higher grade	21					
		Meets criteria for a G/FO at a lower grade		3				
		Does not meet criteria for a G/FO	2					
		Conflicting finding	1	1				
		Meets criteria for a G/FO at a lower grade			8			
		Meets criteria for a G/FO at a lower grade			1			
Subject to policy decision	Meets criteria for a G/FO	Meets criteria for a G/FO at a lower grade			1			
Total			24	4	10	0	0	0
			38			0		0

NOTE: The table includes only those combinations of findings that occurred in the results of our analysis of O-10 positions. In total, there are 80 possible combinations of findings from the structure and organization (eight possible findings), position-by-position (two possible findings), and forced-choice exercise (five possible findings) analyses.

taken into account in the methodology developed for this research—but some of the considerations that go into such decisions are not. Thus, it is not surprising that our results and the service decisions do not perfectly align. But the systematic, repeatable, and transparent method we have developed provides a starting point for deliberations and a way to identify the positions for which there is strong evidence for filling with a G/FO, for which there is weakest justification, which require broader policy decisions, and which require further investigation due to conflicting results.

Table 7.4
Overall Results for O-9 Positions

Structure and Organization Finding	Position-by-Position Finding	Forced-Choice Exercise Finding	Consolidated Result					
			Meets Criteria for a G/FO at Current or Higher Grade	Meets Criteria for a G/FO, Neutral on Grade	Meets Criteria for a G/FO at a Lower Grade	Does Not Meet Criteria for G/FO	Conflicting Findings	Subject to Policy Decision
Meets criteria for a G/FO at current or higher grade	Meets criteria for a G/FO	Meets criteria for a G/FO at current or higher grade	55					
		Meets criteria for a G/FO at a lower grade		26				
		Does not meet criteria for a G/FO	3					
	Does not meet criteria for a G/FO	Meets criteria for a G/FO at current or higher grade	3					
		Meets criteria for a G/FO at a lower grade		4				
Meets criteria for a G/FO at a lower grade	Meets criteria for a G/FO	Meets criteria for a G/FO at current or higher grade		3				
		Meets criteria for a G/FO at a lower grade			21			
		Does not meet criteria for a G/FO			2			
		Conflicting finding			1			
	Does not meet criteria for a G/FO	Meets criteria for a G/FO at a lower grade			2			
Meets criteria for a G/FO, neutral on grade	Meets criteria for a G/FO	Meets criteria for a G/FO at current or higher grade	5					
		Meets criteria for a G/FO at a lower grade			6			
	Does not meet criteria for a G/FO	Meets criteria for a G/FO at a lower grade			2			
Neutral	Meets criteria for a G/FO	Meets criteria for a G/FO at a lower grade			1			

Table 7.4—Continued

Structure and Organization Finding	Position-by-Position Finding	Forced-Choice Exercise Finding	Consolidated Result					
			Meets Criteria for a G/FO at Current or Higher Grade	Meets Criteria for a G/FO, Neutral on Grade	Meets Criteria for a G/FO at a Lower Grade	Does Not Meet Criteria for G/FO	Conflicting Findings	Subject to Policy Decision
Does not meet criteria for a G/FO	Does not meet criteria for a G/FO	Meets criteria for a G/FO at a lower grade				3		
Subject to policy decision	Meets criteria for a G/FO	Meets criteria for a G/FO at a lower grade			2			
	Does not meet criteria for a G/FO	Meets criteria for a G/FO at a lower grade						1
		Conflicting finding					1	
Not reviewed	Meets criteria for a G/FO	Meets criteria for a G/FO at current or higher grade	4					
		Meets criteria for a G/FO at a lower grade			2			
	Does not meet criteria for a G/FO	Meets criteria for a G/FO at a lower grade					2	
Total			70	33	39	4	2	1
			142			4	3	

NOTE: The table includes only those combinations of findings that occurred in the results of our analysis of O-9 positions. In total, there are 80 possible combinations of findings from the structure and organization (eight possible findings), position-by-position (two possible findings), and forced-choice exercise (five possible findings) analyses.

We envision that the department might use the RAND analysis in the following way. Begin by accepting the combined result for the 615 positions that satisfy the criteria for a G/FO requirement (or whatever number of positions an analysis like this might produce). As for the positions that did not meet the combined criteria (132 positions in this analysis), these should be investigated by asking more seriously why they need to be filled by a G/FO and what other alternatives might be used to fill the requirement—such as a senior civilian or lower grade military officer—or whether the requirement might be eliminated. Additional investigation might uncover that the data provided for the position, and on which the RAND analysis is based, is incorrect

Table 7.5
Overall Results for O-8 Positions

Structure and Organization Finding	Position-by-Position Finding	Meets Criteria for a G/FO at Current or Higher Grade	Meets Criteria for a G/FO, Neutral on Grade	Meets Criteria for a G/FO at a Lower Grade	Does Not Meet Criteria for G/FO	Conflicting Findings	Subject to Policy Decision
Meets criteria for a G/FO at current or higher grade	Meets criteria for a G/FO	129					
	Does not meet criteria for a G/FO					57	
Meets criteria for a G/FO at a lower grade	Meets criteria for a G/FO			51			
	Does not meet criteria for a G/FO					28	
Meets criteria for a G/FO, neutral on grade	Meets criteria for a G/FO		14				
	Does not meet criteria for a G/FO					7	
Neutral	Meets criteria for a G/FO		5				
	Does not meet criteria for a G/FO				2		
Does not meet criteria for a G/FO	Meets criteria for a G/FO					11	
	Does not meet criteria for a G/FO				14		
Conflicting findings	Meets criteria for a G/FO		1	6			
	Does not meet criteria for a G/FO				11		
Subject to policy decision	Meets criteria for a G/FO						26
	Does not meet criteria for a G/FO						4
Not reviewed	Meets criteria for a G/FO		17				
	Does not meet criteria for a G/FO						6
Total		129	37	57	27	109	30
		223			27	139	

Table 7.6
Overall Results for O-7 Positions

Structure and Organization Finding	Position-by-Position Finding	Consolidated Result					
		Meets Criteria for a G/FO at Current or Higher Grade	Meets Criteria for a G/FO, Neutral on Grade	Meets Criteria for a G/FO at a Lower Grade	Does Not Meet Criteria for G/FO	Conflicting Findings	Subject to Policy Decision
Meets criteria for a G/FO at current or higher grade	Meets criteria for a G/FO	174					
	Does not meet criteria for a G/FO					94	
Meets criteria for a G/FO, neutral on grade	Meets criteria for a G/FO		6				
	Does not meet criteria for a G/FO					18	
Neutral	Meets criteria for a G/FO		7				
	Does not meet criteria for a G/FO				9		
Does not meet criteria for a G/FO	Meets criteria for a G/FO					59	
	Does not meet criteria for a G/FO				92		
Conflicting findings	Meets criteria for a G/FO	1					
Subject to policy decision	Meets criteria for a G/FO						36
	Does not meet criteria for a G/FO						12
Not reviewed	Meets criteria for a G/FO		24				
	Does not meet criteria for a G/FO					5	
Total		175	37	0	101	176	48
		212			101	224	

NOTE: The table includes only those combinations of findings that occurred in the results of our analysis of O-7 positions. In total, there are 16 possible combinations of findings from the structure and organization (eight possible findings) and position-by-position (two possible findings) analyses.

or incomplete, or that the description of the position does not adequately represent the importance of the position to the readiness or operational capability of a service or joint organization.

Upon further investigation, the services may determine that eliminating the 35 positions with worsening position pyramids would have detrimental impacts on these pyramids and should be retained. Or they may decide that there are sufficient management alternatives (e.g., cross-flowing G/FOs from other pyramids) that would allow for the positions to be eliminated, filled with an O-6, or filled with a senior civilian. There also may be other considerations, such as emerging needs or plans for future capabilities, that were not included in RAND's assessment. Any of these factors might have changed the results of the RAND analysis, had different information been provided in the requirements data received from OSD and, thus, may well be adequate justification for maintaining the G/FO requirement. On the other hand, service and joint senior leaders may, in fact, decide that some of these 132 positions should be downgraded to O-6, eliminated completely, or converted to civilian.

An overall result of "conflicting findings" was given to 287 positions for which the findings of the individual approaches did not agree. Of these 287, only two were O-9 positions. The participants in the forced-choice exercise agreed that one of these positions could be downgraded to O-8 while one of them should be retained as an O-9. The finding for the position-by-position analysis, however, was "does not meet the criteria for a G/FO position." It might be the case that there was significant information about these positions that was left out of the data provided to RAND but that the forced-choice exercise participants were aware of. Still, these positions should be reviewed for potential action. The remaining 285 positions with a result of conflicting findings were O-7 and O-8 positions, and for these the structure and organization and position-by-position findings disagreed. Table 7.7 shows how these various findings align.

The majority (75 percent) of the conflicting findings are cases where the requirement met the structure and organization criteria but failed to meet the criteria for the position-by-position review. This means the analysis validated an organizational need for the position—that is, it was consistent across like organizations, it was not duplicative, etc.—however, the position did not meet the G/FO criteria employed in the filtering criteria for the position-by-position approach.

Table 7.7
Combined Result of Conflicting Findings, O-7 and O-8 Positions (Structure and Organization, Position-by-Position Approaches)

		Structure and Organization Findings			
		Meets the Criteria for a G/FO at Current or Higher Grade	Meets the Criteria for a G/FO, Neutral on Grade	Meets the Criteria for a G/FO at a Lower Grade	Does Not Meet the Criteria for a G/FO	Not Reviewed
Position-by-Position Findings	Meets the criteria for a G/FO				70	
	Does not meet the criteria for a G/FO	151	25	28		11

**Table 7.8
Percentage of Requirements Submitted with
a Result of "Conflicting Findings"**

Army	25%
Navy	16%
Air Force	35%
Marine Corps	14%
Joint	28%

Table 7.8 compares the number of positions with conflicting findings as a percentage of the total requirements submitted by each of the services and the joint community. We posit two likely primary causes for the differences across the services: the differences in the accuracy and completeness of data for the positions, and difference in the clarity of the organizational structures and the nomenclature used for organization names and position titles. OSD General and Flag Officer Management reported that the service and joint G/FO management offices used various means to collect the data for each position—some had significant portions of the information "on the shelf," some handled the information collection centrally assigning a single action officer, some tasked the offices of the general and flag officers currently in the position to individually collect the data. Further, it can be difficult to completely sort out the complex wiring diagrams of organizations, to understand how the positions within an organization fit together, and to understand how responsibilities are distributed. We found that the services differed in the clarity of their organizational structures; some have very easy to understand organizational structures with clearly defined echelons and reporting chains, while others do not.

If updated or corrected data is obtained for a position, or if corrections and clarifications are obtained for organizations and structures, then a revised assessment may lead to different findings and, in turn, to different combined results. With updated information, combined results for a position may change from inconclusive to a conclusive result, with more positions classified as either meeting the criteria for a G/FO or not.

The final consolidated result category, "subject to policy decision," is unique among the results categories in that it is an outcome driven only by the structure and organizational analysis. These 79 positions, that cluster in a small number of groups, deserve particular attention by senior decisionmakers, as discussed in detail in Chapter Three. In our judgment, a decision on whether these positions meet the criteria for a G/FO requirement should be made based on a policy decision governing the positions as a group—for example, whether the most senior military officers should hold positions in an organization such as OSD or whether and under what circumstances G/FOs should lead JTFs.

The management of G/FO requirements across an enterprise of the size and diversity of the DoD is a complex and dynamic undertaking. The data used for the analysis presented here was collected in March 2017, and since then, there have assuredly been changes in military strategy, service priorities, organizational structures, and G/FO job characteristics. Despite these dynamics, the combined results highlight a group of positions that are not well defended as G/FO requirements. These results also show how to apply the RAND-developed methodology that we believe DoD should employ.

Once the department identifies a group of positions for elimination, it is necessary to evaluate the implications of the proposed decision. For example, how would eliminating a group of positions affect career paths and experiences of officers, specifically joint experiences that officers may or may not be able to acquire? RAND's Military Career Model, described in the next chapter, can be used to conduct these assessments, and we illustrate the type of results that can be obtained. In addition, there is value in evaluating communities of G/FOs and the implications of reductions that are targeted to particular groups of officers. There will also be a need in the future to consider emerging requirements for G/FOs that result from organizational change. Another RAND-developed tool, the Command Chain Application, described and employed in Chapter Nine, can support such analyses.

CHAPTER EIGHT

Career Paths, Experiences, and the Military Career Model

The RAND Military Career Model (MCM) is a computer-based simulation model designed to analyze alternative military personnel management policies. Originally, the model was developed to examine how changes to the Defense Officer Personnel Management Act of 1980 (DOPMA) might affect officer career paths.[1] It was also used for an earlier project on G/FO requirements to study the effects of proposals for the 2009 National Defense Authorization Act.[2] Since then, the model has been adapted for a variety of military personnel applications.[3]

The MCM is a vacancy-based simulation model that creates simulated officers and runs over discrete time intervals. Hundreds of simulated officers are individually assigned to different positions, promoted to new grades, and either separate or retire. Assignments can be managed on a position-by-position basis, with very specific rules for required and desired qualifications for each position. For example, one can specify that a service chief position should not be filled by an O-9 newly promoted to O-10 but must, instead, be filled by someone already in another position as an O-10. One can also specify rules with more complexity; for instance, that only certain officers may have a second joint job in the same grade. Assignment lengths can also be manipulated, for example with 18-month durations for some, 24 for others, and 36 for others. In previous work, the MCM has been used to examine policy alternatives such as changes to promotion and eligibility, changes to career lengths, and implementation details of the joint pool.

During the simulation, the model records the entire history of assignments, promotions, and retention behavior for all simulated officer careers. With the MCM, it

---

[1] Peter Schirmer et al., *Challenging Time in DOPMA: Flexible and Contemporary Military Officer Management*, Santa Monica, Calif.: RAND Corporation, MG-451-OSD, 2006.

[2] Peter Schirmer, *Computer Simulation of General and Flag Officer Management: Model Description and Results*, Santa Monica, Calif.: RAND Corporation, TR-702-OSD, 2009.

[3] See Kevin O'Neill, *Sustaining the US Air Force's Force Support Career Field Through Officer Workforce Planning*, Santa Monica, Calif.: RAND Corporation, RGSD-302, 2012; Shanthi Nataraj et al., *Options for Department of Defense Total Workforce Supply and Demand Analysis: Potential Approaches and Available Data Sources*, Santa Monica, Calif.: RAND Corporation, RR-543-OSD, 2014; Alexander D. Rothenberg et al., *Using RAND's Military Career Model to Evaluate the Impact of Institutional Requirements on the Air Force Space Officer Career Field*, Santa Monica, Calif.: RAND Corporation, RR-1302-AF, 2017.

is, thus, possible to analyze the records of simulated officers just as one would analyze the records of real officers, and it is also possible to measure system-wide outcomes. By changing the parameters of the model to mimic potential policy changes, researchers can study how specific policy changes may impact different aspects of a career field's health. Although the model operates at the individual level, assignments are given to each simulated officer in sequence; the model is not equipped to make predictions about an actual individual's career.

In this chapter, we describe how we use the MCM to evaluate several personnel management outcomes due to reductions in the number of positions filled by G/FOs, including the extent to which the positions are filled, the impact on the joint experiences officers acquire, and the extent to which positions within a career group are consistently filled by officers with in-career group experience. The first section of this chapter explains how we develop illustrative baseline and reduced requirements scenarios for the set of positions considered by the model. The next section describes how we calibrated the MCM model and chose different model parameters in the different scenario runs. The final set of sections presents results illustrating the model's capabilities.

This analysis makes a variety of simplifying assumptions to model the logic of all positions across the entire G/FO system. Careful and accurate modeling of all aspects of every G/FO position and officers who fill those positions across the DoD would be a massive undertaking. As a consequence, the results we present should not be taken as prescriptive and should, instead, be considered as illustrative of modeling capabilities that could be used to evaluate future proposed changes to the set of G/FO requirements. Any changes to the various parameters that specify positions or officers in the model would generate different results.

Developing Illustrative Scenarios

For this study, we demonstrate how the MCM could be used to examine the impacts of reductions in particular G/FO positions. To perform an illustrative analysis, we develop two scenarios, a "Baseline 1,044" scenario and a "Reduced 795" scenario. We examine both pyramid health and career experience differences across these scenarios using the pyramid calculator tools introduced in Chapter Six as well as the MCM. Figure 8.1 provides an overview of how the baseline and reduced scenarios are generated from the database of G/FO requirements. The database contained 1,113 G/FO requirements, which were compiled based on data received from the project sponsor.[4] From these requirements, we select a subset of 1,044 single-hatted or "primary"-hatted jobs, thus approximating the number of individuals that would comprise a pyramid

---

[4] Chapter One and Appendix A contain more details on our data sources for the list of positions.

Figure 8.1
Baseline and Reduced Scenario Generation

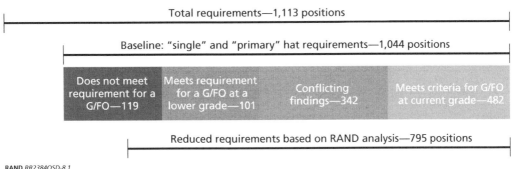

RAND *RR2384OSD-8.1*

that fully fills these requirements. This baseline is referred to as the Baseline 1,044 scenario throughout the rest of the chapter.

From the Baseline 1,044 scenario, we generate an example alternative pyramid of postelimination, postdowngrade requirements as suggested by RAND's integrated analysis. Of the 1,044 primary and single hat requirements, 119 do not meet the criteria for G/FO requirements and, thus, are flagged for elimination. An additional 101 positions meet the criteria for G/FO requirements but at a lower grade and are slated for downgrade. We assume that downgrading these jobs, in turn, causes all subordinate positions to be downgraded in a cascading manner, flagging another 202 requirements to be downgraded. Of the 202 "cascading" downgrades, 130 cause an O-7 position to be downgraded to O-6, removing it from the general and flag officer pyramid. This results in a new total of 795 general and flag officer jobs, which we term the Reduced 795 scenario.

Effects of Reductions on Pyramid Size and Shape

The pyramid resulting from the set of requirements in the Baseline 1,044 scenario is displayed in Figure 8.2. This pyramid directly reflects the requirements data, with a fair-sharing of joint positions based on the proportion of in-service positions held by each service at a given grade as described in Chapter Six. The overall pyramid appears to have a relatively healthy shape.

The pyramid calculator tool introduced in Chapter Six allows us to look at specific pieces of the requirements set. In doing so, we identify several areas where pyramid health concerns may exist under the current set of requirements. As noted, the set of positions in Baseline 1,044 is rooted in job requirements in the data received by RAND rather than actual individuals filling positions today. However, imbalances in

Figure 8.2
Overall Pyramid (Baseline 1,044)

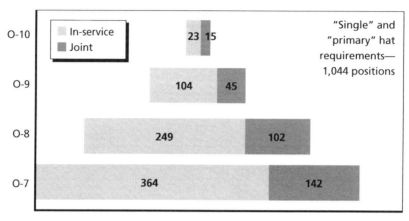

the requirements could highlight areas for further investigation as well as areas that deserve special interest when considering a set of changes. Each individual service's overall pyramid is relatively well balanced in the baseline case, as shown in Figure 8.3. The exception is the Marine Corps, which has a very large number of in-service O-8 positions in the requirements dataset, and this imbalance is further accentuated by the fair-sharing approach to allocating joint positions described in Chapter Six.

Simple pyramid analysis further allows us to comment on pyramids in individual specialty areas. For example, Figure 8.4 highlights the Intelligence and Legal communities. The Intelligence community relies very heavily on joint positions across all grades, possibly making it harder for the services to control career paths and development for the officers in this pyramid. The Legal community is very small and has no joint requirements above the O-7 level. A steep reduction in requirements as officers move from O-7 to O-8, coupled with almost no reductions in requirements from O-8 to O-9, could lead to bench strength issues for selection to O-9.

Figure 8.5 introduces the pyramids for the Reduced 795 scenario obtained from the RAND-analysis-based set of eliminations and reductions described. The healthy shape of the pyramid as seen in the Baseline scenario is preserved even though the size of the overall pyramid is reduced. The set of eliminations and downgrades suggested by RAND's analysis actually improves the general shape of the Marine Corps pyramid, resulting in relatively balanced overall pyramids across all four services, as shown in the lower portion of Figure 8.5. The challenges in the Legal and Intelligence pyramid highlighted in the previous section continue to be seen in the Reduced 795 scenario.

Detailed assessment of individual services, grades, and pyramid categories are possible within the pyramid calculator tool and could enable comparison of specific areas of interest before and after a proposed set of changes.

Figure 8.3
Pyramids by Service (Baseline 1,044)

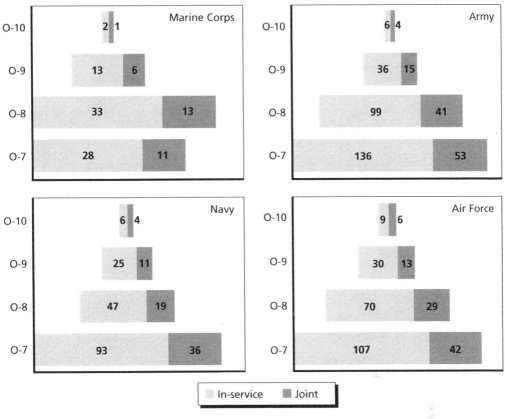

RAND *RR2384OSD-8.3*

Figure 8.4
Intelligence and Legal Sub-Pyramids (Baseline 1,044)

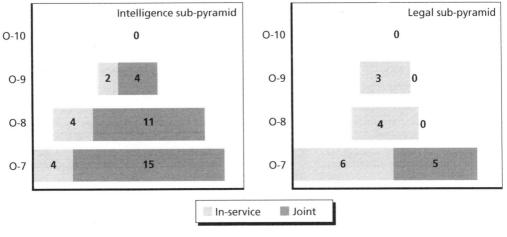

RAND *RR2384OSD-8.4*

Figure 8.5
Pyramid Results from the Reduced 795 Scenario

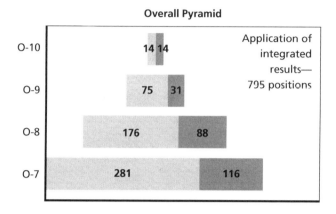

Overall Pyramid

Pyramids by Service

Further Analysis Using the Military Career Model

Specifying Positions

To gain additional insights into the paths of individual officers through the pyramid, the rest of this chapter presents results of illustrative analyses using RAND's Military Career Model. To specify the positions held by G/FOs in the model, we used several different data sources. Key position characteristics and the data sources we used to calibrate them are described below:

- *Grade:* The sponsor provided data from the services and Joint Staff on the current authorized grade for each position in the model. In the Reduced 795 scenario, the grade was changed for those positions that meet the requirements for a G/FO at a lower grade and for all subordinate positions. Otherwise, it was the same as the grade authorized in the Baseline 1,044 scenario. Note that when filling positions, the model discourages but does not prohibit grade substitution.[5]
- *Size:* The total number of positions for each job in the model was set in proportion to the number of positions in the FY 2014 Manpower Programming and Execution System data. However, because the model is a steady state model, the grade distribution of the FY 2014 positions was imbalanced and unsustainable (as discussed previously). We rescaled position totals to correspond to what they would be in a steady state, with the proportions of total jobs by grade set to match this distribution.
- *Duration:* For each G/FO position in the model, we used Blue Book[6] data to determine the preferred duration of each position. We then allowed a buffer of six months to specify the minimum and maximum duration allowed for an officer to hold the position.
- *Fill priority:* In the MCM, a position's fill priority determines the order in which positions are filled. All G/FO positions were coded as "must fill" positions, with the exception of holding jobs. Holding jobs, described later, are filled only after all other "must fill" positions that can be filled are filled.

---

[5]   To assign officers to jobs, the model begins by creating a list of available (unassigned) individuals who can possibly fill a particular job. It then selects officers to fill that position from the list. Depending on the requirements specified for the job in the model, certain characteristics (such as experience) may prevent officers from appearing on an assignment list because they do not satisfy the requirements. For those who do satisfy requirements, the assignment list is sorted; officers with characteristics that are discouraged will appear lower on the list. If officers do not meet the grade requirements for a job, they are still eligible, but they will be ranked below officers who do meet the grade requirements.

[6]   Commonly referred to as the Blue Book, the *General/Flag Officer Joint/Outside-Service Positions of Interest to the Joint Chiefs of Staff* is published quarterly by the Joint Staff and lists all G/FO positions identified on the Joint Duty Assignment List (JDAL). The book is divided into eight sections and reflects all pertinent data applicable to the position and the incumbent. It is designed to be a management tool for the Joint Staff, service chiefs, OSD, and their respective staffs. The list of G/FO positions is governed by CJCSI 1331.01. During the course of our analyses, we were provided with two restricted-access spreadsheet versions of the Blue Book for our use, one dated November 2016 and the other dated July 31, 2017.

- *Experience qualifications:* Certain positions require previous experiences, and these prerequisites were coded in the model. For example, in certain areas, staff jobs had to be filled by individuals with operational experience in the same areas. To code experience qualifications, we used several different in-service data sources, some of which contained information about joint positions. For the Air Force, we used position-level competency data from Air Force General Officer Management Office (AF/DPG). For the Navy, we used the history and biographies of G/FOs from the Navy Personnel Command, using monthly vintages of data from April 2013 to the present.[7] For the Army, we had discussions with subject matter experts to identify stepping-stone positions and requirements for a small number of key jobs. In the event that detailed experience prerequisites were not available, we used specialty logic to ensure that it was preferred that a position in a specific category be filled by someone who already had in-category experience.
- *Holding jobs:* The MCM requires officers be employed in a position for them to be retained. To minimize the impact of transitory unemployment on retention, we created 20 holding positions at O-7 and ten holding positions at O-8 for each service. As described, these positions are filled only if all other positions have been filled, and we also required these positions be filled by someone who had already served in that grade (so that the holding jobs could not impact promotions).

We demonstrate the model's capabilities for analyzing how eliminating positions might impact a variety of different G/FO manpower outcomes. These include: (1) the extent to which positions go unfilled in equilibrium; (2) the extent to which services fall below or exceed their joint ceilings; (3) the impact of eliminating positions on the joint experience of senior officers; (4) the percentage of positions filled with fully qualified personnel; (5) the extent to which career-group pyramids are staffed by officers with only in-group experiences and (6) effects on the intelligence pyramid.

Effects of Reducing Positions on Position Fills

For every position in both the Baseline 1,044 scenario and the Reduced 795 scenario, fill rates were typically over 95 percent. Nearly 90 percent of the positions in both scenarios were always filled. Eliminating positions did not affect fill rates, largely because the experience requirements set in the model were flexible enough to accommodate a reduced number of positions and no positions were removed that were the only possible prerequisites for other positions. These results would change with different scenario inputs to the model. For example, if one position had a single required prerequisite, and if that prerequisite position were eliminated in a scenario, the model would prevent that position from being filled.

---

[7] As of December 29, 2017, the current month's roster data are available here: http://www.public.navy.mil/bupers-npc/officer/Detailing/flagofficer/FlagMgmt/Pages/RostersPublications.aspx

Service-Specific Joint Ceilings

The MCM implementation allows the user to specify the joint ceilings that represent the maximum allowable number of officers from each grade and service that can serve in joint positions at any one time. Figure 8.6 plots the number of officers from each of the services that fill joint positions during each period (quarter) of the simulation. Separate panels are drawn for each of the services, and separate lines indicate the number of joint positions filled during the Baseline 1,044 (blue line) and Reduced 795

Figure 8.6
Joint Ceilings and Floors

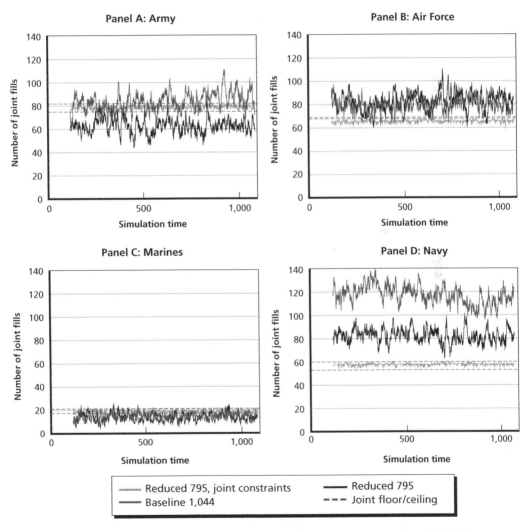

NOTE: These figures depict the counts of the number of officers from the Army (Panel A), Air Force (Panel B), Marines (Panel C), and Navy (Panel D) who serve in joint positions during each period of the model. New service-specific joint ceilings and floors are depicted in red dashed lines.

RAND *RR2384OSD-8.6*

(black line) scenarios. These simulations were relatively flexible, and we did not impose any stringent joint ceilings. We also ran a third scenario, the Reduced 795 Joint Constraints (gold line) simulation, which imposed joint ceilings that correspond to new statutory language.[8] Red dashed lines indicate these new service-specific joint ceilings and floors—which, in the case of the Air Force, is an extremely narrow band.

Despite the significant fluctuations in the black lines, which show the services' share of the joint pool when the shares are not actively managed in the Reduced 795 scenario, once the floors and ceilings—the constraints—are implemented, all but the Air Force are able to stay within these narrow ranges (for the Air Force, the gold line falls below the joint floor). For the Army, Navy, and Marine Corps the floor is between 9 percent and 20 percent below the ceiling; for the Air Force the floor is only 1.5 percent below. The problem for the Air Force is that the floor is 68 and the ceiling is 69. In fact, the challenge for the Air Force isn't to stay below the ceiling but above the floor—but the range is far too narrow. The 2017 NDAA reduced the floors by anywhere from 12 percent to 20 percent for the other three services, but only reduced the floor by 7 percent for the Air Force. Had the Air Force reduction been more in line with the others, it would have been 63 or 64 instead of 68, and this is a much more feasible floor, as Figure 8.6 illustrates.

Effects of Reducing Positions in the Joint Pool on Joint Experience

When joint G/FO positions are eliminated, there are fewer opportunities for G/FOs to obtain joint experience. If some G/FO positions require generalized or specific joint experience, this could lead to undesirable consequences. However, if the joint G/FO positions that are eliminated are "dead end" jobs, which typically terminate officer careers or restrict promotion opportunities, joint experience for G/FOs could actually increase. Figure 8.7 shows a histogram of the number of years O-10s serve in joint G/FO positions for the two different position scenarios.

On average, in the Baseline 1,044 simulation, O-10s accumulated 1.53 years of joint experience from O-7 to O-9. In the Reduced 795 simulation, this average increases slightly to 1.63 years of joint experience. Of note, the increase in joint experience tends to happen on the right tail of the distribution. In particular, in the 1,044 simulation, 18.4 percent of officers had four or more years of joint experience from O-7 to O-9. These numbers increase to 20.9 percent in the 795 simulation.

On the whole, however, in our notional modeling exercise, the joint experience effects we document do not seem to be very large. Eliminating different positions may result in larger and more significant reductions in joint pool experience, and the model could be used to quantify those impacts more precisely.

---

[8]   National Defense Authorization Act for Fiscal Year 2017, Sec. 501(a)(3).

Figure 8.7
Number of Years Served in Joint G/FO Positions for O-10 Officers

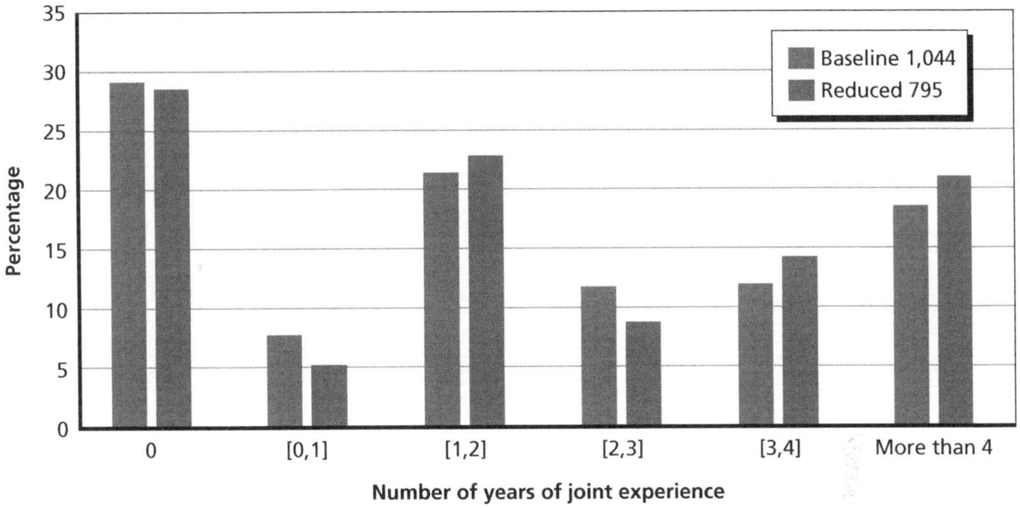

NOTE: These figures depict the proportion of O-10 officers who have different levels of joint experience in both the Baseline 1,044 scenario (blue bars) and the Reduced 795 scenario (red bars). This histogram was created using the entire simulation history of O-10 position fills. The Baseline 1,044 scenario results are a percentage of the 38 total O-10s in that scenario. Similarly, the Reduced 795 results are a percentage of the 28 O-10s in that scenario.

RAND RR2384OSD-8.7

Effects of Reducing Positions on Desired Experiences

If some junior positions are prerequisites for more senior positions, when those junior prerequisite jobs are eliminated, it could affect the extent to which senior positions are filled by individuals with desired experiences. These prerequisite positions could be established proactively by the services and the joint community or based on the career paths of those who have previously filled the position.

To explore these effects, we examine how the G/FO position reductions impact the share of officers who have desired experiences for several example senior G/FO positions in the services and joint commands. As shown in Table 8.1, these positions include: (1) Commanding General, United States Army Forces Command, an O-10 operations position; (2) N2/N6, Vice Admiral for Information Dominance, one of the chief intelligence positions in the Navy; (3) Commander, Air Force Materiel Command; (4) Commanding General, United States Army Materiel Command; (5) Director, Naval Reactors, Naval Nuclear Propulsion Program; and (6) Commander, United States Transportation Command. Using historical data on individuals who served in these positions and discussions with the G/FO management offices, we established a set of desired experiences for each of these positions. These desired experiences could

Table 8.1
Impact of Position Reductions on Percent of G/FOs with Desired Experiences

	Baseline 1,044: %	Reduced 795: %
Commanding General, United States Army Forces Command	95.2	90.4
N2/N6	90.3	88.0
Commander, Air Force Materiel Command	85.2	79.7
Commanding General, United States Army Materiel Command	98.3	94.7
Director, Naval Reactors, Naval Nuclear Propulsion Program	89.7	80.5
Commander, United States Transportation Command	87.6	86.2

NOTE: The percentages are calculated over the entire simulation history of position fills.

be adjusted based on the needs of the service and the analysis repeated. The focus here is on the change in the percentage of officers with prerequisite positions in the baseline and reduced cases.

For this sampling of positions, in the Reduced 795 case the share of officers filling positions with desired prerequisites is somewhat lower, but for most positions the impacts are small. The model can be used to further examine prerequisites for specific positions and to identify which positions would be more difficult to fill as a consequence of the reductions.

Effects of Reducing Positions on Pyramid Consistency

Reductions in the number of positions could affect the extent to which officers' careers are well rounded with experiences in many different types of career fields or whether they are narrowly focused on a single or a small number of functional areas. For each simulation run and each position, we calculated the fraction of positions that are filled with officers who held only other positions in that same career field, who held positions in that same field more than 50 percent of the time, who held positions in that field between 20 percent and 50 percent of the time, or who spent less than 20 percent of their G/FO career in those types of positions. As examples, we examine pyramid consistency for operations and intelligence positions.

In Figure 8.8, we plot the fraction of O-10 operations positions filled with people who have had different types of experiences during their careers. Of these O-10 operations positions, in the Baseline 1,044 scenario, 13.5 percent of positions were filled by officers who spent their entire career in operations positions. With positions reduced to 795, the share increases to 14.7 percent. Similarly, the share of O-10 operations positions filled by officers who have spent less than 20 percent of their career in operations

Figure 8.8
Operations Positions Consistency (O-10)

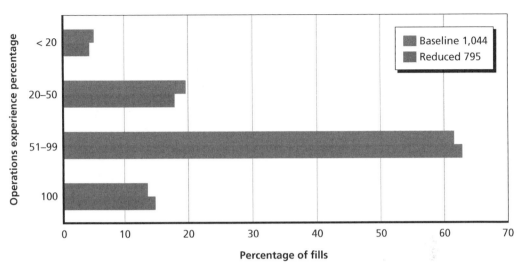

NOTE: These figures depict the proportion of O-10 operations officers who have operations experience in both the Baseline 1,044 scenario (blue bars) and the Reduced 795 scenario (red bars). This histogram was created using the entire simulation history of O-10 position fills. The Baseline 1,044 scenario results are a percentage of the 34 total O-10 operations positions in that scenario. Similarly, the Reduced 795 results are a percentage of the 26 O-10 operations positions in that scenario.
RAND *RR2384OSD-8.8*

positions, or between 20 percent and 50 percent of their careers in operations positions, falls as positions are reduced.

Turning to the intelligence pyramid, the Baseline 1,044 scenario contained 40 intelligence positions. In the Reduced 795 scenario, seven positions at O-7 (mostly director and staff positions) and three positions at O-8 ([1], Assistant Deputy Chief of Staff Intelligence, Surveillance, and Reconnaissance, AF/A2, [2] Military Deputy to the Director, Defense Intelligence Agency, and [3] Assistant Director of National Intelligence for Partner Engagement, Office of the Director of National Intelligence) did not meet the criteria for a G/FO requirement. This left 30 intelligence positions.

Figure 8.9 depicts how the remaining positions change the consistency of the intelligence pyramid. The three panels show the percentage of intelligence positions that are filled by officers with different levels of intelligence experience. In the Baseline 1,044 simulation, most O-7 intelligence positions are filled by people who spend less than 20 percent of their career in intelligence, and this does not change substantially with the position reductions (Panel A). At the grade of O-8, more intelligence positions are being filled by people who have spent between 20 percent and 50 percent of their career in intelligence, as shown in Panel B. As positions are reduced, this proportion increases, and the share of positions being filled by officers who have spent less than

Figure 8.9
Intelligence Pyramid Consistency

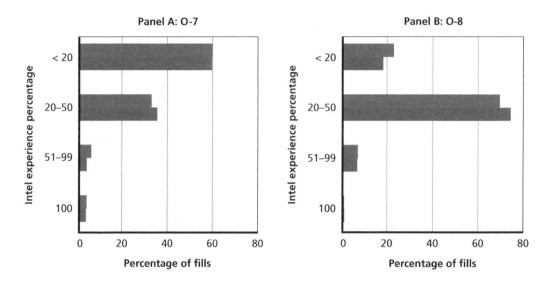

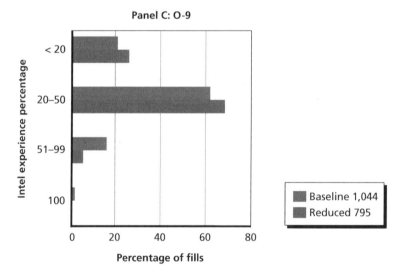

NOTE: These figures depict the proportion of officers holding intelligence positions at each grade who have spent various percentages of their career in the intelligence sub-pyramid in the Baseline 1,044 scenario (blue bars) and the Reduced 795 scenario (red bars). This histogram was created using the entire simulation history of intelligence position fills. The Baseline 1,044 scenario results are a percentage of the 19 O-7, 15 O-8, and 6 O-9 intelligence positions in that scenario. Similarly, the Reduced 795 results are a percentage of the 14 O-7, 14 O-8, and 2 O-9 intelligence positions in that scenario.

RAND *RR2384OSD-8.9*

20 percent of their career in intelligence falls. For O-9s, in Panel C, the share of intelligence positions that are being filled by officers spending more than half their career in intelligence falls from 15.6 percent in the Baseline 1,044 to 4.6 percent in the Reduced 767 scenario.

Conclusion

In this chapter, we have described how to use RAND's MCM to examine the effects of proposed reductions in G/FO positions on various aspects of officer career experience and position fills. In particular, when positions are eliminated it may impact joint experiences that officers are able to obtain, and this, in turn, could have implications for the extent to which different positions are filled by fully qualified officers. Position reductions may also affect the extent to which different career groups are staffed by officers who have spent their entire careers in the same career group. This analysis illustrates modeling capabilities that the G/FO management offices should use to highlight the implications of eliminating specific G/FO positions.

CHAPTER NINE

Managing General and Flag Officers Beyond the Mandated Review

The previous chapters described the methodology and results of RAND's review of general and flag officer requirements as mandated by Congress. This review examined requirements as of a point in time, March 2017, based on information provided by the services and joint community, and determined whether existing requirements for general and flag officers stand up to scrutiny. But managing the corps of general and flag officers is an ongoing endeavor for DoD, and the approaches used in this review, most centrally the factors and guidelines used to make the myriad decisions concerning whether existing positions do, in fact, meet reasonable criteria for a G/FO requirement, can be employed on an ongoing basis.

This chapter explores how the RAND methodology can be used to (1) focus on general and flag officer communities of interest, to determine whether current positions meet criteria of a G/FO requirement or to identify where DoD might be willing to take some risk and, (2) guide decisions regarding G/FO leadership requirements as a result of organizational changes, such as if the department needs to establish a new combatant command or functional organization. These types of assessments can be conducted in tandem. Given the limitations on G/FO authorizations, it is often the case that new G/FO requirements are met by moving and eliminating positions elsewhere in the department. Analyzing requirements within various communities can offer insights into where such positions might be drawn from.

Evaluating General and Flag Officer Communities

In our discussions with G/FO management offices and during the forced-choice exercise, certain categories of positions were often identified as "the first place to look" or "ideas that are always on the table" when G/FO reductions are required. Thus, DoD may want to study particular groups of positions to understand the impacts of reductions or to harvest G/FO positions for other uses. To illustrate how our methodology can support this type of targeted analysis, we identified select communities of interest and, based on RAND's integrated results, considered the implications of potential policy decisions on the G/FO corps. Using the RAND-developed G/FO Command Chain Application,[1] we assessed, for example, the implications of policy decisions such as limiting the number of O-9 positions in joint and service headquarter staffs, restructuring professional career fields, or converting positions in certain career fields from a G/FO to a senior civilian official.

In this section, we consider general and flag officer positions in the following communities of interest:

- OSD and DoD agencies
- Joint and service headquarter staffs
- Limiting service four-star positions
- Professional career fields
- Academies, PME institutions, and training organizations.

For each of these communities, we provide results of potential policy decisions by grade and by service of the positions affected in the three basic RAND integrated results classifications—meets criteria for a G/FO requirement, does not meet criteria for a G/FO requirement, and inconclusive. Our conclusions provide insight into which positions or groups of positions are least well defended as G/FO requirements.

OSD and DoD Agencies

The OSD and DoD agencies have 66 G/FO positions, as summarized by grade and organization in Table 9.1 (including suborganizations when that information was available in the Blue Book). All these positions are in the joint pool. Of note is the inclusion of defense attachés and senior defense officials in the DIA totals. Among these positions, we include one from the Track Four Efficiency Study, namely the defense attaché to Mexico.

Table 9.2 summarizes the integrated RAND results by organization and grade for these agencies. Almost one-third of the positions were assessed as meeting the criteria of a G/FO requirement while almost half had an inconclusive result. For the inconclusive results to lead to actual reductions in the number of G/FO positions, there would have to be agency restructuring and reorganization. However, this summary provides a rough indication of the maximum number of general and flag officer positions that would be affected by focusing on positions within OSD and DoD agencies.

Joint and Service Headquarters Staffs

One method for reducing the number of G/FO positions on headquarter staffs could be to cap the number of O-9 positions. The services have already consolidated to some degree by combining functions such as the operations staff (A/G/N/S3) and the plans staff (A/G/N/S5) or the logistics staff (A/G/N/S4) and the military education and

---

[1]   Appendix B contains a description of the Command Chain Application.

Table 9.1
General and Flag Officer Positions in OSD and DoD Agencies

Organization	O-10	O-9	O-8	O-7
Secretary of Defense (SECDEF)		1		1
Cost Assessment and Program Evaluation (CAPE)		1		
Chief Information Officer (CIO)			1	
Defense Information Systems Agency (DISA)		1	1	1
Defense Legal Services Agency (DLSA)				2
Total		3	2	4
Under Secretary of Defense for Acquisition, Technology, and Logistics (USD [AT&L])		1	2	2
Defense Contract Management Agency (DCMA)		1		1
Defense Logistics Agency (DLA)		1	3	4
Defense Threat Reduction Agency (DTRA)		1	1	3
Missile Defense Agency (MDA)		1	3	1
Total		5	9	11
Under Secretary of Defense for Intelligence (USD [I])		1		
Defense Intelligence Agency (DIA)		1	4	10
National Security Agency (NSA)	1		3	
Total	1	2	7	10
Under Secretary of Defense for Personnel and Readiness (USD [P&R])		1	1	
Defense Health Agency (DHA)		1	2	2
Total		2	3	2
Under Secretary of Defense for Policy (USD [P])				4
Defense Security Cooperation Agency (DSCA)		1		
Total		1		4
Grand Total	1	13	21	31

SOURCE: Blue Book.

Table 9.2
RAND Integrated Results for OSD and DoD Agencies

	Meets Criteria of a G/FO Requirement				Does Not Meet Criteria of a G/FO Requirement				Inconclusive			
	O-10	O-9	O-8	O-7	O-10	O-9	O-8	O-7	O-10	O-9	O-8	O-7
SECDEF		2		2			1			1	1	2
USD (AT&L)		4	1	4		1	1	5			7	2
USD (I)	1	2	2				1	1			4	9
USD (P&R)		1	1			1	1	1			1	1
USD (P)		1										4
Total	1	10	4	6	0	2	4	7	0	1	13	18
	21				13				32			

training staff (A/G/N/S7).[2] Table 9.3 lists the O-9 staff positions included in this pos-sible consolidation effort, which includes the joint staff.

Table 9.4 displays a tabulation of these positions and all subordinate positions. In this and subsequent tables the cells are color-coded to indicate the joint pool (purple), the Air Force (light blue), the Army (light green), the Navy (dark blue), and the Marine Corps (red). No O-10 positions are included in this group. We note that the Army Commanding General, Installation Management Command is an O-9 position that reports to the Director of the Army Staff. This accounts for another Army O-9 in addi-tion to those listed in the table. These staff organizations make up approximately 15 percent of the overall general and flag officer positions. The RAND integrated results concluded that a little less than half of these positions meet the criteria for a G/FO requirement and about 15 percent do not.

If, for example, a policy decision were made to limit the number of O-9s in each staff to three positions, about 60 percent of the O-9s would need to be reduced in grade or eliminated. The ripple effect of this type of reduction could also cause 45 to 50 O-7s to be downgraded and, therefore, eliminated from the G/FO force.

Limiting Service Four-Stars

Limits could be placed on the number of O-10 positions each service retains within their officer corps. As an extreme, we evaluated a scenario where each service retains only two O-10 positions, namely the chief and vice chief of staff, or assistant comman-

---

[2]   Under the general staff system, each staff position in a headquarters is assigned a letter-prefix corresponding to the formation's element (joint organizations [J], Army [G], Navy [N], Air Force [A]) and one or more numbers specifying a role. The staff numbers are generally: 1 for manpower or personnel, 2 for intelligence, 3 for opera-tions, 4 for logistics, 5 for plans, 6 for communications, 7 for military education and training, and 8 for resource management. Staff numbers beyond 8 are assigned to element-specific roles.

Table 9.3
General and Flag Officer Positions on Joint and Service Headquarter Staffs

Organization	O-9 Positions
Joint Staff	Assistant to the Chairman Director of the Joint Staff J3 J4 J5 J6 J7 J8
Army	Director of the Army Staff G1 G2 G3/5/7 G4 G6 G8
Air Force	Assistant Vice Chief of Staff A1 A2 A3/5 A4/7 A6 A8 A10
Navy	Director of the Navy Staff N1 N2/6 N3/5 N8 N9
Marine Corps	Director of the Marine Corps Staff Deputy Commandants for • Manpower and Reserve Affairs • Installations Logistics • Plans, Policies and Operations • Programs and Resources • Aviation

dant for the Marine Corps. All the other O-10 positions in service (not joint) commands would then be downgraded to O-9. This would include seven in the Air Force, four in the Army, and four in the Navy. Table 9.5 shows a summary of these officers by service along with all their subordinates. Assuming that a reduction in grade would trickle down, 199 O-7 positions could be affected. In the RAND integrated results, 35 of these O-7 positions did not meet the criteria for a G/FO requirement and 67 had an inconclusive result. The restructuring that would occur as a result of downgrading these service O-10 positions would, undoubtedly, affect a large percentage of these O-7 positions.

Table 9.4
RAND Integrated Results for Joint and Service Headquarter Staffs

	Meets Criteria of a G/FO Requirement		Does Not Meet Criteria of a G/FO Requirement		Inconclusive		Total		Total
O-9	8						8		36
	8	8					8	8	
	6	5	1				6	6	
O-8	1		5		4		10		62
	3	8	2	3	6	7	11	18	
	9	6	2	2	1	3	12	11	
O-7	2		2		19		23		79
		7	2	2	11	8	13	17	
	9	4	5	2	3	3	17	9	
Total	11		7		23		41		177
	11	23	4	5	17	15	32	43	
	24	15	7	5	4	6	35	26	
	84		28		65		177		

Legend: Joint ▪ Air Force ▪ Army ▪ Navy ▪ Marine Corps

Professional Career Fields

Restructuring the professional career fields, namely the health professionals, legal, and chaplains, would create an opportunity to downgrade or eliminate some positions. Table 9.6 shows all the current positions by grade. There are no O-10 positions in this group. The integrated RAND results concluded that approximately one-third of these positions did not meet the criteria for a G/FO requirement. Results for a little more than 40 percent of the positions were inconclusive and would depend on the objectives for restructuring these career fields.

Academies, Professional Military Education Institutions, and Training Organizations

In some cases, civilians may be able to assume the responsibilities now held by G/FOs within the service academies, professional military education (PME) institutions, and training organizations. Table 9.7 shows the current set of positions in this category. RAND's integrated results concluded that only three of the 70 positions did not meet

Table 9.5
RAND Integrated Results for O-10 Positions in Service Commands

	Meets Criteria of a G/FO Requirement	Does Not Meet Criteria of a G/FO Requirement	Inconclusive	Total	
O-10	7, 4, 4			7, 4, 4	15
O-9	5, 9, 12, 6			5, 9, 12, 6	32
O-8	1, 24, 39, 10		1, 12, 7, 2	2, 36, 46, 12	96
O-7	19, 45, 33	2, 20, 9, 4	6, 33, 21, 7	8, 72, 75, 44	199
Total	6, 59, 100, 53	2, 20, 9, 4	7, 45, 28, 9	15, 124, 137, 66	342
	218	35	89	342	

Legend: ▮ Joint   ▮ Air Force   ▮ Army   ▮ Navy   ▮ Marine Corps

criteria for a G/FO requirement. Just as important, a large number of the positions, 70 percent, were assessed as meeting the criteria for a G/FO requirement. It is noteworthy that the services organize and perform training somewhat differently. For example, the Air Force provides a significant amount of training in a decentralized fashion within its operational organizations, whereas the Army has a more centralized approach. This accounts for the larger number of general officers in the Army's training organizations, which exceeds all the other services combined.[3]

---

[3] The Army training portion of the total includes all the subordinates to the Commander of the Training and Doctrine Command except for Recruiting Command and the Army Futures/Army Capability Integration Center.

Table 9.6
RAND Integrated Results for Professional Career Fields

	Meets Criteria of a G/FO Requirement		Does Not Meet Criteria of a G/FO Requirement		Inconclusive		Total		
O-9	1						1		7
	2	2					2	2	
	2						2		
O-8	2		1		1		4		27
	2	2		4	3	7	5	13	
		1			3	1	4	1	
O-7	2				2		4		39
		2	6	11	4	6	10	19	
	1		2		3		6		
Total	5		1		3		9		73
	4	6	6	15	7	13	17	34	
	3		3		6	1	12	1	
	18		25		30		73		

Legend: ■ Joint   ■ Air Force   ■ Army   ■ Navy   ■ Marine Corps

Summary

The five cases just considered include 665 total positions with 63 in two cases and the other 602 positions in only one of the cases. Among the 63 positions in two cases are 39 positions in the Army Training and Doctrine Command, which are included in the case reducing the services to two O-10 positions and the case with academies, PME institutions, and training organizations. RAND integrated results determined that across these five cases, 355 (54 percent) of the 665 positions meet the criteria for a G/FO requirement. If DoD determined that all five of these categories were areas where reductions should be aimed, then RAND's integrated result suggests that 95 of these positions do not meet the criteria for a G/FO requirement. Additional analysis would be required to ensure that positions that might be eliminated, downgraded, or converted to a civilian do not introduce concerns relative to the organizational hierarchy or the ability to develop G/FOs for the most senior positions.

Table 9.7
RAND Integrated Results for Academies, PME Institutions, and Training Organizations

	Meets Criteria of a G/FO Requirement		Does Not Meet Criteria of a G/FO Requirement		Inconclusive		Total		
O-10		1						1	1
O-9	3	4					3	4	8
	1						1		
O-8		1				1		2	
	1	11	1			1	2	12	21
	2	3					2	3	
O-7		1		1		3		5	
		18	1		4	7	5	25	42
	2	3			2		4	3	
Total		2		1		4		7	
	4	34	2		4	8	10	42	72
	5	6			2		7	6	
	51		3		18		72		

Joint   Air Force   Army
         Navy   Marine Corps

Potential Demand for Additional General and Flag Officers

Organizational changes in the Department of Defense can affect the use and number of G/FOs. If new organizations are established to meet current or future requirements, DoD may need to make room for G/FO leadership positions within them if statutory authorizations are not increased. In this section, we explore several potential organizational changes and how they may influence the G/FO force. These explorations provide only rough estimates, derived from simple, first-order comparisons to existing organizations, of what additional demands for G/FOs might be. These estimates do not represent formal analyses of requirements or the numbers of G/FOs that will be required. Nor do we wish to imply these organizational changes (except for those already announced) will happen or should happen. Instead, they serve as examples through which to illustrate approximate planning factors for potential additional G/FO requirements.

Growth of U.S. European Command

There has been speculation that the increased military activity in U.S. European Command (USEUCOM) would require additional G/FO positions as the combatant command increases its number of military forces. To consider how and whether G/FO positions might increase at USEUCOM, we examined U.S. Pacific Command (USPACOM), another large combatant command in terms of scope and activity.

Although the two combatant commands have nearly the same number of authorized G/FO positions, ten for USEUCOM and 11 for USPACOM, the grade distribution is slightly different, with USPACOM employing two more O-8s and one fewer O-7 than USEUCOM. USPACOM uses O-8s to lead its J2 and J4 organizations compared to USEUCOM O-7s. USPACOM is the only geographical combatant command to have an O-8 J2 director, and only USPACOM and U.S. Central Command (USCENTCOM) have O-8 J4 directors. As its mission increases, USEUCOM may consider elevating one or both of these positions to O-8.

Furthermore, both USEUCOM and USPACOM employ several other types of G/FOs, including CRPs, individual mobilization augmentees (IMA), foreign officers, international rotational officers, or other G/FOs. Both USEUCOM and USPACOM rely on CRPs and IMAs (five for USEUCOM and six for USPACOM), and we expect significant impacts to the combatant commands if these G/FOs are eliminated without considering how to adapt the organization or its responsibilities to meet these ongoing requirements. From the information provided to us, the nature of the work done by USPACOM's foreign G/FOs is unclear. We identified at least three foreign G/FOs, and at least one of these positions rotates to the United States, but it is not currently held by a U.S. G/FO. Without knowing if these foreign G/FOs are filling U.S. requirements or if their work is more in support of their home country, we cannot determine if USEUCOM would benefit from a similar cadre of foreign G/FOs.

Service component commands provided by each of the services also give support to the combatant command. But there are differences between the service component commands' headquarters staff for USEUCOM and USPACOM. First, the Navy, Marine Corps, and Air Force all dual-hat their USEUCOM service component command G/FOs with their counterparts in U.S. Africa Command (USAFRICOM). Second, as can be seen in Table 9.8, there are more G/FOs supporting USPACOM than USEUCOM, and they also are of a higher grade. The higher G/FO numbers are driven by Pacific Fleet, since Pacific Fleet is also the Navy's west-coast force provider. While we have attempted to disentangle the force-provider and component functions, we estimate the differences are almost entirely attributable to the force-provider functions and not representative of potential future G/FO demands for Naval Forces Europe. These tables count the number of G/FOs in the headquarters staff of the respective service component commands, including country-specific G/FOs; they

Table 9.8
General and Flag Officers at U.S. European and Pacific Commands

Service Component	O-10	O-9	O-8	O-7	Total
U.S. European Command					
Army Europe	0	1	1	3	5
Naval Forces Europe	1	1[a]	1	1	4
Marine Corps Forces Europe	0	0	1	0	1
Air Forces in Europe	1	0	2	3	6
Total	2	2	5	7	16
U.S. Pacific Command					
Army Pacific	1	0	2	1	4
Pacific Fleet	1	3	3	16	23[b]
Marine Corps Forces Pacific	0	1	1	0	2
Pacific Air Forces	1	0	2	3	6
Total	3	4	8	20	35

[a] This position, "Commander, SIXTH Fleet/Commander, Task Force SIX/Commander, Striking and Support Forces NATO/Deputy Commander, United States Naval Forces Europe/Deputy Commander, United States Naval Forces Africa/Joint Force Maritime Component Commander Europe," is technically a joint position but because of its multiple responsibilities within the naval command chain, we include it here.

[b] We attribute the disproportionately large number of Pacific Fleet G/FOs compared to other service component commands to Pacific Fleet's role as the Navy's west-coast force provider. We do not consider this larger number representative of potential future G/FO demands for Naval Forces Europe.

do not include subordinate combatant commands, such as Alaskan Command, U.S. Forces Japan, and U.S. Forces Korea, nor do they include operational forces.

If attention and priorities continue to shift toward USEUCOM and if we assume USEUCOM needs to grow to roughly match USPACOM in number and grade of G/FOs, we estimate that USEUCOM would need to add three to four G/FOs, along with possible upgrades for USEUCOM J2 and J4 directors from O-7 to O-8.

Elevation of U.S. Cyber Command to a Unified Combatant Command

With support from the Department of Defense, the National Defense Authorization Act for Fiscal Year 2017 requires the President to "establish . . . a unified combatant command for cyber operations forces."[4] Following this direction, in August 2017, the President elevated USCYBERCOM, previously a subordinate unified combatant command of U.S. Strategic Command (USSTRATCOM), to a full and independent unified combatant command.

---

[4]   10 U.S. Code § 167b—Unified combatant command for cyber operations (a).

The USCYBERCOM combatant commander is already serving at the grade of O-10. We do not expect growth in the number and grade of G/FOs in the headquarters staffs, since the command already has as many G/FOs at the same grades as USSTRATCOM and USAFRICOM (and more G/FOs than both U.S. Southern Command [USSOUTHCOM] and U.S. Transportation Command [USTRANSCOM]). However, if USCYBERCOM finds additional requirements for a G/FO, it could offset an increase by civilianizing the J8 director. In every other combatant command (except for U.S. Special Operations Command [USSOCOM], which has service-like responsibilities and uses an O-8), the J8 director is a civilian, making USCYBERCOM's J8 G/FO director stand out as an anomaly.

As we understand it, when USCYBERCOM becomes a unified combatant command, the commander will no longer be dual-hatted as the NSA/CSS director. If the dual-hatting is eliminated, the director of NSA/CSS could be civilian; however, this change is not certain. If the director is military (this option seems more likely at the time this report is being written), we assume the director of NSA/CSS would revert to O-9, the grade the position had prior to becoming dual-hatted. Should the final decision be to continue to dual-hat the commander of USCYBERCOM as the director of NSA/CSS, there are no additional G/FO requirements.

As it transforms to a unified combatant command, we assume all of USCYBERCOM's current elements will remain under them, including Cyber National Mission Force (CNMF), Joint Force Headquarters Department of Defense Information Networks (JFHQ-DODIN), and DISA. We foresee that the current joint force cyber coordination elements at the various combatant commands will evolve into formal joint force cyberspace component commanders (JFCCCs) and will change in grade from O-6 to O-7, which could add up to nine additional new G/FO positions, one for each unified combatant command (and perhaps another for USFK). Because the service component commands to USCYBERCOM are well established, we believe these are unlikely to change as a result of the transition and that no additional G/FO requirements would arise from these.

In total, if USCYBERCOM emerges to match other functional unified combatant commands, we estimate that the elevation of USCYBERCOM to a unified command could add nine or more G/FOs.

Establishing or Eliminating a Unified Combatant Command

Many hypothetical ideas have floated around to include the notion of either creating new combatant commands or disestablishing old ones.[5] To garner a rough understanding of the G/FO requirement for such changes, we examined the average size of the G/FO staff in the current unified combatant commands' "J-code" headquarters. For the

---

[5] See, for example, Kathleen J. McInnis, *Goldwater-Nichols at 30: Defense Reform and Issues for Congress*, Congressional Research Service, June 2, 2016.

geographical combatant commands, their G/FO general staff ranges from as few as six G/FOs (USSOUTHCOM) up to 12 G/FOs (USCENTCOM), with the most common size being nine (USAFRICOM and U.S. Northern Command [USNORTHCOM]) and ten (USEUCOM and USPACOM).[6] Functional combatant commands range from five G/FOs (USTRANSCOM) to nine (USSTRATCOM). USSOCOM, a functional unified combatant command with service-like responsibilities, has seven G/FOs. The combatant commands that use fewer G/FOs rely more on civilians or combine directorates, such as creating a J5/8 or J4/5.

Depending on the expected size and mission of a potential combatant command, we estimate the J-code G/FO staff could range between five and 12 G/FOs. This G/FO general staff could look something like the following:

- O-10 commander
- O-9 deputy commander
- O-8 chief of staff
- O-7 J2 director
- O-8 J3 director
- O-7 J3 deputy director
- O-7 J4 director (more commonly used for geographical combatant commands; functional combatant commands frequently use a non-G/FO)
- O-8 J5 director
- O-7 J5 deputy director (more commonly used for geographical combatant commands; functional combatant commands frequently use a non-G/FO)
- O-7 J6 director.

In addition to tailoring the J-code staff, a combatant command may also require additional G/FOs to fulfill specific missions unique to the command. For example, USPACOM uses an O-7 as the Commander Pacific Representative to Guam, while USCENTCOM has several G/FOs to help coordinate activities with foreign nations in its area of responsibility. Furthermore, functional unified combatant commands tend to have a nontrivial number of G/FO-led subcommands. USSOCOM, for example, has several G/FOs to lead their theater special operations commands (TSOC). Both types of combatant commands may also have subordinate unified commands, joint task forces (JTFs), and joint functional components. A new combatant command may need these bespoke G/FOs and subcommands to help it meet its mission, and the magnitude of these positions or organizations cannot be predicted.

Similarly, establishing a unified combatant command could impact the number of service G/FOs. Frequently, a service will stand up a service component command to

---

[6] While USPACOM submitted 11 G/FOs to us in the data, ten of these G/FOs are within USPACOM's J-code structure.

support the combatant command. However, services can choose to dual-hat a G/FO to serve in two separate organizations, such as the Air Force general who serves as both the commander of U.S. Air Forces Africa and the commander of U.S. Air Forces Europe or the commander of First Air Force and the commander of Air Forces Northern (in support of USNORTHCOM). In this way there is no net increase in the number of service G/FOs for the service component commands. A service component command usually has between one and seven G/FOs in its headquarters staff, but there can also be no net increase in the number of G/FOs if the G/FOs are multi-hatted with existing positions. The service may also provide a specific operational force or a single service force to support the unified combatant command.

On the other hand, eliminating a combatant command will not necessarily eliminate all G/FOs in the command. Since many of its missions are likely to continue after the abolishment of a combatant command, the missions, along with a subset of its G/FOs, are likely to be transferred to another entity, such as another combatant command. And, because most service components associated with combatant commands are dual-hatted, their elimination is also unlikely to lead to many reductions in service G/FOs.

As part of the forced-choice exercise, for example, the participants suggested the possibility of consolidating combatant commands, thereby eliminating some of the staff positions. In particular, the players discussed two possible consolidations: USAF-RICOM and USEUCOM, and USNORTHCOM and USSOUTHCOM. Table 9.9 shows a comparison between the USAFRICOM and USEUCOM headquarters staff positions. Currently, each contains the same positions and at the same grade except

Table 9.9
Comparison Between USAFRICOM and USEUCOM Headquarter Staff G/FOs

	Headquarter Staff	
Grade	USAFRICOM	USEUCOM
O-10	Commander	Commander
O-9	Deputy Commander	Deputy Commander
O-8	Chief of Staff	Chief of Staff
O-7	Director J2	Director J2
O-8	Director J3	Director J3
O-7	Deputy Director J3	Deputy Director J3
O-7	Director J4	Director J4
O-8	Director J5	Director J5
O-7	Deputy Director J5	Deputy Director J5
O-7		Director J6

for a J6 in USEUCOM but not USAFRICOM. Consolidating these two staffs would eliminate the following positions:

- One O-10 commander
- One O-9 deputy commander
- Three O-8 chief of staff, director J3, director J5
- Four O-7 director J2, deputy director J3, director J4, deputy director J5.

Additionally, while the Air Force and Navy component commanders are dual-hatted in USAFRICOM and USEUCOM, the Army and Marine component commanders are not. Assuming the two O-8 Marine Force Commanders would be consolidated and that the O-8 Army Africa Commander would be consolidated with the O-9 Army Europe Commander, two O-8 positions could be eliminated. Finally, the O-8 Africa Special Operations Commander could be absorbed into the O-9 Europe Special Operations Commander. We assume that all other positions and commands (defense attachés, supreme allied headquarters, allied force headquarters, and joint task force headquarters) would not be changed. In total, one O-10, one O-9, six O-8, and four O-7 G/FO requirements might be eliminated.

Table 9.10 shows a comparison between the USNORTHCOM/NORAD and USSOUTHCOM Headquarter staff G/FOs. While the USNORTHCOM/NORAD Commander is a single G/FO requirement, headquarter subordinates Chief of Staff,

Table 9.10
Comparison Between USNORTHCOM and USSOUTHCOM Headquarter Staff G/FOs

Grade	USNORTHCOM	NORAD	USSOUTHCOM
O-10	Commander		Commander
O-9	Deputy Commander		Deputy Commander
O-7		Deputy Commander Canadian NORAD Region	
O-8	Chief of Staff (Dual Hat)		Chief of Staff
O-7	Director J2 (Dual Hat)		Director J2
O-8	Director J3		
O-7			Director J3[a]
O-7	Deputy Director J3[a]		
O-7	Deputy Director J3 (Protection)		
O-8	Director J5 (Dual Hat)		Director J5
O-7	Director Cyberspace Operations (Dual Hat)		

[a] Coast Guard positions.

Director J2, Director J5, and Director Cyberspace Operations are dual-hatted, with each hat as a separate G/FO requirement. Also of note are the Coast Guard positions, USNORTHCOM Deputy Director J3 and the USSOUTHCOM Director J3. How these staffs might be affected by a combined USNORTHCOM/USSOUTHCOM is uncertain.

If we consider just the staff positions that USNORTHCOM and USSOUTHCOM have in common at the same grade (Commander, Deputy Commander, Chief of Staff, Director J2, Director J5), the G/FO requirement could be reduced by:

- One O-10
- One O-9
- Two O-8
- One O-7.

Combining the J3s would depend on resolution of the Coast Guard positions. Furthermore, if the USNORTHCOM and NORAD dual-hatted positions (each as two requirements) were consolidated into a single requirement, two O-8 and two O-7 G/FO requirements would be eliminated. Additionally, component commanders in USSOUTHCOM could be absorbed into their USNORTHCOM counterparts with a reduction of one O-9, two O-8s, and one O-7.[7] Beyond these consolidations we assume that other subordinate commands (Joint Interagency Task Force South and Alaska Command) would remain intact.

In summary, the consolidation of USAFRICOM and USEUCOM as well as USNORTHCOM and USSOUTHCOM might lead to eliminating the following total G/FO requirements:

- Two O-10
- Three O-9
- Twelve O-8
- Eight O-7.

Formation of a "Space Corps" or a U.S. Space Command Unified Combatant Command

With growing attention and strategic value placed on space, there is consideration being given to elevating the space function currently within the U.S. Air Force to a Space Corps or a reconstituted U.S Space Command.[8] Either option could increase G/FO requirements.

---

[7]   The USSOUTHCOM Air Force component commander is an O-9 with an O-7 vice commander. The other component commanders have no G/FO subordinates.

[8]   The United States Space Command (USSPACECOM) was a unified combatant command created in 1985 and merged with USSTRATCOM in 2002.

Space Corps

Creation of a Space Corps is intended to be a new armed service to man, train, and equip "spacemen." We presume a modest start to the potential Space Corps, making the Marine Corps organization the closest service comparison for estimating G/FO staff sizes. We project G/FO requirements for this new service would arise in the following ways:

- The new service secretariat
- The new service chief, vice chief, and service headquarters staff
- Some number of Space Corps major commands, with a minimum of three: one to command space operations, one to manage space materiel and systems, and one to oversee the recruiting and training of Space Corps officers and enlisted
- The creation of Space Corps service component commands to combatant commands.

Some of the initial structure for the Space Corps can be transferred from existing organizations throughout the Department of Defense. However, the Space Corps would likely need additional structure to build out the organization, and any gaps in leadership would need to be complemented with new G/FO requirements. We list here the G/FO positions that we hypothesize, based on the small service U.S. Marine Corps template, that the new service would need. Note that we list here the G/FO positions without regard as to whether they would be new or transferred G/FOs; we subsequently address the number of these positions that are likely to be transferred from other services.

- A Secretary of Space and a corresponding secretariat staff that is primarily civilian, with perhaps five to ten G/FOs serving in positions such as the inspector general, legislative liaison, chief information officer, public affairs, and assistants/deputies to the Secretary of Space. If there is a secretariat staff, we predict that new G/FO positions will be provided, with an increase of about five to ten G/FOs. Notionally, this change would be one or two O-9 positions (such as for an inspector general, chief information officer, and/or an acquisition director), two or three O-8 positions, and two to five O-7 positions.
- A new Space Corps service headquarters led by a chief and vice chief with a traditional general staff, which we will identify using "X" prefixes, analogous to the Headquarters of the Air Force's current "A" prefixes. The Space Corps chief and vice chief would be O-10 positions. One of these would be taken from the current O-10 position corresponding to the commander of Air Force Space Command (this organization would become an O-9-led Space Corps major command; see below), but the other O-10 position would be a new requirement. Following the Marine Corps template, we assume O-9s would serve as directors of the X-code headquarters staff (X1, X3/5, X4, X6, X8, X9) and estimate a total of six O-9s, ten

O-8s, and seven O-7s for the directorate staffs as a whole. We presume the current Air Force A11 directorate would transfer to the Space Corps headquarters staff.

- We assume the new service would have three major commands: a Space Operations Command, a Space Materiel/Systems Command, and a Space Recruiting/Training Command. We estimate these would require approximately 20 to 30 G/FO positions.

  - Space Operations Command. For purposes of discussion, we assume the current Air Force Space Command (AFSPC) would become the Space Operations Command. All of AFSPC's subordinate commands would also transfer and become subordinates of Space Operations Command. The commander of Space Operations Command would be an O-9 (recall the O-10 position was used for the service chief position). The transferred organizational structure comprises 11 G/FO positions (five O-8s[9] and six O-7s), in addition to the new O-9 commander position).

  - Space Systems and Materiel Command. Based on the Marine Corps template, this organization would require a single O-8 commander and no other G/FOs. However, space-related systems and materiel are particularly costly and complex, especially as compared to Marine Corps systems. In this instance, the Marine Corps template may not apply. If the Air Force Materiel Command (and its subordinates) is a better representation of the requirements, this could be as large as 25 G/FOs, including a few O-9s and a half-dozen O-8s, with the correct answer for Space probably somewhere between. For our purpose, we assume an O-9 commander and maybe five to ten additional G/FOs (say two to four O-8s and three to seven O-7s).

  - Space Recruiting and Training Command. Following the Marine Corps model, this command (and subordinates) would add about five to ten G/FOs (potentially spread across subordinate organizations), notionally an O-9 commander, two to four O-8s, and two to four O-7s.

- Space Corps service component commands to each of the nine unified combatant commands (except for USTRANSCOM) as well as for the subordinated unified combatant commands of USCYBERCOM and USFK. To staff these commands, we estimate that the Space Corps would require ten new G/FOs to serve as service component commanders. For simplicity, we assume these commanders would be authorized as O-7s, but it is possible the authorized grades may be higher. As a comparison, the Marine Corps' service component commanders are authorized O-8 or O-9, with only the service component commander to USSOUTHCOM authorized at O-7.

---

[9]   We assume the two currently subordinate O-9 positions in AFSPC would be downgraded to O-8s if the organization transferred under the Space Corps with an O-9 commander. This change would make available two O-9 positions for elsewhere in the Space Corps.

In summary, we estimate a Space Corps service might require a total of 64 to 79 positions distributed as follows:

- Two O-10s (the service chief and vice chief)
- Ten to 11 O-9s (one or two in the Secretariat, six in the service headquarters, and three as commanders of major commands)
- 21 to 26 O-8s
- 31 to 40 O-7s.

We assume that not all of these positions would be new. As highlighted previously, we assume AFSPC and all its subordinate commands, the Air Force HQ A11 directorate, and a few other disparate organizations (including, possibly, from the Army and Navy) would transfer to the new Space Corps. From these organizations, we estimate a total of about 30 G/FO positions would transfer to the Space Corps, which leaves a net requirement for about 35 to 50 more G/FO positions over the existing G/FO requirements. This addition would include one new O-10 position (one O-10 position would transfer and be repurposed from present AFSPC), and seven to eight new O-9 positions (three existing O-9 positions would transfer and be repurposed from USAF HQ A11 and AFSPC subordinate commands).

U.S. Space Command

If the decision were made to, instead, create a combatant command for space, for example, USSPACECOM, then USCYBERCOM is a relevant comparison as a functional combatant command.[10] Overall additional requirements for G/FOs would come from the following:

- Creation of USSPACECOM headquarters staff
- Creation of a subordinate unified combatant command under USSPACECOM, analogous to the Joint Special Operations Command or Cyber National Mission Force
- Creation of USSPACECOM joint force functional component commands to other combatant commands (or vice versa) (could add up to nine additional new G/FO positions, one for each unified combatant command, and perhaps two more for USCYBERCOM and USFK)
- Creation of service component commands to USSPACECOM.

---

[10] We considered using the disestablished U.S. Space Command as a comparative organization for a newly formed U.S. Space Command, but decided it was not a good template. Combatant commands have changed dramatically since 2002, becoming much larger and more complex. For example, in 2002, there were approximately five G/FOs serving in U.S. Southern Command headquarters, either as part of the J-staff or subordinate organizations; today there are approximately 13.

Based on USCYBERCOM as a model, USSPACECOM would require nine G/FOs to lead its headquarters general staff:

- One O-10 (commander)
- One O-9 (deputy commander)
- Three O-8s (chief of staff, J3 director, and J5 director)
- Four O-7s (J2 director, J8 director, and two J3 deputy directors)
- Two J3 deputy directors.

However, USSPACECOM could choose to be like most of the other combatant commands and use a civilian as its J8 director, leaving USSPACECOM to need only eight G/FOs to lead its headquarters.

We assume USSPACECOM would also create a joint operations command as a subordinate unified combatant command for space, which we notionally call National Space Operations Command. Further, we assume the National Space Operations Command would be based on a renamed Joint Functional Component Command (JFCC)-Space and, therefore, would require one O-9 and one O-7.

Similar to USCYBERCOM's potential to develop joint force cyberspace component commands at each of the combatant commands, we assume that USSPACECOM will also establish a functional component command for each of the unified combatant commands (and perhaps for USFK). We expect each of these functional component commands will be led by an O-7, for a total of ten to eleven new G/FOs.

Similarly, we predict each of the four services will set up a service component command to support a USSPACECOM. We assume these commands would be roughly equivalent to the current service component commands to USCYBERCOM, as shown in Table 9.11.

Based on these rough estimates, the creation of USSPACECOM as a functional unified combatant command could potentially create requirements for the following G/FO positions:

- One O-10
- Four O-9s
- Five O-8s
- 18 to 19 O-7s.

Not all these positions would be new; some number of existing positions would transfer to USSPACECOM. However, it is much harder to estimate the number transferred than in the case of creating Space Corps as a new service, since the man, train, and equip responsibilities associated with space remain with the services (predominately with the Air Force). Therefore, AFSPC and USAF HQ-11 would not automatically transition entirely to USSPACECOM. Nevertheless, some selected elements or portions of existing commands would likely transfer functionality to USSPACECOM and, accordingly, some G/FO positions as well.

Table 9.11
Potential G/FO Positions for Service Component Commands to a Possible USSPACECOM

Grade	ARSPACE (based on Army Cyber)	NAVSPACE (based on 10th Fleet)	MARSPACE (based on Marine Corps Cyberspace Command)	SPACEAF (based on 24th Air Force)	Total
O-9	1	1			2
O-8			1	1	2
O-7	1	1		1	3
Total	2	2	1	2	7

NOTE: Based on service component commands to USCYBERCOM.

It is somewhat uncertain if the services have existing space-related commands that could be dual-hatted to fill the service component command needs. The Air Force could dual-hat AFSPC as the Air Force service component to USSPACECOM, and perhaps the Army would dual-hat Army Space and Missile Defense Command as its service component. We assume the Navy and Marine Corps would, again, multi-hat their current USSTRATCOM components to also serve as components to USSPACE-COM. In any case we assume all service components' demands would be satisfied by dual-hatting and no new G/FO requirements would actually arise from the service component commands to USSPACECOM.

In summary, for purposes of estimating the number of existing G/FOs, we assume that:

- One O-8 and two O-7 positions from AFSPC transfer to USSPACECOM
- JFCC-Space with its O-9 and O-7 positions transfers in its entirety under USSPACECOM, becoming the new the National Space Operations Command
- All service component commands' requirements are met from existing commands and G/FO positions.

This leaves a potential net requirement for:

- One O-10
- One O-9
- Three O-8s
- 12 to 13 O-7s.

In total, this is close to 20 additional G/FO positions over existing G/FO requirements.

Future Management Challenges

This chapter demonstrates how the methodologies developed in RAND's review of G/FO requirements can be used to support the management of the department's G/FO force in a practical way. The ongoing and dynamic decisions required to manage this force ensure the services and joint commands have the uniformed senior leaders needed to support the mission while remaining within congressionally mandated limits on G/FO authorizations. Deliberations within the department on which positions require G/FO leadership should be systematic and transparent. They should also be made in a way that acknowledges the fact that very senior decisionmakers cannot review the characteristics of more than a thousand requirements or the needs of hundreds of organizations. Examining meaningful communities of positions can be a more manageable approach to providing insight into the decisionmaking process.

Nonetheless, service equities, readiness considerations, and management challenges mean that distributing limited G/FO authorizations among the requirements for leadership positions will always be a challenging endeavor, and any approach for helping the department arrive at such decisions in a more systematic way must take this into account. The analyses presented in this chapter illustrate the types of information that can be produced to inform decisions.

Using RAND's integrated results and themes uncovered in the forced-choice exercise, the subordinate relationships in the Command Chain Application illustrate the potential number of positions to be harvested from communities of positions often considered for reduction. Using these methods in this way demonstrates that across OSD and DoD agencies, joint and service headquarters, service component commands, professional career fields, and academic and training organizations, approximately 100 positions did not meet the criteria for a G/FO requirement. Should reductions in the number of G/FO positions be mandated now or in the future, RAND recommends these positions be reviewed for consideration along with additional positions that could be identified due to the ripple effect of downgrades.

In addition, the characteristics of organizations uncovered during the structural and organizational analysis coupled with deliberations during the forced-choice exercise illustrate how G/FO staffing decisions must be considered when new organizations are needed for mission requirements or new requirements are mandated. Conventional wisdom often suggests that organizational restructuring can lead to a significant change in the requirements for leadership positions, but our analyses indicate that is not always the case. A shift in priorities toward USEUCOM and consolidation of combatant commands yielded relatively few additions or savings in G/FO requirements; elevating USCYBERCOM to a unified command could result in a moderate increase in G/FO requirements. On the other hand, standing up a new organization, such as a Department of Space, substantially increases requirements for G/FO leadership positions and would require careful study as to where these positions would be drawn from should the authorization caps remain unchanged. The type of analysis underlying these results can play a role in future G/FO management.

CHAPTER TEN

Policy and Management Recommendations

In the previous chapters, we described a systematic process for reviewing G/FO requirements and implemented that process using a dataset of 1,113 service and joint requirements provided to RAND (as of March 2017). Using data from that date and sets of criteria, guidelines, and assumptions that we described in detail, we illustrated the types of results that are possible. The findings in this report can assist DoD in making choices among G/FO requirements in response to congressional directives. However, the primary purpose of this study was to develop a rigorous and systematic approach for making such choices. In that vein, our recommendations center on steps the department should take to ensure G/FO requirements meet current needs and are well justified in the future. The recommendations are divided into two groups, policy and management.

Policy Recommendations

Holistic Approach to Filling Leadership Requirements
Establish a philosophy for using all available workforce talent to fill DoD leadership requirements—active and reserve component general and flag officers, senior civilians, officers at the grade of O-6 or below. (USD [P&R] and the service secretaries)

In the past, the services and joint organizations responded to ever-pressing constraints on the total number of G/FOs by "trimming along the edges" rather than conducting a comprehensive and global evaluation of requirements that most need to be filled by G/FOs. Trimming along the edges may result in an allocation of limited G/FO resources that is suboptimal. We observed in our point-in-time analysis that there were opportunities for converting G/FO positions to senior civilian positions, filling positions with O-6s, and consolidating organizations and duties so as to eliminate the need for a G/FO in a position. This does not mean our analysis concludes that there are excess G/FO authorizations; rather, we conclude that G/FOs may not be filling the most strongly justified positions.

DoD needs to take a holistic approach to filling leadership positions that draws on talent from all parts of the workforce—active and reserve component G/FOs, senior civil servants, and officers at the grade of O-6 and below. We recommend that OSD establish an overarching philosophy and guidelines for using all available talent, and especially cases where the use of non-G/FO personnel is justified. To add flexibility, and thus enable a holistic approach, the department could consider coding some senior leadership positions for multiple sectors of the workforce—civilian and military, active and reserve, as appropriate. In doing so, selection would be dependent on the best qualified individual with consideration also given to the current national security environment, the current state of the organization, and workforce constraints (G/FO authorizations or civilian Senior Executive Service [SES] caps).

Strategic Guidance

Issue overarching policy guidance related to G/FO leadership roles and requirements. (Secretary of Defense)

A significant challenge in conducting this review, and which the department has faced more broadly in responding to periodic congressional inquiries regarding the appropriate number of G/FOs, is the lack of formal policy guidance regarding what constitutes a G/FO requirement and how these requirements should be prioritized in the face of limited G/FO resources. While highly prescriptive policy guidance would be inappropriate and counterproductive, the complete lack of policy on G/FO requirements exposes the department to continued questioning about this issue by outside organizations, fails to counter repeated use of G/FO-to-troop ratios as the "defining" metric, and contributes to poorly or inconsistently written job descriptions for G/FO positions—which in turn unnecessarily exposes the department to challenges and undermines confidence in DoD's G/FO management processes.

We recommend the Secretary of Defense issue overarching policy guidance that:

- Identifies the G/FO leadership roles in the department.
- Highlights some of the most important characteristics that identify most G/FO requirements while acknowledging that other factors beyond those explicitly listed may also play a role in certain cases.
- Emphasizes that just as the proverbial corporal is called upon not only to be tactical but also "strategic,"[1] so, too, the department's leaders are increasingly called upon to be not only operational experts but also motivating leaders, strategic thinkers, capable diplomats, reliable financial stewards, effective interlocutors in dealings with the executive and legislative branches, and savvy in interacting with international counterparts and the media. For this reason, many positions held by non-G/FOs in the past require skills associated with G/FOs today. Simplistic

---

[1]   Charles C. Krulak, "The Strategic Corporal: Leadership in the Three Block War," *Marines Magazine*, Air University, 1999.

G/FO-to-troop ratios are an inappropriate and anachronistic representation of current requirements.

* Makes clear that G/FOs are a limited resource—a high-demand, low-density asset—and identifies broad principles for prioritizing how valuable G/FO resources should be assigned and effectively managed.

We further recommend that the Chairman of the Joint Chiefs of Staff (for joint requirements) and the service secretariats and chiefs (for the service requirements) issue corresponding guidance that nests under and appropriately refines the Secretary's guidance, highlights joint- or service-specific factors and priorities, and expands the Secretary of Defense's priorities for developing, managing, and assigning G/FOs.

Guidance such as this would go a long way toward defusing outside criticism, establish a basis for future reviews, and serve as guidance for developing effective, well-justified G/FO requirements.

Periodically Evaluate G/FO Requirements

Establish a standing central body for vetting G/FO requirements in accordance with Secretary of Defense strategic guidelines and with up-to-date and on-the-shelf data. (USD [P&R], lead)

We recommend that the department use the methodology described here to conduct reviews of G/FO requirements on a periodic basis. Key to an effective review process is the establishment of a standing (as opposed to ad hoc) central body for vetting requirements in accordance with strategic guidelines set by the Secretary of Defense and with up-to-date and on-the-shelf data (as recommended in the management section). This body should include representatives from the services and joint community to include subject matter experts from the G/FO management offices, representatives from the service secretariat Manpower and Reserve Affairs organizations, and when necessary, senior leaders with knowledge of operational, readiness, and management policies impacting current and future G/FO requirements.

Departmental mandates to review categories of G/FO requirements over time will encourage discussion and engagement among the members and help reduce service-centric perspectives. A standing body means the participants will accumulate knowledge on G/FO requirements and avoid the significant time required to understand G/FO related statutes, requirements considerations, and management processes typical of ad hoc arrangements.

The intent of such a body is not to limit service secretary, service chief, or joint senior leader prerogative to establish G/FO requirements. Instead, the aim is to ensure more consistency across the services in identifying true requirements, have a means to prioritize among competing requirements, share opportunities for efficiencies, and ensure the department speaks with one voice about the priorities for uniformed senior executives.

Management Recommendations

Targeted Reviews of G/FO Positions

Conduct targeted reviews of G/FO positions to determine the need for G/FO requirements and provide guidance to clarify apparent inconsistencies in the use of G/FOs within each group today. (OUSD [P&R], Joint Staff, and service secretaries)

In conducting this review, we identified groups of positions for which we recommend DoD and the services (as appropriate) conduct internal reviews. The reasons for this recommendation varied. In some cases, there is an overarching policy decision needed for whether such positions are appropriate uses of G/FOs. In other cases, there are gross inconsistencies across G/FO positions that are notionally equivalent. In yet other cases, job descriptions are uniformly unsatisfactory across a group of positions. We recommend the following targeted reviews.

G/FO Positions Within OSD

The fundamental issue is a policy question for DoD to answer: What is the appropriate role of G/FO positions within the Office of the Secretary of Defense and for civilian organizations outside of DoD? The question is whether the benefits justify the opportunity cost of filling these positions with a G/FO. We assess the pros of such assignments to be:

- These G/FOs bring senior military experience and perspectives to a civilian organization.
- The assignments provide valuable experience and understanding of OSD and interdepartmental and interagency to G/FOs who may go on to even more senior positions within DoD.
- The individual serves as a critical liaison between OSD and other agencies and the uniformed military.

The cons of such assignments include:

- The presence of these G/FOs may bypass OSD's formal and official mechanisms for reaching out to the Joint Staff, the services, or any of the combatant commands to obtain military advice and perspectives.
- These assignments put a senior military person in a civilian government agency (e.g., the Department of State) outside DoD.
- In some cases, these assignments place a senior military G/FO in the command chain of a department outside DoD.
- They potentially result in a perceived conflict of interest by putting a senior military person in OSD, an organization specifically charged to provide civilian guidance to and oversight of the military.
- They use a limited G/FO resource so that it cannot be employed elsewhere in DoD.

In our judgment, neither the pros nor the cons are entirely compelling. We recommend the Department of Defense conduct a review of these G/FO positions to provide overarching guidance on the appropriate uses of G/FO positions within OSD; review the existing G/FO positions within OSD to identify those that are consistent with said guidance and meet the criteria for a G/FO and transition to civilian positions those that are not; and review, especially in conjunction with the Department of State, the appropriateness and necessity of G/FO positions assigned to the Department of State.

G/FOs Assigned as Defense Attachés

It was not evident in our analysis why certain defense attaché (DATT) positions merited a G/FO of the grade specified as compared to other DATT positions around the world. Nor could we identify the criteria for determining the appropriate grade of a G/FO DATT and/or how many of the available G/FO resources should be dedicated to DATT missions. We recommend DoD conduct a review of all DATT G/FO positions to determine, based on systematic criteria, when G/FOs are needed in DATT positions, the countries that should be assigned G/FO DATTs, and the appropriate grades for these positions.

Contingency G/FO Positions and G/FOs in Joint Task Forces

We recommend a review of all contingency G/FO positions to determine whether the requirement for these positions still exists. Furthermore, we recommend such a review occur at regular periodic intervals as contingency operations are always evolving. In addition, four JTFs are currently led by G/FOs (and many more are not led by G/FOs). These organizations were a target for the Track Four Efficiency Initiatives Decisions from March 14, 2011, with the transformation of ten joint task forces and two Joint Interagency Task Forces (JIATF) into a total of six JIATFs. We recommend that the department review not only which JTF's merit G/FO leadership but also if they are structured and organized appropriately.

G/FOs in Combatant Commands

There is significant variation in the roles of G/FOs within combatant command (CCMD) staffs. To a large extent this reflects the varying missions, scopes, and scales of the different CCMDs. Nevertheless, given the pressures being applied to reduce the number of G/FO positions in the joint pool and the number of these positions within CCMD staffs, we recommend the department review this group of positions to ensure valuable G/FO resources are applied where they are most needed within the CCMDs.

G/FOs in Numbered Air Forces

The commanders and vice-commanders of numbered air forces currently vary in grade, with no correlation between the two. It is evident neither from the type of numbered air force nor the position description why positions have particular grades. We, therefore, recommend that the Air Force review these positions and articulate clear principles as to which numbered air forces merit an O-9 or O-8 commander (and which merit an O-7 or O-6 vice commander).

G/FOs in Deputy, Vice, and Assistant Positions

These terms are not consistently assigned to positions in the service or joint community. For example, *deputy* in some cases is used for someone whose primary job is to
"stand in for" the immediate senior (i.e., a traditional deputy commander). In other
cases, *deputy* is used for a senior subordinate with a specific and significant portfolio
of duties and functions (deputy chief of staff for an organization). In yet other cases
deputies more deeply buried within headquarter staffs often have job descriptions that
resemble a high-end administrative assistant. These latter are particularly challenging
to justify as G/FO positions. There are even G/FO positions titled *deputy deputy*—
with position descriptions that, unsurprisingly, make it difficult to justify as a G/FO
position. *Assistant* also is used for positions with an equally broad and diverse set of
functions, some clearly meriting a G/FO, many less obviously so. In view of this, we
recommend the department review positions with such titles, attempt to standardize
their use, and ensure that all are valid G/FO requirements.

Management of G/FO Positions

*To facilitate management and review of G/FO requirements, maintain updated, well-
defined position descriptions; assign standardized job titles and position identifiers; and
compile and maintain a repository of organization charts with standardized nomenclature
for defining organizational relationships. (The military services and Joint Staff)*

Our methodology for analyzing the general and flag officer force relied on critical information supplied by the services to OSD. The detailed position descriptions
were paramount. These descriptions not only define the roles and missions associated with the positions, but the span of control, managed resources, authorities, and
organizational relationships subordinate and superior to each position. We found that
although many positions had such a position description, most were considerably out
of date. Because of this, OSD's first task focused on creating or significantly updating
almost all general and flag officer position descriptions. This task proved to require
a substantial amount of effort and time. To improve the overall management of general and flag officers, we recommend that updated, well-defined position descriptions
be maintained. Because positions frequently change due to organizational changes or
world events, the regularity of the update should occur at prescribed intervals so as to
ensure that position descriptions are current. Further, the specific data items collected
should be consistent across position descriptions with clear specification of the information required. The data defined and collected by OSD for this study and organized
by RAND could be used as a point of departure on managing the position descriptions
in the future.

Additionally, two key parts of the position description are the position title and
the organizational relationships associated with a position. Position titles are often used
as a primary method for identifying a position. Changes in a title occur frequently and
can represent fundamental modifications to the position or simply a refining or alter-

native method of specifying the position. Additionally, because most titles are lengthy, various abbreviations or identifiers are often used as substitutes for the title. These different methods for labeling a position can cause confusion both in appropriately interpreting the label and in comparing or matching the label among multiple position lists over time and across services. Because of this, we recommend a systematic list of job titles and unique identifiers be complied and updated. For historical purposes, a pedigree of these labels should be maintained and not reused to reference different positions.

The organizational relationships of a position provide additional insight into the function and importance of the position. However, capturing these relationships is a difficult task. These associations are an additional dimension to the other elements of the position description representing not just the encapsulating organization but also reporting authorities, subordination, and lateral associations. The reporting authorities alone can include a wide range of potential relations from day-to-day administrative duties to operational responsibilities. Communicating these associations is often done using organizational charts. During the course of this project, we found gaps in the available organizational charts and a variety of approaches to the design and level of detail of the organizational charts that were available. Thus, we recommend that the department standardize the nomenclature for defining the organizational relationships and that a repository of organizational charts for senior leaders be compiled and maintained.

Improving the currency and standardization of general and flag officer job titles, position descriptions, and organizational charts will give OSD an ability to better manage and justify positions held by general and flag officers.

Leadership Needs for Emerging Requirements
Adopt a systematic approach to identifying leadership needs for organizational changes (creating or dissolving) in response to emerging requirements so they are well understood before changes are adopted. (USD [P&R] and Joint Staff, co-lead)

Deliberations within the department on which positions require G/FO leadership should be systematic and transparent. The tools developed in RAND's review of G/FO requirements can be used to evaluate leadership requirements when organizational change is needed in response to emerging needs—either to establish a new organization or dissolve an existing one. Evaluating communities of positions to support such changes offers a transparent way to identify the leadership requirements (or savings) associated with organizational change. Moreover, conventional wisdom often suggests that organizational restructuring can lead to a significant change in the requirements for leadership positions, but our analysis indicates that is not always the case.

Our analysis of a shift in priorities toward USEUCOM and consolidation of combatant commands yielded relatively few additions or savings in G/FO requirements; elevating USCYBERCOM to a unified command could result in a moderate increase in G/FO requirements. On the other hand, our analysis of standing up a new organization, such as a Department of Space, substantially increases requirements for G/FO leadership positions and would require careful study as to where these positions would be drawn from should the authorization caps remain unchanged. The type of analysis underlying these results can play a role in future G/FO management and inform decisionmaking in response to emerging requirements.

As the department makes decisions on organizational change or must do so in response to congressional mandate, it is important to make the implications of these changes more transparent so that leadership needs (from a strategic perspective) are well understood. Plans for organizational change should include the specific number and level of G/FO and SES leadership positions affected; DoD should then report implementation results once the organization is established or dissolved.

Implication of New Joint Pool Specifications for Each Service

Evaluate whether to seek lower joint pool floors and the elimination of joint pool ceilings to ensure the right balance between service control in joint positions and flexibility in managing G/FOs—in particular flexibility in developing G/FOs and ensuring qualified G/FOs are available to serve in joint positions. (OUSD [P&R])

The purpose and implications of §501(a)(2)(E) of the 2017 NDAA are unclear to us. That subparagraph not only lowers the joint pool authorization to 232 positions but also apportions the entire number to the services: 82 to the Army, 60 to the Navy, 69 to the Air Force, and 21 to the Marine Corps. However, the U.S. Code is not amended to reflect this apportionment. U.S. Code § 526a(b)(2) does, however, specify minimum numbers of G/FOs expected to serve in joint pool positions. These floors were introduced with the creation of the joint pool in the 2009 NDAA, and the 2017 NDAA lowered them in keeping with the smaller size of the joint pool. Those statutory floors, as amended, are 75 for the Army, 53 for the Navy, 68 for the Air Force, and 17 for the Marine Corps. However, those floors will be superseded if the apportionment of the full 232 joint pool positions in the 2017 NDAA is binding. The rationale might be that the apportionments effectively become floors when taking into account that there are up to 30 additional OCO positions that could go to any service. But the OCO positions may disappear, there may be fewer than 232 positions designated for the joint pool, and a service may not have the appropriate officers in the appropriate grades to fill every position in its joint pool apportionment, in which case it is unclear how the apportionments apply, if at all.

The introduction of joint pool floors ensured that each service would have a minimum number of G/FOs over and above its authorized end strength, while still allowing some variability and flexibility for the system to select the best person for the job. The 2009 NDAA originally established a joint pool of up to 324 G/FO positions, and the initial minimums summed to 243, or exactly 75 percent of the total size of the joint pool. When the maximum size of the joint pool was lowered to 310, the Air Force floor was lowered slightly, too, and the sum total of the minimums equaled 77 percent of the total size of the joint pool. The new minimums now total 213 positions, which will be 92 percent of the joint pool once it reaches the 232 total. If we treat the 82/60/69/21 allocations by service in the 2017 NDAA as minimums, they will equal 100 percent of the 232 joint pool and 86 percent of the joint pool plus 30 OCO.

Higher service-specific floors means less flexibility in managing the joint pool, but the trade-off may be greater predictability for the services in managing end strength.[2] To maintain the balance between flexibility and predictability, it would seem more appropriate to make floors disproportionately lower—in other words, make them a relatively smaller percentage of the total joint pool—as the joint pool gets smaller relative to in-service authorizations. Instead, the opposite appears to have happened with the 2017 NDAA, particularly if the service-specific allocations become binding.

There is a broader issue here, one that is beyond the scope of this study. That is the question of trade-offs in flexibility to choose a person for a position at the time the person is needed versus the ability to develop a person for that position before they are needed. If there were no joint positions, all of this could obviously be left up to the services and there may be no such trade-off because they would manage positions as well as people. With joint positions, it becomes trickier. Allowing the services more control and predictability in managing their people may result in better development and preparation for joint positions. But this comes at a cost of having less flexibility in assigning people to joint positions: the proverbial "right person" may not be available at the "right time" in the "right place." The services should evaluate whether seeking a change to the newer legislative restrictions will ensure the right balance between service control in joint positions and flexibility in managing G/FOs—which could lead to revision of current statutes. This is the only potential change in statute that has emerged in our assessment.

Final Thoughts

DoD needs a more analytic foundation with which to justify its G/FO requirements. RAND has offered such a method that the department could adopt. By undertaking periodic, systematic reviews of G/FO requirements within the context of senior leader strategic guidance and comprehensive leadership needs, the department is less likely to be issued congressional cuts, beyond those mandated for 2022, that are potentially detrimental. Our results suggest that at this time, with the requirements information provided, there are positions that should not be filled by G/FOs and it is possible to achieve the 110 reduction mandated by Congress while retaining sufficient senior

---

[2] To illustrate the point, end strength predictability was not much of an issue before 2009 when the exclusion for joint duty requirements was 12.

uniformed leadership. However, in the future, with a smaller G/FO population and potential emerging requirements, it will be much more difficult to identify reductions in the G/FO corps. Continuing to respond to pressures to reduce the number of G/FOs serving in leadership positions in the department by "counting stars" rather than systematically evaluating and establishing requirements that are well justified will be unsustainable.

Data Collection Protocol

This appendix describes the general and flag officer requirements data collected from the services by the OSD G/FO Management Office and provided to RAND. RAND assisted in development of the data collection protocol, included at the end of this appendix, so that the protocol would cover the totality of information required to conduct the RAND review. RAND also took care to review the data and ensure errors were corrected before conducting its analysis; that process is also described.

Developing the Data Collection Protocol

Taking into account the strengths and weaknesses of previous studies, RAND developed an electronic data protocol for use by OSD in gathering information on G/FO positions. The protocol was designed to include all G/FO positions that were counted against active component authorized strength, including all G/FO requirements that were not currently filled by a G/FO due to rotation scheduling, limited authorizations, or other management constraints.[1] The instrument includes 29 questions broken into seven categories: background, general information, nature of the responsibilities, magnitude of responsibilities, role in general/flag officer development, historical manning of the position, and concluding questions.

These categories, and their 29 component questions, were heavily informed by prior study efforts, particularly RAND's 2016 study of reserve G/FO requirements, which itself drew on the 16 established factors used in designating G/FO requirements, and the data protocols used by Kapos Associates Inc. and the Logistics Management Institute.[2] Background, general information, and conclusion provided general information about the position. Nature of the responsibilities and magnitude of responsibilities included question groupings similar to the Kapos study.

---

[1] The list of submitted G/FO positions included requirements that had not been filled by a G/FO following implementation of DoD's 2010–2011 Track Four Efficiency Initiatives.

[2] For more discussion of these factors and studies, see Harrington et al., 2016.

Role in general/flag officer development was a category added to the reserve general and flag officer study, which helped analyze the potential of the position in developing G/FOs for future positions (health of the pyramid). These questions also improved upon historical studies that were criticized for not accounting for emerging needs and requirements. Historical manning was another category included in the reserve general and flag officer study that improved upon previous studies as these questions accounted for dual-hatted positions and "workarounds" and assisted in identifying opportunities for military-to-civilian conversions.

Previous studies were criticized for being subjective and allowing for different interpretations of questions and their responses by the various services. To mitigate these criticisms, the data collection protocol was reviewed by each of the services and the Joint Staff; RAND also set aside time for a feedback period to ensure questions were well understood and appropriate. The services and Joint Staff also "pretested" the instrument against a sample of their requirements and recommended changes to the question wording. An exemplary real-life position was completed in coordination with the Joint Staff to provide an example for the services and Joint Staff to follow.

OSD collected data in an electronic format to standardize responses and aid in consistency for analysis. The DoD G/FO Working Group reviewed the final data collection form and process and approved it as sufficient in defining, capturing, and reflecting G/FO requirements.

Data Quality and Cleanup

To the maximum extent possible, the respective general/flag officer management office for each service attempted to prepopulate responses to questions. These offices had basic descriptive information that considerably improved data standardization and quality as well as minimized the data collection requirements for the individual completing the protocol. The instructions were for the individual serving in the position to review and edit the prepopulated responses as well as provide inputs for all other questions. Some G/FOs used their staffs to assist in the data completion process, and then they reviewed all responses prior to submission.

During the course of the data collection process, RAND responded to questions from the service and Joint Staff action officers concerning issues with and interpretation of the data collection protocol. Data codebooks were developed documenting acceptable responses for each question as well as serving as the basis for business intelligence checks of data quality. Additional explanations, guidance, lists of acceptable responses, and question clarifications were provided to assist in both G/FOs completing the protocol and action officers who were responsible for data quality and consistency of their service responses. Before data were provided to RAND, the respective

G/FO management offices conducted a quality and consistency check of their individual submissions both within their major command structures as well as the service as a whole.

RAND reviewed the data submissions for each individual position provided. This review focused on data consistency and completeness, with particular attention paid to survey questions that could be interpreted inconsistently by respondents. When survey responses were found to be inconsistent or blank, RAND flagged this for correction and, where sufficient information was available, proposed an alternative response. RAND maintained data resolution logs to ensure that all data issues were documented, addressed, and resolved. The revised dataset was given back to OSD to obtain the missing information from the services and review and revise RAND proposed corrections.

Separate quality control procedures were applied to multi-hatted positions to confirm the uniqueness of responsibilities. Such requirements were treated as separate data entries with information reflecting the separate and distinct aspects of the multiple roles. A few of the requirements originally submitted by the services and Joint Staff were determined not to be multi-hatted requirements but rather "additional duties" under a single requirement. These submissions were designated as duplicates and after confirmation by the services and Joint Staff were deleted from the final dataset. RAND also removed a small number of reserve component requirements that were included in the original data submission following verification of their status.

To further ensure data completeness, RAND checked the service and joint submissions against four sources: (a) the Blue Books from multiple dates, (b) service-submitted authorized strength reports, (c) organization charts received from the services and other sources, and (d) protocol responses on superiors and subordinate G/FOs. In cases where a missing G/FO requirement was found, RAND contacted the OSD G/FO management office to request a full data protocol submission. After final validation of the original submissions, including deletion of duplicate positions, the dataset included survey data for 1,148 requirements.

Some of the 1,148 individual requirements were part of a larger multi-hatted set of requirements that have generally been filled by a single G/FO. RAND combined all the O-10 and O-9 multi-hatted requirements into a single row in the dataset, due to these positions having been validated as a single consolidated requirement during the Senate confirmation process. The O-8 and O-7 multi-hatted requirements, which are not subject to the same position-specific review during the Senate confirmation process, were left as separate rows in the dataset to be considered individually. Consolidation of O-9 and O-10 multi-hatted positions reduced the number of requirements in the dataset by 35, for a total of 1,113. This final dataset of 1,113 positions was used as the basis for each of the analytical efforts detailed in the report.

Instrument

Instructions

The data collection worksheet is administered via Excel and consists of two tabs. The first tab contains these general instructions for completing the database; the second tab contains the questions that require completion. You are only required to complete tab 2.

Tab 2, the data template, consists of 29 questions. You will find the questions in column A. Column B consists of an exemplar response to assist you in answering the questions. Responses for each position will be input in a single column. For example, responses for your first position will go in Column C, the second position in Column D and so on. If a position is multi-hatted you will complete a column for each of the positions ("hats") held. Please fill out a column for each general/flag officer in your purview.

Answers will be either free text, answers restricted to drop-down boxes, or specifically formatted. These variations are color coded—blank indicates free text, yellow indicates restricted to drop-down menus, and green indicates numeric format. Copying and pasting is allowed in the free text answer boxes. Please do not add any additional choices to the drop-down menus, nor make any changes to the questions. These cells will be locked. Please ensure all cells contain an entry even if the response is N/A. Rows that are shaded blue do not require responses.

When copying and pasting information into this worksheet from another source it is IMPORTANT that you follow these directions: either (1) choose "paste special" and then choose "text," or (2) choose "Match Destination Formatting" when you paste. If you do not choose either of these options when you paste it will lock the cell and you will be unable to edit the cell when you click out of it.

Further instructions may be provided by each Service's Action Officer for this data collection effort. Their contact information is provided separately.

Table A.1
Data Collection Protocol

General Information	Exemplar Responses
1. Position/duty/billet title *(make a complete and separate entry for any dual-hatted position, gapped billet, or lesser grade-filled assignments—a later section will collect additional information on these unique circumstances.)*	Commander, Director, Chief of Staff, J4, etc.
2. Authorized grade for position.	O-7 to O-10
3. Unique position identifier.	Joint position ID, Service-specific position identifier (e.g., Air Force Master ID, Navy Billet ID)
4. Organization name (please identify at the lowest organizational level appropriate, not the parent unit)	351st Civil Affairs Command, II MEF, PACAF, OPNAV N98
5. Unit Identification Code (UIC)	WYBKAA, PE3KFC11, 53824
6. Location (of the immediate/lowest organization, later question will address area of responsibility/ area supported).	Fort Bragg, NC; Stuttgart, Germany; Washington, D.C.

Background

7. What is the job description of the billet? (Official Description) (Please describe the primary functions of the job as listed in an official billet description or similar source.)	Write out billet description
8. The billet is currently accounted for under which statutory authority?	Title 10 USC 526 (a) or 526 (b); Title 10 USC 152
a. Is this billet currently exempt under the provisions of Title 10, USC, Section 527 or 528?	Yes/No
9. Position within operational chain of command.	For example, a Division/Wing commander would list subordinate Brigades/Squadrons; a Chief of Staff would list the 1-digit codes managed.
a. Within the operational chain of command, what are the grades and positions of the billets directly above and two levels above this position? Include all superiors in cases of dual-hatted positions.	The O-7 CENTCOM J33 would list: O-8 CENTCOM J3; and O-10 CENTCOM Commander
b. Within the operational chain of command, what are the GO/FO/SES and principal O-6/GS-15 grades and positions of the billets directly below and two levels below this position? (Please keep answers to permanent GO/FO/ SES subordinate positions and O-6 principal subordinates. Ignore temporary positions. There may be instances where "none" is an appropriate answer.)	The O-8 CENTCOM J3 would list: O-7 CENTCOM J33 and O-7 CENTCOM J39; would also list O-6 CENTCOM J32 and O-6 CENTCOM J35; and any principal O-6s subordinate to the first level named.
c. List all GO/FO/SES positions at the same level of this position within the operational chain of command. Include multiple lists of peers in the case of dual-hatting.	USARCENT would list USNAVCENT, USAFCENT, etc., under superior USCENTCOM. CENTCOM J5 would list all other CENTCOM J-code principals *regardless of rank.*

Table A.1—Continued

General Information	Exemplar Responses
Nature of the Responsibilities	
10. What is the mission of the organization? Include any additional objectives and goals that are not captured in the organizational mission statement. (Please provide the explicit stated mission of the organization in which the billet exists, not the parent organization.)	Write out unit mission statement. Other objectives may include promote regional stability or caring for the families of subordinates—peacetime activities versus just wartime orientation.
11. Characteristics of the organization (Please choose from the dropdown choices. If "other" is chosen, please identify the organization in the designated box.)	Type of organization
a. This position is in which type of organization? (Choose one)	
i. National	NSC, DIA
ii. OSD	OSD Staff, Under Secretary Staffs, Assistant Secretary Staffs
iii. Service Secretariat	SECARMY, SECNAV, SECAF
iv. Joint Staff	Joint Staff, J1, J2
v. Combatant Command	USCENTCOM, USPACOM, USCYBERCOM
vi. Service Chief Staff Headquarters	OPNAV, HQDA, Air Staff, HQMC
vii. Major Commands/Service Commands	TRADOC, ACC, COMNAVAIRFOR, Marine Corps Combat Development Command
viii. Theater	ISAF, USFOR-A, NATO, CJTF-HOA
ix. Service Component Command	ARCENT, NAVCENT, AFCENT
x. Operating Forces	Numbered Air Forces, Numbered Fleets, Armies, MAGTFs
xi. Direct reporting unit/Shore-based bureaus/Acquisition Activity/Supporting Establishment/Field Operating Agencies	USAF Academy, Naval Air Systems Command, U.S. Army Corps of Engineers, Capabilities Development Directorate
xii. Defense, Joint, or Service Agency	DISA, JPRA
xiii Other	Other
12. Characteristics of billet function. The following two questions establish the type and role of the position.	*For example, Commander of the Supply Corps would choose "commander" for part (a) and "Materiel and Logistics" for part (b).*
a. What is the nature of the billet position?	
i. Commander	1st Brigade Commander; Commander
ii. Deputy or Vice Commander	Deputy CG of I MEF
iii. Director	Director, Joint Staff
iv. Deputy Director	Deputy Director
v. Chief of Staff	Chief of Staff
vi. General/Flag Staff	J1, J2, J3

Table A.1—Continued

General Information	Exemplar Responses
vii. Program Executive Officer/Deputy PEO	PEO, DPEO
viii. Other	Other
b. What is the role of the position? (For Commanders/Directors this should be the same as the role of the organization. For other positions identify the specific function or role of the position within the organization.)	
i. Manpower and Personnel	J1; Deputy Chief of Staff for Personnel
ii. Intelligence	J2; Director, DIA
iii. Military Operations	J3; Commanding General, 2nd Army; Commander, 8th Air Force
iv. Materiel and Logistics	J4; Director, Defense Logistics Agency; Commander of the Supply Corps
v. C4I	J6; Deputy Chief of Staff for C4I
vi. Force Management, Development, Education and Training	Commanding General, Recruiting Command; Superintendent of the Naval Academy; Commanding General, Combat Development Center
vii. Strategic Plans and Policy	J5; Deputy Chief of Staff for Plans and Policies
viii. Acquisition/Research and Development	Program Executive Officer for F-35
ix. Special Staff (Legal, Medical, Public Affairs, Chaplain, Congressional Affairs)	Legislative Assistant; Judge Advocate General; Chief of Information; Commanding General, U.S. Army Medical Command
x. Capabilities Development/Integration	DC, CD&I; Navy Integration Office
xi. Program Management/Financial Management	J8; Director of the Army Budget
xii. Security	Chief of Security
xiii. Engineer	Chief of Engineers
xiv. Other	Other
13. Over the course of a typical month, what is the billet's role at the national and international level? (Please complete all boxes, even if they are all "N/A.")	*These entries do not include routine operational, administrative, or day-to-day responsibilities and therefore the totals do not necessarily sum to 100%. This question simply reflects the percent of time generally associated with these various audiences.*
Nature of Engagement with Each Type of Audience	
Primary (>50%) Frequent (25–50%) Occasional (5–24%) Rarely (<5%)	

Table A.1—Continued

General Information	Exemplar Responses
a. Senior Government Officials	OSD, State Department
b. Senior Political Officials	White House, Congress, Congressional Staff
c. State/Local authorities	Governors
d. Foreign government/Foreign military leaders	MoD
e. Nongovernmental organization senior leadership	USAID
f. Press, national level	Press, national level

Magnitude of Responsibilities

14. Resources managed and employed on an annual basis (including operational control, administrative control, and immediate staff).

(Please round to whole numbers. For personnel break out commissioned officers/warrant officers/ enlisted/civilian. For value of equipment, total obligation authority, and Working Capital Fund please provide response in $ million)

a. Direct reporting units. (Number and type of units normally assigned or programmed)	Military Units: 7th CSC: 15 units (including 5x O-6 commands); 21st TSC: 40 units
b. Personnel. (Number of authorized personnel by commissioned officer, warrant officer, enlisted, and civilian)	Personnel: 12,000; 7th CSC: 318/38/658/12; 21st TSC: 691/0/125/6807
c. Value of equipment and properties— annual. (Total value of equipment, supplies, and real property displayed in $ million or N/A)	Value of equipment: $21 million
d. Total obligation authority—annual. (record in $ million or N/A)	Total Obligation Authority: $23 million
e. Working Capital Fund—annual. (Record in $ million or N/A)	$189M, N/A
f. Other important resources—annual (including foreign resources, contracting support, overseas contingency operations). (Record in $ million or N/A)	$27M, N/A
15. Does the position set or direct specific areas of policy and doctrine development? If yes, identify which specific areas.	Budget, program, communications, manpower, supporting the "x" command, "y" service, or "z" COCOM
16. Does the position have authority to negotiate commitments or international agreements with foreign nations on behalf of the United States? If yes, please articulate under what circumstances, if able to do so in an UNCLASSIFIED manner.	Yes; supports CONPLAN 4299/4269
17. Geographical area of responsibility (including the size, location, and if appropriate, the criticality of the land, sea, or air spaces involved).	145.6 square miles in Oklahoma, 2,059 buildings

Table A.1—Continued

General Information	Exemplar Responses
18. Span of decisionmaking—describe specific areas of such independence of decisionmaking.	Provide examples of range of decisions autonomously made; making independent choices free from immediate direction; authority to formulate, affect, interpret, and implement policies and practices; authority to commit significant resources; authority to waive or deviate from established policies and practices without prior approval.
19. Are there any other unique attributes or authorities associated with this position that we should know about? (Specifically identify why there is a need for a General or Flag Officer in this position.)	The position requires the coordination of 6 O-6 level commands, or 90% of meetings that the individual attends are GO/FO-level meetings requiring commensurate level participation.

Role in General/Flag Officer Development

General Information	Exemplar Responses
20. **What prior experiences do you bring to your current role?** What special qualifications, if any, required by the position are essential to the proper execution of positional responsibilities? Please specify if each qualification is required by statue, policy, precedence, or some other factor (fill all that apply and identify the particular education, training, experience, etc. that is required; if they do not apply enter "N/A").	
a. Specific Training needed for this billet.	Specific branch or specialty (e.g., Chaplain, Seabee), language training for DAT
b. Prior Experience	Operational experience in the NAVCENT AOR; legislative experience; joint acquisition experience
c. Previous assignments recommended/ required to do your current job	MG Command; Joint billet
d. Other	Language skills
21. **What experiences will you gain in your current role?** What aspects of this position are key in developing incumbents for advancement to more-senior general and flag officer positions? Please specify if each qualification is required by statute, policy, precedence, or some other factor (fill all that apply and identify the particular education, training, experience etc. that will be gained; if they do not apply, enter "N/A").	HQ level experience particularly interactions with Congress and White House
a. Does this billet provide specific training?	Specific branch or specialty (e.g., Chaplain, Seabee); language training for DAT
b. Relevant skill-specific experience?	Operational experience in the NAVCENT AOR; legislative experience; joint acquisition experience
c. Relevant HQ experience?	HQ level experience particularly interactions with Congress and White House

Table A.1—Continued

General Information	Exemplar Responses
22. Does the position afford an opportunity to acquire significant joint experience?	Yes/No
a. Yes or no?	
b. If yes, please elaborate.	
c. Is the position identified as a Critical Joint Duty Assignment (CJDA)?	
Historical Manning of the Position	
23. Current grade of incumbent	O-6 to O-10 or potentially SES or vacant/gapped
a. Is the current incumbent frocked?	Yes/No
24. Is this position a buffer or temporary billet? (Service specific needs, emerging or contingent requirements of 2 years or less that are not renewable)	Yes/No
25. Does a general or flag officer currently fill this position?	Yes/No
a. Going back as far as available records permit, has a lesser grade ever been assigned to (filled) this billet?	Yes/No
Data not available	
Never	
Yes	
b. Does the lower grade of the individual currently filling the position impact the ability of the organization to perform its mission? If yes, please explain why, and address whether the assignment of promotable/selected O-6s does or does not mitigate the challenges.	Yes. Interaction with all Acquisition Flags is a routine event. Specifically, with NAVAIR peers, this billet is instrumental in working requirements for support in a dynamic and ever-changing environment. An O-6 would simply not have the institutional "horsepower" to affect change when needed. Lacks proper legal authority to execute OPLAN.
26. Going back as far as available records permit, approximately what percentage of the time has the position been filled by:	Provide answers in percentage, does not need to equal 100%
a. Gapped	
b. An officer of a higher grade	None
c. An officer of a lesser grade	10%
d. An SES	None

Table A.1—Continued

General Information	Exemplar Responses
27. Is this a dual-hatted or multi-hatted position? *(This includes holding two different positions, as well as a second "title" with corresponding functions, but not a separate billet. Explain both functions (hats) in the same line because they are filled by one person)*	
a. Yes/No	Yes/No
b. If yes, identify grade and title of other position(s)	Director, National Security Agency
c. If yes, identify precedence for dual-hatting of position	Precedence
i. Statute	
ii. Policy	
iii. Precedence	
iv. Some other factor	
28. To the extent that data is available, was this position split out from another position?	
a. Yes/No. If yes:	Yes/No
b. What position did this one originate from?	Title of position
c. What other positions were split out of it? (Please focus on what functions/positions may need to be codified in authorizations.)	Title of position
Conclusion	
29. Is there anything else specific to this billet that you wish to add that was not covered?	There is a similar SES position, no requirement for both a GO and SES position of the same nature

Command Chain Application

The Command Chain Application was designed to provide a way to organize, manage, and visualize the relationships between general and flag officer positions within the military chain of command. In this appendix, we describe how the Command Chain Application operates, how to install it, and some additions that could extend its capabilities.

Command Chains

When the Command Chain Application opens, the screen shown in Figure B.1 is displayed. Circled red numbers indicate specific portions of the display. The bulk of the display, indicated by red 1, portrays the command hierarchy starting with the political leadership, such as the President of the United States. This portion of the display can be expanded to follow specific command lines of authority. More on this part of the interface will be discussed after this initial overview.

The red 2 in the top left of the opening display shows the path to the database that maintains the command chain information. At the very bottom of the page, the red 3 shows two tabs containing two window options. The first window option, Command Chain, is the display shown in the figure. The second window, Position Search, contains an interface for searching through all the general and flag officer positions. The red 4 is placed just to the right of a tally of all of the general and flag officer positions in the command chain (1,113). Since civilian, foreign, and U.S. Coast Guard positions are also included in the command chain when at least one general or flag officer position is subordinate at some level below the position, a tally of all the positions is also given (1,196). To the right of the red 4 is a button that displays a designator for the position used in the database. For general and flag officers, these designators were supplied by the Joint Staff and the services. Two buttons at the bottom-middle are to the right of red 5. These buttons either save changes (Save Tree Changes) made by the user or cancels the changes (Cancel Changes). Finally, to the right of red 6 is a text box for typing in a value to search within the tree and resetting the text box. To submit a

Figure B.1
Opening Display for the Command Chain Application

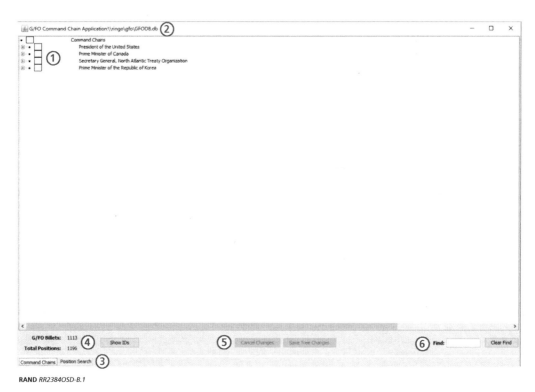

text search, type in the desired text and hit return. The display will then open the command chain to every position title that matches that set of text.

The next two figures (B.2 and B.3) show a close-up of the command chain. In Figure B.2, the command chain has been opened to Commander, Marine Forces Africa. Each line of the command chain represents one G/FO requirement. Symbology is used as a prefix to each position title to navigate the command chain and to describe the position. The navigation symbols ⊞ and ⊟ in front of positions are used to navigate through the hierarchy. The ⊞ symbol indicates that there are subordinate positions that have not been displaced. Clicking on this symbol will display the subordinate positions indented from their superior. By clicking ⊟, the list of subordinates retracts, showing just the superior position. When no box appears, the position does not have any subordinates.

After the navigation symbols, a small solid black box appears for all positions and then a larger colored box indicating association for the position. This includes:

• Purple for joint positions
• Light blue for Air Force positions

Figure B.2
Close-Up of the Opened Command Chain

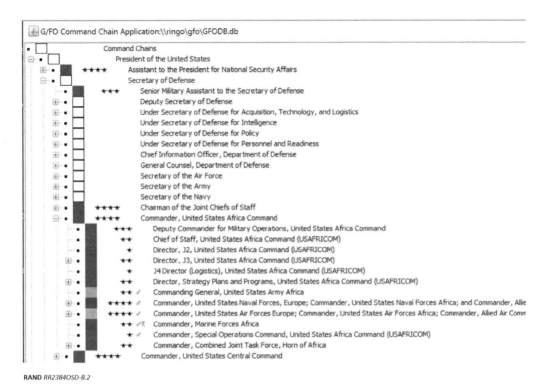

- Light green for Army positions
- Dark blue for Navy positions
- Dark red for Marine Corps positions
- White for civilian positions (U.S. or foreign)
- Bright red for Coast Guard positions
- Salmon for foreign general or flag officer positions.

After the association are stars indicating the authorized grade for G/FO positions. Between the stars and the position title, two small red symbols may appear. The symbol *&* indicates that this position occurs in other portions of the command chain. These are positions that report to multiple superiors based on various roles or conditions (such as administrative versus operation chain of command). For example, the Commander, Marine Corps Forces Africa is not only subordinate to the Commander, United States Africa Command but also the Commandant of the Marine Corps. The other symbol that might appear, $\bar{\chi}$, means that this position is multiple-hatted with other positions. For example, the Commander, Marine Corps Forces Africa is dual-hatted with the Commander, Marine Corps Forces Europe.

Positions in the command chain can be moved in sequence or under different superiors. This is done by clicking and holding the left mouse button. While holding, the position can then be dragged to the desired location and dropped (by releasing the mouse button). Dropping the selected position on another position will place the selected position last in the list of subordinates to the other position. Dropping the selected position between other positions inserts the selected position between the other positions. As the position is moved, a black line will appear as the mouse moves between positions. The drag-and-drop feature in the Command Chain Application requires that the command chain be opened to both the location of the selected position and the location where it is to be inserted.

Additional functions that can be performed for a position are shown in Figure B.3. By right-clicking a position, a menu appears. This menu currently contains functions that are available now and functions planned for future versions of the application. These include:

- Duplicate position (current): Replicated the position title and places it immediately below the selected title. This function is convenient for managing positions with multiple superiors.
- Delete position (current): Removes this particular instance of the position from the command chain.

Figure B.3
Menu of Options for a Position

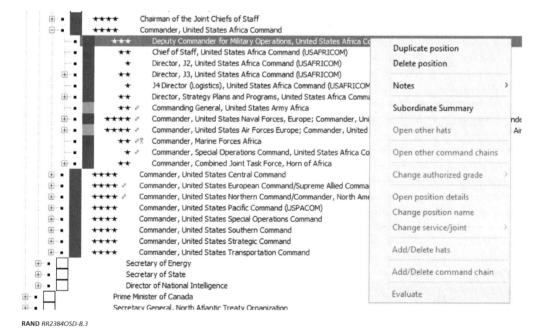

- Notes (current): Free-form comments can be added to any position or to any position/superior link in the command chain.
- Subordinate Summary (current): This option opens an Excel workbook that creates a tally and list of the positions subordinate to the selected position.
- Open other hats (current): Opens the command chain to all the positions that are multi-hatted with the selected position.
- Open other command chains (current): Opens the command chain to any multiple occurrences of this position reporting to other senior officers.
- Change authorized grade (future): Allows the user to change the authorized grade for the position.
- Open position details (future): This selection would pop up a screen with position details contained in the underlying database. Many of these details are shown in the position search screen described in the next section. Additional details collected by OSD or provided by the services could also be added.
- Change position name (future): Allows the position title to be altered.
- Change service/joint (future): Allows the position association to a desired service or to joint.
- Add/Delete hats (future): Connects/disconnects the selected position to/from other positions in a multi-hatted relationship.
- Add/Delete command chain (future): Adds/deletes the selected position to/from other organizations in the command chain.
- Evaluate (future): Tool for determining the status of the selected position.

Additional functionality that could be added to the Command Chain Application is discussed at the conclusion of this appendix.

Position Search

The second tab in the Command Chain Application, Position Search (as shown in Figure B.1, red 3), is used to find particular positions or groups of positions within the command chain. The interface is shown in Figure B.4. Along the left side of the window is a set of options for filtering positions. After clicking the "Search" button at the bottom left, a list of qualifying positions appears in the upper portion of the main window. Beneath the list of positions is a tally of the number of positions overall and by grade for the positions in the upper portion. Selecting a position in the upper window will cause details for the position to be displayed in the lower portion of the window.

The example in Figure B.4 shows the selection of filters that would include all the general and flag officer positions in the professional career fields (health professions, legal, and chaplains) that are classified as "Meets the criteria for a G/FO at current or higher grade" in the RAND integrated results. If a subset of these positions for particular services or grades is desired, the boxes near the top of the filter list can

Figure B.4
Position Search Interface

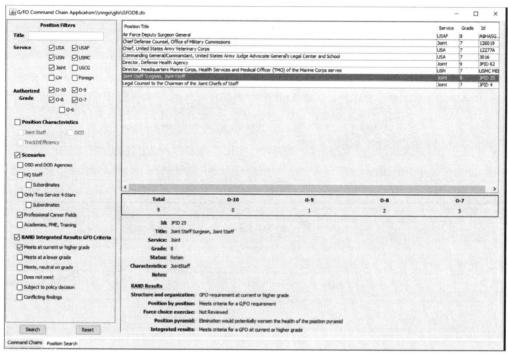

be unchecked. Boxes checked within one of the categories in bold type (Title, Service, Authorized Grade, Position Characteristics, Scenarios, and Position Status) will include positions with any of these characteristics. This is equivalent to an "or" condition among these values, such as O-7, O-8, O-9, or O-10 as selected in Figure B.4. Between categories in bold type, positions must satisfy all the criteria. This is equivalent to an "and" condition, such as positions in the Professional Career Fields and judged as "retain" in RAND's integrated results.

The qualifying position list contains four key characteristics associated with the position: position title, associated service, authorized grade, and the unique identifier supplied by the services. These columns can be sorted by clicking on the column designator at the top. Additionally, the columns can be moved in sequence by clicking and holding on the column designator, and then dragging and dropping the column in the desired order.

When a position is selected in the upper window, additional characteristics are shown below. The position identifier, position title, associated service, and authorized grade are repeated. Additionally, RAND's integrated results are shown after the status designator. The characteristic attribute indicates that the selected position is health related. The details also include any notes available for the position. Findings from RAND's four primary analytic approaches are then presented. For example, for this position, the structural analysis concluded that the position should be a G/FO requirement at current or higher grade. The position-by-position analysis concluded that the position meets the criteria for a G/FO requirement. The position was not reviewed as part of the Forced-Choice Exercise since it is an O-8 authorized position and the exercise covered only O-9 and O-10 positions. Finally, the pyramid analysis showed that elimination of this position would potentially worsen the health of the position pyramid. Overall, RAND's integrated results were that the position meets the criteria of a G/FO requirement at the current or higher grade.

Installing the Command Chain Application

The Command Chain Application consists of the following files:

- GFO_Command_Chain.jar
- sqlite-jdbc-3.16.1.jar
- sqliteodbc.exe
- SubordinateSummary.xlsm
- GFODB.db.

The first step in installing the application is to install the sqliteodbc.exe driver. Two drivers are available depending on whether the target computer is 32- or 64-bit. Select the version of the driver installer compatible with the computer being used. Starting this file will initiate the setup for the ODBC driver. Step through each of the screens. Install the SQLite 2 Drivers and the SQLite +TCC components.

Once the driver is installed, the GFO_Command_Chain.jar and GFODB.db files should be placed in a directory. Create a "lib" directory, and place sqlite-jdbc-3.16.1.jar and SubordinateSummary.xlsm in that directory. Once that is completed, opening the GFO_Command_Chain.jar file will open the application as explained above.

Possible Improvements

This first version of the Command Chain Application demonstrates some of the initial features used to better visualize and understand command linkages and position characteristics. The features completed in this version were useful in analyzing various aspects of general and flag officer position requirements. As shown previously, some additional features were planned for the command chains interface but not completed in this version. These include:

- Display of position details
- Changing position name
- Changing authorized grade
- Changing service affiliation
- Adding/deleting multiple hats
- Adding/deleting multiple command relationships
- Functions for evaluating position requirements.

Additional improvements to the command chain interface could include:

- Adding the position incumbent
- Specifying other characteristics or groupings for a position.

Improvements could also be made to the position search interface, including:

- Creating a more flexible set of filter options
- In the position list, display other characteristics
- For a selected position, optionally list multiple hats, superiors, and type of relationship (e.g., other leadership, staff, component commander, force provider, functional commander), and a tally of subordinates by grade.

Movement between the command chain interface and the position search interface could also improve the functionality of the application.

Statutes Governing General and Flag Officers

This appendix contains section-by-section language of relevant Title 10 authorizations relating to G/FO authorizations and positions. Table C.1 identifies statutes pertaining to the authorized number of general and flag officers, which includes sections 525 (General and Flag Officer Grade Distributions), 526 (General and Flag Officer Caps and Exemptions), 526a (General and Flag Officer Caps and Exemptions Starting 2023), 527 (Presidential Authority to Suspend Caps), 528 (Exemptions of Intelligence Positions from Caps), and 3210 and 8210, which stipulate the authorized strength for general officers in the Regular Army and Regular Air Force, respectively.

Table C.2 contains statutes related to specific G/FO positions in the joint community and within the military services. The following positions are covered:

- Chairman of the Joint Chiefs of Staff
- Vice Chairman of the Joint Chiefs of Staff
- Commanders of Combatant Commands: Assignment; Powers and Duties
- Commander, U.S. Special Operations Command
- Commander, U.S. Cyber Command
- Chief of Staff of the Army
- Vice Chief of Staff of the Army
- Deputy Chiefs of Staff and Assistant Chiefs of Staff of the Army
- Chief of Army Reserve
- Chief of Veterinary Corps of the Army
- Chief of Naval Operations
- Vice Chief of Naval Operations
- Chief of Navy Reserve
- Commandant of the Marine Corps
- Assistant Commandant of the Marine Corps
- Commander, Marine Forces Reserve
- Chief of Staff of the Air Force
- Vice Chief of Staff of the Air Force
- Deputy Chiefs of Staff and Assistant Chiefs of Staff of the Air Force
- Chief of Air Force Reserve

- Chief of the National Guard Bureau
- Three- and four-star positions
- Joint Requirements Oversight Council
- Director of the National Geospatial-Intelligence Agency (if held by an officer of the armed forces)
- Dean of the Academic Board of the United States Military Academy
- Communications Security Review and Advisory Board.

Table C.1
Statutes Pertaining to the Authorized Number of General and Flag Officers

Authorization and Section	Text
General and Flag Officer Grade Distributions *Section 525*	(a) For purposes of the applicable limitation in section 526(a) of this title on general and flag officers on active duty, no appointment of an officer on the active duty list may be made as follows: (1) in the Army, if that appointment would result in more than— (A) 7 officers in the grade of general; (B) 46 officers in a grade above the grade of major general; or (C) 90 officers in the grade of major general; (2) in the Air Force, if that appointment would result in more than— (A) 9 officers in the grade of general; (B) 44 officers in a grade above the grade of major general; or (C) 73 officers in the grade of major general; (3) in the Navy, if that appointment would result in more than— (A) 6 officers in the grade of admiral; (B) 33 officers in a grade above the grade of rear admiral; or (C) 50 officers in the grade of rear admiral; (4) in the Marine Corps, if that appointment would result in more than— (A) 2 officers in the grade of general; (B) 17 officers in a grade above the grade of major general; or (C) 22 officers in the grade of major general. (b) The limitations of subsection (a) do not include the following: (1) An officer released from a joint duty assignment, but only during the 60-day period beginning on the date the officer departs the joint duty assignment, except that the Secretary of Defense may authorize the Secretary of a military department to extend the 60-day period by an additional 120 days, but no more than three officers from each armed forces may be on active duty who are excluded under this paragraph. (2) The number of officers required to serve in joint duty assignments as authorized by the Secretary of Defense under section 526(b) for each military service. (c)(1) Subject to paragraph (3), the President— (A) may make appointments in the Army, Air Force, and Marine Corps in the grades of lieutenant general and general in excess of the applicable numbers determined under this section if each such appointment is made in conjunction with an offsetting reduction under paragraph (2); and (B) may make appointments in the Navy in the grades of vice admiral and admiral in excess of the applicable numbers determined under this section if each such appointment is made in conjunction with an offsetting reduction under paragraph (2). (2) For each appointment made under the authority of paragraph (1) in the Army, Air Force, or Marine Corps in the grade of lieutenant general or general or in the Navy in the grade of vice admiral or admiral, the number of appointments that may be made in the equivalent grade in one of the other armed forces (other than the Coast Guard) shall be reduced by one. When such an appointment is made, the President shall specify the armed force in which the reduction required by this paragraph is to be made.

Table C.1—Continued

Authorization and Section	Text
	(3)(A) The number of officers that may be serving on active duty in the grades of lieutenant general and vice admiral by reason of appointments made under the authority of paragraph (1) may not exceed 15. (B) The number of officers that may be serving on active duty in the grades of general and admiral by reason of appointments made under the authority of paragraph (1) may not exceed 5. (4) Upon the termination of the appointment of an officer in the grade of lieutenant general or vice admiral or general or admiral that was made in connection with an increase under paragraph (1) in the number of officers that may be serving on active duty in that armed force in that grade, the reduction made under paragraph (2) in the number of appointments permitted in such grade in another armed force by reason of that increase shall no longer be in effect. (d) An officer continuing to hold the grade of general or admiral under section 601(b) (5) of this title after relief from the position of Chairman of the Joint Chiefs of Staff, Chief of Staff of the Army, Chief of Naval Operations, Chief of Staff of the Air Force, or Commandant of the Marine Corps shall not be counted for purposes of this section. (e) The following officers shall not be counted for purposes of this section: (1) An officer of that armed force in the grade of brigadier general or above or, in the case of the Navy, in the grade of rear admiral (lower half) or above, who is on leave pending the retirement, separation, or release of that officer from active duty, but only during the 60-day period beginning on the date of the commencement of such leave of such officer. (2) At the discretion of the Secretary of Defense, an officer of that armed force who has been relieved from a position designated under section 601(a) of this title or by law to carry one of the grades specified in such section, but only during the 60-day period beginning on the date on which the assignment of the officer to the first position is terminated or until the officer is assigned to a second such position, whichever occurs first. (f) An officer while serving as Attending Physician to the Congress is in addition to the number that would otherwise be permitted for that officer's armed force for officers serving on active duty in grades above brigadier general or rear admiral (lower half) under subsection (a). (g)(1) The limitations of this section do not apply to a reserve component general or flag officer who is on active duty for a period in excess of 365 days, but not to exceed three years, except that the number of officers from each reserve component who are covered by this subsection and are not serving in a position that is a joint duty assignment for purposes of chapter 38 of this title may not exceed 5 per component, unless authorized by the Secretary of Defense. (2) Not later than 30 days after authorizing a number of reserve component general or flag officers in excess of the number specified in paragraph (1), the Secretary of Defense shall notify the Committees on Armed Services of the Senate and the House of Representatives of such authorization, and shall include with such notice a statement of the reason for such authorization.
General and Flag Officer Caps and Exemptions *Section 526*	(a) Limitations.—The number of general officers on active duty in the Army, Air Force, and Marine Corps, and the number of flag officers on active duty in the Navy, may not exceed the number specified for the armed force concerned as follows: (1) For the Army, 231. (2) For the Navy, 162. (3) For the Air Force, 198. (4) For the Marine Corps, 62. (b) Limited Exclusion for Joint Duty Requirements.— (1) The Secretary of Defense may designate up to 310 general officer and flag officer positions that are joint duty assignments for purposes of chapter 38 of this title for exclusion from the limitations in subsection (a). The Secretary of Defense shall allocate those exclusions to the armed forces based on the number of general or flag officers required from each armed force for assignment to these designated positions.

Table C.1—Continued

Authorization and Section	Text
	(2) Unless the Secretary of Defense determines that a lower number is in the best interest of the Department, the minimum number of officers serving in positions designated under paragraph (1) for each armed force shall be as follows:
	(A) For the Army, 85.
	(B) For the Navy, 61.
	(C) For the Air Force, 73.
	(D) For the Marine Corps, 21.
	(3) The number excluded under paragraph (1) and serving in positions designated under that paragraph—
	(A) in the grade of general or admiral may not exceed 20;
	(B) in a grade above the grade of major general or rear admiral may not exceed 68; and
	(C) in the grade of major general or rear admiral may not exceed 144.
	(4) Not later than 30 days after determining to raise or lower a number specified in paragraph (2), the Secretary of Defense shall notify the Committees on Armed Services of the Senate and the House of Representatives of such determination.
	(5)(A) The Chairman of the Joint Chiefs of Staff may designate up to 15 general and flag officer positions in the unified and specified combatant commands, and up to three general and flag officer positions on the Joint Staff, as positions to be held only by reserve component officers who are in a general or flag officer grade below lieutenant general or vice admiral. Each position so designated shall be considered to be a joint duty assignment position for purposes of chapter 38 of this title.
	(B) A reserve component officer serving in a position designated under subparagraph (A) while on active duty under a call or order to active duty that does not specify a period of 180 days or less shall not be counted for the purposes of the limitations under subsection (a) and under section 525 of this title if the officer was selected for service in that position in accordance with the procedures specified in subparagraph (C).
	(C) Whenever a vacancy occurs, or is anticipated to occur, in a position designated under subparagraph (A)—
	(i) the Secretary of Defense shall require the Secretary of the Army to submit the name of at least one Army reserve component officer, the Secretary of the Navy to submit the name of at least one Navy Reserve officer and the name of at least one Marine Corps Reserve officer, and the Secretary of the Air Force to submit the name of at least one Air Force reserve component officer for consideration by the Secretary for assignment to that position; and
	(ii) the Chairman of the Joint Chiefs of Staff may submit to the Secretary of Defense the name of one or more officers (in addition to the officers whose names are submitted pursuant to clause (i)) for consideration by the Secretary for assignment to that position.
	(D) Whenever the Secretaries of the military departments are required to submit the names of officers under subparagraph (C)(i), the Chairman of the Joint Chiefs of Staff shall submit to the Secretary of Defense the Chairman's evaluation of the performance of each officer whose name is submitted under that subparagraph (and of any officer whose name the Chairman submits to the Secretary under subparagraph (C)(ii) for consideration for the same vacancy).
	(E) Subparagraph (B) does not apply in the case of an officer serving in a position designated under subparagraph (A) if the Secretary of Defense, when considering officers for assignment to fill the vacancy in that position which was filled by that officer, did not have a recommendation for that assignment from each Secretary of a military department who (pursuant to subparagraph (C)) was required to make such a recommendation.
	(c) Exclusion of Certain Reserve Officers.—
	(1) The limitations of this section do not apply to a reserve component general or flag officer who is on active duty for training or who is on active duty under a call or order specifying a period of less than 180 days.
	(2) The limitations of this section also do not apply to a number, as specified by the Secretary of the military department concerned, of reserve component general or flag officers authorized to serve on active duty for a period of not more than 365 days. The number so specified for an armed force may not exceed the number equal to 10 percent of the authorized number of general or flag officers, as the case may be, of that armed force under section 12004 of this title. In determining such number, any fraction shall be rounded down to the next whole number, except that such number shall be at least one.

Table C.1—Continued

Authorization and Section	Text
	(3) The limitations of this section do not apply to a reserve component general or flag officer who is on active duty for a period in excess of 365 days but not to exceed three years, except that the number of such officers from each reserve component who are covered by this paragraph and not serving in a position that is a joint duty assignment for purposes of chapter 38 of this title may not exceed 5 per component, unless authorized by the Secretary of Defense.
	(d) Exclusion of Certain Officers Pending Separation or Retirement or Between Senior Positions.—
	The limitations of this section do not apply to a general or flag officer who is covered by an exclusion under section 525(e) of this title.
	(e) Exclusion of Attending Physician to the Congress.—
	The limitations of this section do not apply to the general or flag officer who is serving as Attending Physician to the Congress.
	(f) Temporary Exclusion for Assignment to Certain Temporary Billets.—
	(1) The limitations in subsection (a) and in section 525(a) of this title do not apply to a general or flag officer assigned to a temporary joint duty assignment designated by the Secretary of Defense.
	(2) A general or flag officer assigned to a temporary joint duty assignment as described in paragraph (1) may not be excluded under this subsection from the limitations in subsection (a) for a period of longer than one year.
	(g) Exclusion of Officers Departing From Joint Duty Assignments.—
	The limitations in subsection (a) do not apply to an officer released from a joint duty assignment, but only during the 60-day period beginning on the date the officer departs the joint duty assignment. The Secretary of Defense may authorize the Secretary of a military department to extend the 60-day period by an additional 120 days, except that not more than three officers on active duty from each armed force may be covered by an extension under this sentence at the same time.
	(h) Active-duty Baseline.—
	(1) Notice and wait requirement.—
	If the Secretary of a military department proposes an action that would increase above the baseline the number of general officers or flag officers of an armed force under the jurisdiction of that Secretary who would be on active duty and would count against the statutory limit applicable to that armed force under subsection (a), the action shall not take effect until after the end of the 60-calendar day period beginning on the date on which the Secretary provides notice of the proposed action, including the rationale for the action, to the Committees on Armed Services of the House of Representatives and the Senate.
	(2) Baseline defined.—For purposes of paragraph (1), the term "baseline" for an armed force means the lower of—
	(A) the statutory limit of general officers or flag officers of that armed force under subsection (a); or
	(B) the actual number of general officers or flag officers of that armed force who, as of January 1, 2014, counted toward the statutory limit of general officers or flag officers of that armed force under subsection (a).
	(3) Limitation.—
	If, at any time, the actual number of general officers or flag officers of an armed force who count toward the statutory limit of general officers or flag officers of that armed force under subsection (a) exceeds such statutory limit, then no increase described in paragraph (1) for that armed force may occur until the general officer or flag officer total for that armed force is reduced below such statutory limit.
	(i) Joint Duty Assignment Baseline.—
	(1) Notice and wait requirement.—
	If the Secretary of Defense, the Secretary of a military department, or the Chairman of the Joint Chiefs of Staff proposes an action that would increase above the baseline the number of general officers and flag officers of the armed forces in joint duty assignments who count against the statutory limit under subsection (b)(1), the action shall not take effect until after the end of the 60-calendar day period beginning on the date on which the Secretary or Chairman, as the case may be, provides notice of the proposed action, including the rationale for the action, to the Committees on Armed Services of the House of Representatives and the Senate.

Table C.1—Continued

Authorization and Section	Text
	(2) Baseline defined.—For purposes of paragraph (1), the term "baseline" means the lower of—
	(A) the statutory limit on general officer and flag officer positions that are joint duty assignments under subsection (b)(1); or
	(B) the actual number of general officers and flag officers who, as of January 1, 2014, were in joint duty assignments counted toward the statutory limit under subsection (b)(1).
	(3) Limitation.—
	If, at any time, the actual number of general officers and flag officers in joint duty assignments counted toward the statutory limit under subsection (b)(1) exceeds such statutory limit, then no increase described in paragraph (1) may occur until the number of general officers and flag officers in joint duty assignments is reduced below such statutory limit.
	(j) Annual Report on General Officer and Flag Officer Numbers.—Not later than March 1, 2015, and each March 1 thereafter, the Secretary of Defense shall submit to the Committees on Armed Services of the House of Representatives and the Senate a report specifying—
	(1) the numbers of general officers and flag officers who, as of January 1 of the calendar year in which the report is submitted, counted toward the service-specific limits of subsection (a); and
	(2) the number of general officers and flag officers in joint duty assignments who, as of such January 1, counted toward the statutory limit under subsection (b)(1).
	(k) Cessation of Applicability.—
	The provisions of this section shall not apply to number [1] of general officers and flag officers in the armed forces after December 31, 2022. For provisions applicable to the number of such officers after that date, see section 526a of this title.
General and Flag Officer Caps and Exemptions starting 2023 *Section 526a*	(a) Limitations.—The number of general officers on active duty in the Army, Air Force, and Marine Corps, and the number of flag officers on active duty in the Navy, after December 31, 2022, may not exceed the number specified for the armed force concerned as follows:
	(1) For the Army, 220.
	(2) For the Navy, 151.
	(3) For the Air Force, 187.
	(4) For the Marine Corps, 62.
	(b) Limited Exclusion for Joint Duty Requirements.—
	(1) In general.—
	The Secretary of Defense may designate up to 232 general officer and flag officer positions that are joint duty assignments for purposes of chapter 38 of this title for exclusion from the limitations in subsection (a).
	(2) Minimum number.—Unless the Secretary of Defense determines that a lower number is in the best interest of the Department of Defense, the minimum number of officers serving in positions designated under paragraph (1) for each armed force shall be as follows:
	(A) For the Army, 75.
	(B) For the Navy, 53.
	(C) For the Air Force, 68.
	(D) For the Marine Corps, 17.
	(c) Exclusion of Certain Officers Pending Separation or Retirement or Between Senior Positions.—The limitations of this section do not apply to—
	(1) an officer of an armed force in the grade of brigadier general or above or, in the case of the Navy, in the grade of rear admiral (lower half) or above, who is on leave pending the retirement, separation, or release of that officer from active duty, but only during the 60-day period beginning on the date of the commencement of such leave of such officer; or
	(2) an officer of an armed force who has been relieved from a position designated under section 601(a) of this title or by law to carry one of the grades specified in such section, but only during the 60-day period beginning on the date on which the assignment of the officer to the first position is terminated or until the officer is assigned to a second such position, whichever occurs first.
	(d) Temporary Exclusion for Assignment to Certain Temporary Billets.—

Table C.1—Continued

Authorization and Section	Text
	(1) In general.—

The limitations in subsection (a) do not apply to a general officer or flag officer assigned to a temporary joint duty assignment designated by the Secretary of Defense.

(2) Duration of exclusion.—

A general officer or flag officer assigned to a temporary joint duty assignment as described in paragraph (1) may not be excluded under this subsection from the limitations in subsection (a) for a period of longer than one year.

(e) Exclusion of Officers Departing From Joint Duty Assignments.—

The limitations in subsection (a) do not apply to an officer released from a joint duty assignment, but only during the 60-day period beginning on the date the officer departs the joint duty assignment. The Secretary of Defense may authorize the Secretary of a military department to extend the 60-day period by an additional 120 days, except that not more than three officers on active duty from each armed force may be covered by the additional extension at the same time.

(f) Active-Duty Baseline.—

(1) Notice and wait requirements.—

If the Secretary of a military department proposes an action that would increase above the baseline the number of general officers or flag officers of an armed force under the jurisdiction of that Secretary who would be on active duty and would count against the statutory limit applicable to that armed force under subsection (a), the action shall not take effect until after the end of the 60-calendar day period beginning on the date on which the Secretary provides notice of the proposed action, including the rationale for the action, to the Committees on Armed Services of the Senate and the House of Representatives.

(2) Baseline defined.—In paragraph (1), the term "baseline" for an armed force means the lower of—

(A) the statutory limit of general officers or flag officers of that armed force under subsection (a); or

(B) the actual number of general officers or flag officers of that armed force who, as of January 1, 2023, counted toward the statutory limit of general officers or flag officers of that armed force under subsection (a).

(g) Joint Duty Assignment Baseline.—

(1) Notice and wait requirement.—

If the Secretary of Defense, the Secretary of a military department, or the Chairman of the Joint Chiefs of Staff proposes an action that would increase above the baseline the number of general officers and flag officers of the armed forces in joint duty assignments who count against the statutory limit under subsection (b)(1), the action shall not take effect until after the end of the 60-calendar day period beginning on the date on which such Secretary or the Chairman, as the case may be, provides notice of the proposed action, including the rationale for the action, to the Committees on Armed Services of the Senate and the House of Representatives.

(2) Baseline defined.—In paragraph (1), the term "baseline" means the lower of—

(A) the statutory limit on general officer and flag officer positions that are joint duty assignments under subsection (b)(1); or

(B) the actual number of general officers and flag officers who, as of January 1, 2023, were in joint duty assignments counted toward the statutory limit under subsection (b)(1).

(h) Annual Report.—Not later than March 1 each year, the Secretary of Defense shall submit to the Committees on Armed Services of the Senate and the House of Representatives a report specifying the following:

(1) The numbers of general officers and flag officers who, as of January 1 of the calendar year in which the report is submitted, counted toward the service-specific limits of subsection (a).

(2) The number of general officers and flag officers in joint duty assignments who, as of such January 1, counted toward the statutory limit under subsection (b)(1).

Table C.1—Continued

Authorization and Section	Text
Presidential Authority to Suspend Caps *Section 527*	In time of war, or of national emergency declared by Congress or the President after November 30, 1980, the President may suspend the operation of any provision of section 523, 525, or 526 of this title. So long as such war or national emergency continues, any such suspension may be extended by the President. Any such suspension shall, if not sooner ended, end on the last day of the two-year period beginning on the date on which the suspension (or the last extension thereof) takes effect or on the last day of the one-year period beginning on the date of the termination of the war or national emergency, whichever occurs first. With respect to the end of any such suspension, the preceding sentence supersedes the provisions of title II of the National Emergencies Act (50 U.S.C. 1621–1622) which provide that powers or authorities exercised by reason of a national emergency shall cease to be exercised after the date of the termination of the emergency.
Exceptions of intelligence positions from caps *Section 528*	(a) Military Status.—An officer of the armed forces, while serving in a position covered by this section— (1) shall not be subject to supervision or control by the Secretary of Defense or any other officer or employee of the Department of Defense, except as directed by the Secretary of Defense concerning reassignment from such position; and (2) may not exercise, by reason of the officer's status as an officer, any supervision or control with respect to any of the military or civilian personnel of the Department of Defense except as otherwise authorized by law. (b) Director and Deputy Director of CIA.— When the position of Director or Deputy Director of the Central Intelligence Agency is held by an officer of the armed forces, the position, so long as the officer serves in the position, shall be designated, pursuant to subsection (b) of section 526 of this title, as one of the general officer and flag officer positions to be excluded from the limitations in subsection (a) of such section. (c) Associate Director of Military Affairs, CIA.— When the position of Associate Director of Military Affairs, Central Intelligence Agency, or any successor position, is held by an officer of the armed forces, the position, so long as the officer serves in the position, shall be designated, pursuant to subsection (b) of section 526 of this title, as one of the general officer and flag officer positions to be excluded from the limitations in subsection (a) of such section. (d) Officers Serving in Office of DNI.— When a position in the Office of the Director of National Intelligence designated by agreement between the Secretary of Defense and the Director of National Intelligence is held by a general officer or flag officer of the armed forces, the position, so long as the officer serves in the position, shall be designated, pursuant to subsection (b) of section 526 of this title, as one of the general officer and flag officer positions to be excluded from the limitations in subsection (a) of such section. However, not more than five of such positions may be included among the excluded positions at any time. (e) Effect of Appointment.—Except as provided in subsection (a), the appointment or assignment of an officer of the armed forces to a position covered by this section shall not affect— (1) the status, position, rank, or grade of such officer in the armed forces; or (2) any emolument, perquisite, right, privilege, or benefit incident to or arising out of such status, position, rank, or grade. (f) Military Pay and Allowances.— (1) An officer of the armed forces on active duty who is appointed or assigned to a position covered by this section shall, while serving in such position and while remaining on active duty, continue to receive military pay and allowances and shall not receive the pay prescribed for such position. (2) Funds from which pay and allowances under paragraph (1) are paid to an officer while so serving shall be reimbursed as follows: (A) For an officer serving in a position within the Central Intelligence Agency, such reimbursement shall be made from funds available to the Director of the Central Intelligence Agency.

Table C.1—Continued

Authorization and Section	Text
	(B) For an officer serving in a position within the Office of the Director of National Intelligence, such reimbursement shall be made from funds available to the Director of National Intelligence. (g) Covered Positions.— The positions covered by this section are the positions specified in subsections (b) and (c) and the positions designated under subsection (d).
Regular Army Strength in Grade, general officers *Section 3210*	(a) Subject to section 526 of this title, the authorized strength of the Regular Army in general officers on the active-duty list is 75/10,000 of the authorized strength of the Regular Army in commissioned officers on the active-duty list. (b) The authorized strength of each of the following branches— (1) each corps of the Army Medical Department; and (2) the Chaplains; in general officers on the active-duty list of the Regular Army is 5/1,000 of the authorized strength of the branch concerned in commissioned officers on the active-duty list of the Regular Army. Not more than one-half of the authorized strength in general officers in such a branch may be in a regular grade above brigadier general. (c) When the application of the percentages and ratios specified in this section results in a fraction, a fraction of one-half or more is counted as one, and a fraction of less than one-half is disregarded.
Regular Air Force Strength in Grade, general officers *Section 8210*	(a) Subject to section 526 of this title, the authorized strength of the Regular Air Force in general officers on the active-duty list is 75/10,000 of the authorized strength of the Regular Air Force in commissioned officers on the active-duty list. Of this authorized strength, not more than one-half may be in a regular grade above brigadier general. (b) When the application of subsection (a) results in a fraction, a fraction of one-half or more is counted as one, and a fraction of less than one-half is disregarded. (c) General officers on the active-duty list of the Regular Air Force who are specifically authorized by law to hold a civil office under the United States, or an instrumentality thereof, are not counted in determining authorized strength under this section.

Table C.2
Statutes Pertaining to Specific General and Flag Officer Positions

Position and Section*	Text
Chairman of the Joint Chiefs of Staff *Section 152*	(a) Appointment; Term of Office.— (1) There is a Chairman of the Joint Chiefs of Staff, appointed by the President, by and with the advice and consent of the Senate, from the officers of the regular components of the armed forces. The Chairman serves at the pleasure of the President for a term of two years, beginning on October 1 of odd-numbered years. Subject to paragraph (3), an officer serving as Chairman may be reappointed in the same manner for two additional terms. However, in time of war there is no limit on the number of reappointments. (2) In the event of the death, retirement, resignation, or reassignment of the officer serving as Chairman before the end of the term for which the officer was appointed, an officer appointed to fill the vacancy shall serve as Chairman only for the remainder of the original term, but may be reappointed as provided in paragraph (1). (3) An officer may not serve as Chairman or Vice Chairman of the Joint Chiefs of Staff if the combined period of service of such officer in such positions exceeds six years. However, the President may extend to eight years the combined period of service an officer may serve in such positions if he determines such action is in the national interest. The limitations of this paragraph do not apply in time of war. (b) Requirement for Appointment.— (1) The President may appoint an officer as Chairman of the Joint Chiefs of Staff only if the officer has served as— (A) the Vice Chairman of the Joint Chiefs of Staff; (B) the Chief of Staff of the Army, the Chief of Naval Operations, the Chief of Staff of the Air Force, or the Commandant of the Marine Corps; or (C) the commander of a unified or specified combatant command. (2) The President may waive paragraph (1) in the case of an officer if the President determines such action is necessary in the national interest. (c) Grade and Rank.— The Chairman, while so serving, holds the grade of general or, in the case of an officer of the Navy, admiral and outranks all other officers of the armed forces. However, he may not exercise military command over the Joint Chiefs of Staff or any of the armed forces.
Vice Chairman of the Joint Chiefs of Staff *Section 154*	(a) Appointment.— (1) There is a Vice Chairman of the Joint Chiefs of Staff, appointed by the President, by and with the advice and consent of the Senate, from the officers of the regular components of the armed forces. (2) The Chairman and Vice Chairman may not be members of the same armed force. However, the President may waive the restriction in the preceding sentence for a limited period of time in order to provide for the orderly transition of officers appointed to serve in the positions of Chairman and Vice Chairman. (3) The Vice Chairman serves at the pleasure of the President for a term of two years and may be reappointed in the same manner for two additional terms. However, in time of war there is no limit on the number of reappointments. (b) Requirement for Appointment.— (1) The President may appoint an officer as Vice Chairman of the Joint Chiefs of Staff only if the officer— (A) has the joint specialty under section 661 of this title; and (B) has completed a full tour of duty in a joint duty assignment (as defined in section 664(f) [1] of this title) as a general or flag officer. (2) The President may waive paragraph (1) in the case of an officer if the President determines such action is necessary in the national interest. (c) Duties.— The Vice Chairman performs the duties prescribed for him as a member of the Joint Chiefs of Staff and such other duties as may be prescribed by the Chairman with the approval of the Secretary of Defense.

Table C.2—Continued

Position and Section*	Text
	(d) Function as Acting Chairman.— When there is a vacancy in the office of Chairman or in the absence or disability of the Chairman, the Vice Chairman acts as Chairman and performs the duties of the Chairman until a successor is appointed or the absence or disability ceases. (e) Succession After Chairman and Vice Chairman.— When there is a vacancy in the offices of both Chairman and Vice Chairman or in the absence or disability of both the Chairman and the Vice Chairman, or when there is a vacancy in one such office and in the absence or disability of the officer holding the other, the President shall designate a member of the Joint Chiefs of Staff to act as and perform the duties of the Chairman until a successor to the Chairman or Vice Chairman is appointed or the absence or disability of the Chairman or Vice Chairman ceases. (f) Grade and Rank.— The Vice Chairman, while so serving, holds the grade of general or, in the case of an officer of the Navy, admiral and outranks all other officers of the armed forces except the Chairman. The Vice Chairman may not exercise military command over the Joint Chiefs of Staff or any of the armed forces.
Commanders of Combatant Commands: Assignment; Powers and Duties *Section 164*	(a) Assignment as Combatant Commander.— (1) The President may assign an officer to serve as the commander of a unified or specified combatant command only if the officer— (A) has the joint specialty under section 661 of this title; and (B) has completed a full tour of duty in a joint duty assignment (as defined in section 664(f) 1 of this title) as a general or flag officer. (2) The President may waive paragraph (1) in the case of an officer if the President determines that such action is necessary in the national interest. (b) Responsibilities of Combatant Commanders.— (1) The commander of a combatant command is responsible to the President and to the Secretary of Defense for the performance of missions assigned to that command by the President or by the Secretary with the approval of the President. (2) Subject to the direction of the President, the commander of a combatant command— (A) performs his duties under the authority, direction, and control of the Secretary of Defense; and (B) is directly responsible to the Secretary for the preparedness of the command to carry out missions assigned to the command. (3) Among the full range of command responsibilities specified in subsection (c) and as provided for in section 161 of this title, the primary duties of the commander of a combatant command shall be as follows: (A) To produce plans for the employment of the armed forces to execute national defense strategies and respond to significant military contingencies. (B) To take actions, as necessary, to deter conflict. (C) To command United States armed forces as directed by the Secretary and approved by the President. (c) Command Authority of Combatant Commanders.— (1) Unless otherwise directed by the President or the Secretary of Defense, the authority, direction, and control of the commander of a combatant command with respect to the commands and forces assigned to that command include the command functions of— (A) giving authoritative direction to subordinate commands and forces necessary to carry out missions assigned to the command, including authoritative direction over all aspects of military operations, joint training, and logistics; (B) prescribing the chain of command to the commands and forces within the command; (C) organizing commands and forces within that command as he considers necessary to carry out missions assigned to the command;

Table C.2—Continued

Position and Section*	Text
	(D) employing forces within that command as he considers necessary to carry out missions assigned to the command;
(E) assigning command functions to subordinate commanders;
(F) coordinating and approving those aspects of administration and support (including control of resources and equipment, internal organization, and training) and discipline necessary to carry out missions assigned to the command; and
(G) exercising the authority with respect to selecting subordinate commanders, selecting combatant command staff, suspending subordinates, and convening courts—martial, as provided in subsections (e), (f), and (g) of this section and section 822(a) of this title, respectively.
(2)(A) The Secretary of Defense shall ensure that a commander of a combatant command has sufficient authority, direction, and control over the commands and forces assigned to the command to exercise effective command over those commands and forces. In carrying out this subparagraph, the Secretary shall consult with the Chairman of the Joint Chiefs of Staff.
(B) The Secretary shall periodically review and, after consultation with the Secretaries of the military departments, the Chairman of the Joint Chiefs of Staff, and the commander of the combatant command, assign authority to the commander of the combatant command for those aspects of administration and support that the Secretary considers necessary to carry out missions assigned to the command.
(3) If a commander of a combatant command at any time considers his authority, direction, or control with respect to any of the commands or forces assigned to the command to be insufficient to command effectively, the commander shall promptly inform the Secretary of Defense.
(d) Authority Over Subordinate Commanders.—Unless otherwise directed by the President or the Secretary of Defense—
(1) commanders of commands and forces assigned to a combatant command are under the authority, direction, and control of, and are responsible to, the commander of the combatant command on all matters for which the commander of the combatant command has been assigned authority under subsection (c);
(2) the commander of a command or force referred to in clause (1) shall communicate with other elements of the Department of Defense on any matter for which the commander of the combatant command has been assigned authority under subsection (c) in accordance with procedures, if any, established by the commander of the combatant command;
(3) other elements of the Department of Defense shall communicate with the commander of a command or force referred to in clause (1) on any matter for which the commander of the combatant command has been assigned authority under subsection (c) in accordance with procedures, if any, established by the commander of the combatant command; and
(4) if directed by the commander of the combatant command, the commander of a command or force referred to in clause (1) shall advise the commander of the combatant command of all communications to and from other elements of the Department of Defense on any matter for which the commander of the combatant command has not been assigned authority under subsection (c).
(e) Selection of Subordinate Commanders.–
(1) An officer may be assigned to a position as the commander of a command directly subordinate to the commander of a combatant command or, in the case of such a position that is designated under section 601 of this title as a position of importance and responsibility, may be recommended to the President for assignment to that position, only—
(A) with the concurrence of the commander of the combatant command; and
(B) in accordance with procedures established by the Secretary of Defense.
(2) The Secretary of Defense may waive the requirement under paragraph (1) for the concurrence of the commander of a combatant command with regard to the assignment (or recommendation for assignment) of a particular officer if the Secretary of Defense determines that such action is in the national interest.

Table C.2—Continued

Position and Section*	Text
.	(3) The commander of a combatant command shall— (A) evaluate the duty performance of each commander of a command directly subordinate to the commander of such combatant command; and (B) submit the evaluation to the Secretary of the military department concerned and the Chairman of the Joint Chiefs of Staff. (4) At least one deputy commander of the combatant command the geographic area of responsibility of which includes the United States shall be a qualified officer of a reserve component of the armed forces who is eligible for promotion to the grade of O–9, unless a reserve component officer is serving as commander of that combatant command. (f) Combatant Command Staff.— (1) Each unified and specified combatant command shall have a staff to assist the commander of the command in carrying out his responsibilities. Positions of responsibility on the combatant command staff shall be filled by officers from each of the armed forces having significant forces assigned to the command. (2) An officer may be assigned to a position on the staff of a combatant command or, in the case of such a position that is designated under section 601 of this title as a position of importance and responsibility, may be recommended to the President for assignment to that position, only— (A) with the concurrence of the commander of such command; and (B) in accordance with procedures established by the Secretary of Defense. (3) The Secretary of Defense may waive the requirement under paragraph (2) for the concurrence of the commander of a combatant command with regard to the assignment (or recommendation for assignment) of a particular officer to serve on the staff of the combatant command if the Secretary of Defense determines that such action is in the national interest. (g) Authority to Suspend Subordinates.—In accordance with procedures established by the Secretary of Defense, the commander of a combatant command may suspend from duty and recommend the reassignment of any officer assigned to such combatant command. (h) Support to Chairman of the Joint Chiefs of Staff.—The commander of a combatant command shall provide such information to the Chairman of the Joint Chiefs of Staff as may be necessary for the Chairman to perform the duties of the Chairman under section 153 of this title.
Commander, U.S. Special Operations Command *Section 167 (c)*	The commander of the special operations command shall hold the grade of general or, in the case of an officer of the Navy, admiral while serving in that position, without vacating his permanent grade. The commander of such command shall be appointed to that grade by the President, by and with the advice and consent of the Senate, for service in that position.
Commander, U.S. Cyber Command *Section 167b (c)*	The commander of the cyber command shall hold the grade of general or, in the case of an officer of the Navy, admiral while serving in that position, without vacating that officer's permanent grade. The commander of such command shall be appointed to that grade by the President, by and with the advice and consent of the Senate, for service in that position.
Chief of Staff of the Army *Section 3033*	(a)(1) There is a Chief of Staff of the Army, appointed for a period of four years by the President, by and with the advice and consent of the Senate, from the general officers of the Army. He serves at the pleasure of the President. In time of war or during a national emergency declared by Congress, he may be reappointed for a term of not more than four years. (2) The President may appoint an officer as Chief of Staff only if— (A) the officer has had significant experience in joint duty assignments; and (B) such experience includes at least one full tour of duty in a joint duty assignment (as defined in section 664(f) [1] of this title) as a general officer.

Table C.2—Continued

Position and Section*	Text
	(3) The President may waive paragraph (2) in the case of an officer if the President determines such action is necessary in the national interest.
	(b) The Chief of Staff, while so serving, has the grade of general without vacating his permanent grade.
	(c) Except as otherwise prescribed by law and subject to section 3013(f) of this title, the Chief of Staff performs his duties under the authority, direction, and control of the Secretary of the Army and is directly responsible to the Secretary.
	(d) Subject to the authority, direction, and control of the Secretary of the Army, the Chief of Staff shall—
	(1) preside over the Army Staff;
	(2) transmit the plans and recommendations of the Army Staff to the Secretary and advise the Secretary with regard to such plans and recommendations;
	(3) after approval of the plans or recommendations of the Army Staff by the Secretary, act as the agent of the Secretary in carrying them into effect;
	(4) exercise supervision, consistent with the authority assigned to commanders of unified or specified combatant commands under chapter 6 of this title, over such of the members and organizations of the Army as the Secretary determines;
	(5) perform the duties prescribed for him by sections 171 and 2547 of this title and other provisions of law; and
	(6) perform such other military duties, not otherwise assigned by law, as are assigned to him by the President, the Secretary of Defense, or the Secretary of the Army.
	(e)(1) The Chief of Staff shall also perform the duties prescribed for him as a member of the Joint Chiefs of Staff under section 151 of this title.
	(2) To the extent that such action does not impair the independence of the Chief of Staff in the performance of his duties as a member of the Joint Chiefs of Staff, the Chief of Staff shall inform the Secretary regarding military advice rendered by members of the Joint Chiefs of Staff on matters affecting the Department of the Army.
	(3) Subject to the authority, direction, and control of the Secretary of Defense, the Chief of Staff shall keep the Secretary of the Army fully informed of significant military operations affecting the duties and responsibilities of the Secretary.
Vice Chief of Staff of the Army *Section 3034*	(a) There is a Vice Chief of Staff of the Army, appointed by the President, by and with the advice and consent of the Senate, from the general officers of the Army.
	(b) The Vice Chief of Staff of the Army, while so serving, has the grade of general without vacating his permanent grade.
	(c) The Vice Chief of Staff has such authority and duties with respect to the Department of the Army as the Chief of Staff, with the approval of the Secretary of the Army, may delegate to or prescribe for him. Orders issued by the Vice Chief of Staff in performing such duties have the same effect as those issued by the Chief of Staff.
	(d) When there is a vacancy in the office of Chief of Staff or during the absence or disability of the Chief of Staff—
	(1) the Vice Chief of Staff shall perform the duties of the Chief of Staff until a successor is appointed or the absence or disability ceases; or
	(2) if there is a vacancy in the office of the Vice Chief of Staff or the Vice Chief of Staff is absent or disabled, unless the President directs otherwise, the most senior officer of the Army in the Army Staff who is not absent or disabled and who is not restricted in performance of duty shall perform the duties of the Chief of Staff until a successor to the Chief of Staff or the Vice Chief of Staff is appointed or until the absence or disability of the Chief of Staff or Vice Chief of Staff ceases, whichever occurs first.
Deputy Chiefs of Staff and Assistant Chiefs of Staff of the Army *Section 3035*	(a) The Deputy Chiefs of Staff and the Assistant Chiefs of Staff shall be general officers detailed to those positions.
	(b) The Secretary of the Army shall prescribe the number of Deputy Chiefs of Staff and Assistant Chiefs of Staff, for a total of not more than eight positions.

Table C.2—Continued

Position and Section*	Text
Chief of Army Reserve *Section 3038*	(a) There is in the executive part of the Department of the Army an Office of the Army Reserve which is headed by a chief who is the adviser to the Chief of Staff on Army Reserve matters. (b) Appointment.— (1) The President, by and with the advice and consent of the Senate, shall appoint the Chief of Army Reserve from general officers of the Army Reserve who have had at least 10 years of commissioned service in the Army Reserve. (2) The Secretary of Defense may not recommend an officer to the President for appointment as Chief of Army Reserve unless the officer— (A) is recommended by the Secretary of the Army; and (B) is determined by the Chairman of the Joint Chiefs of Staff, in accordance with criteria and as a result of a process established by the Chairman, to have significant joint duty experience. (3) An officer on active duty for service as the Chief of Army Reserve shall be counted for purposes of the grade limitations under sections 525 and 526 of this title. (4) Until December 31, 2006, the Secretary of Defense may waive subparagraph (B) of paragraph (2) with respect to the appointment of an officer as Chief of Army Reserve if the Secretary of the Army requests the waiver and, in the judgment of the Secretary of Defense— (A) the officer is qualified for service in the position; and (B) the waiver is necessary for the good of the service. Any such waiver shall be made on a case-by-case basis. (c) Term; Reappointment.— The Chief of Army Reserve is appointed for a period of four years, but may be removed for cause at any time. An officer serving as Chief of Army Reserve may be reappointed for one additional four-year period. (d) Budget.— The Chief of Army Reserve is the official within the executive part of the Department of the Army who, subject to the authority, direction, and control of the Secretary of the Army and the Chief of Staff, is responsible for justification and execution of the personnel, operation and maintenance, and construction budgets for the Army Reserve. As such, the Chief of Army Reserve is the director and functional manager of appropriations made for the Army Reserve in those areas. (e) Full Time Support Program.— The Chief of Army Reserve manages, with respect to the Army Reserve, the personnel program of the Department of Defense known as the Full Time Support Program. (f) Annual Report.— (1) The Chief of Army Reserve shall submit to the Secretary of Defense, through the Secretary of the Army, an annual report on the state of the Army Reserve and the ability of the Army Reserve to meet its missions. The report shall be prepared in conjunction with the Chief of Staff of the Army and may be submitted in classified and unclassified versions. (2) The Secretary of Defense shall transmit the annual report of the Chief of Army Reserve under paragraph (1) to Congress, together with such comments on the report as the Secretary considers appropriate. The report shall be transmitted at the same time each year that the annual report of the Secretary under section 113 of this title is submitted to Congress.
Chief of Veterinary Corps of the Army *Section 3084*	The Chief of the Veterinary Corps of the Army shall be appointed from among officers of the Veterinary Corps. An officer appointed to that position who holds a lower grade shall be appointed in the grade of brigadier general.
Chief of Naval Operations *Section 5033*	(a) (1) There is a Chief of Naval Operations, appointed by the President, by and with the advice and consent of the Senate. The Chief of Naval Operations shall be appointed for a term of four years, from the flag officers of the Navy. He serves at the pleasure of the President. In time of war or during a national emergency declared by Congress, he may be reappointed for a term of not more than four years.

Table C.2—Continued

Position and Section*	Text
	(2) The President may appoint an officer as the Chief of Naval Operations only if— (A) the officer has had significant experience in joint duty assignments; and (B) such experience includes at least one full tour of duty in a joint duty assignment (as defined in section 664(f) 1 of this title) as a flag officer. (3) The President may waive paragraph (2) in the case of an officer if the President determines such action is necessary in the national interest. (b) The Chief of Naval Operations, while so serving, has the grade of admiral without vacating his permanent grade. In the performance of his duties within the Department of the Navy, the Chief of Naval Operations takes precedence above all other officers of the naval service. (c) Except as otherwise prescribed by law and subject to section 5013(f) of this title, the Chief of Naval Operations performs his duties under the authority, direction, and control of the Secretary of the Navy and is directly responsible to the Secretary. (d) Subject to the authority, direction, and control of the Secretary of the Navy, the Chief of Naval Operations shall— (1) preside over the Office of the Chief of Naval Operations; (2) transmit the plans and recommendations of the Office of the Chief of Naval Operations to the Secretary and advise the Secretary with regard to such plans and recommendations; (3) after approval of the plans or recommendations of the Office of the Chief of Naval Operations by the Secretary, act as the agent of the Secretary in carrying them into effect; (4) exercise supervision, consistent with the authority assigned to commanders of unified or specified combatant commands under chapter 6 of this title, over such of the members and organizations of the Navy and the Marine Corps as the Secretary determines; (5) perform the duties prescribed for him by sections 171 and 2547 of this title and other provisions of law; and (6) perform such other military duties, not otherwise assigned by law, as are assigned to him by the President, the Secretary of Defense, or the Secretary of the Navy. (e)(1) The Chief of Naval Operations shall also perform the duties prescribed for him as a member of the Joint Chiefs of Staff under section 151 of this title. (2) To the extent that such action does not impair the independence of the Chief of Naval Operations in the performance of his duties as a member of the Joint Chiefs of Staff, the Chief of Naval Operations shall inform the Secretary regarding military advice rendered by members of the Joint Chiefs of Staff on matters affecting the Department of the Navy. (3) Subject to the authority, direction, and control of the Secretary of Defense, the Chief of Naval Operations shall keep the Secretary of the Navy fully informed of significant military operations affecting the duties and responsibilities of the Secretary.
Vice Chief of Naval Operations *Section 5035*	(a) There is a Vice Chief of Naval Operations, appointed by the President, by and with the advice and consent of the Senate, from officers on the active-duty list in the line of the Navy serving in grades above captain and eligible to command at sea. (b) The Vice Chief of Naval Operations, while so serving, has the grade of admiral without vacating his permanent grade. (c) The Vice Chief of Naval Operations has such authority and duties with respect to the Department of the Navy as the Chief of Naval Operations, with the approval of the Secretary of the Navy, may delegate to or prescribe for him. Orders issued by the Vice Chief of Naval Operations in performing such duties have the same effect as those issued by the Chief of Naval Operations. (d) When there is a vacancy in the office of Chief of Naval Operations or during the absence or disability of the Chief of Naval Operations— (1) the Vice Chief of Naval Operations shall perform the duties of the Chief of Naval Operations until a successor is appointed or the absence or disability ceases; or

Table C.2—Continued

Position and Section*	Text
	(2) if there is a vacancy in the office of the Vice Chief of Naval Operations or the Vice Chief of Naval Operations is absent or disabled, unless the President directs otherwise, the most senior officer of the Navy in the Office of the Chief of Naval Operations who is not absent or disabled and who is not restricted in performance of duty shall perform the duties of the Chief of Naval Operations until a successor to the Chief of Naval Operations or the Vice Chief of Naval Operations is appointed or until the absence or disability of the Chief of Naval Operations or Vice Chief of Naval Operations ceases, whichever occurs first
Chief of Navy Reserve *Section 5143*	(a) Establishment of Office: Chief of Navy Reserve.—There is in the executive part of the Department of the Navy, on the staff of the Chief of Naval Operations, an Office of the Navy Reserve, which is headed by a Chief of Navy Reserve. The Chief of Navy Reserve— (1) is the principal adviser on Navy Reserve matters to the Chief of Naval Operations; and (2) is the commander of the Navy Reserve Force. (b) Appointment.— (1) The President, by and with the advice and consent of the Senate, shall appoint the Chief of Navy Reserve from flag officers of the Navy (as defined in section 5001(1)) who have had at least 10 years of commissioned service. (2) The Secretary of Defense may not recommend an officer to the President for appointment as Chief of Navy Reserve unless the officer— (A) is recommended by the Secretary of the Navy; and (B) is determined by the Chairman of the Joint Chiefs of Staff, in accordance with criteria and as a result of a process established by the Chairman, to have significant joint duty experience. (3) An officer on active duty for service as the Chief of Navy Reserve shall be counted for purposes of the grade limitations under sections 525 and 526 of this title. (4) Until December 31, 2006, the Secretary of Defense may waive subparagraph (B) of paragraph (2) with respect to the appointment of an officer as Chief of Navy Reserve if the Secretary of the Navy requests the waiver and, in the judgment of the Secretary of Defense— (A) the officer is qualified for service in the position; and (B) the waiver is necessary for the good of the service. Any such waiver shall be made on a case-by-case basis. (c) Term; Reappointment.— The Chief of Navy Reserve is appointed for a term determined by the Chief of Naval Operations, normally four years, but may be removed for cause at any time. An officer serving as Chief of Navy Reserve may be reappointed for one additional term of up to four years. (d) Budget.— The Chief of Navy Reserve is the official within the executive part of the Department of the Navy who, subject to the authority, direction, and control of the Secretary of the Navy and the Chief of Naval Operations, is responsible for preparation, justification, and execution of the personnel, operation and maintenance, and construction budgets for the Navy Reserve. As such, the Chief of Navy Reserve is the director and functional manager of appropriations made for the Navy Reserve in those areas.
Commandant of the Marine Corps *Section 5043*	(a)(1) There is a Commandant of the Marine Corps, appointed by the President, by and with the advice and consent of the Senate. The Commandant shall be appointed for a term of four years from the general officers of the Marine Corps. He serves at the pleasure of the President. In time of war or during a national emergency declared by Congress, he may be reappointed for a term of not more than four years. (2) The President may appoint an officer as Commandant of the Marine Corps only if— (A) the officer has had significant experience in joint duty assignments; and (B) such experience includes at least one full tour of duty in a joint duty assignment (as defined in section 664(f) [1] of this title) as a general officer.

Table C.2—Continued

Position and Section*	Text
	(3) The President may waive paragraph (2) in the case of an officer if the President determines such action is necessary in the national interest.
	(b) The Commandant of the Marine Corps, while so serving, has the grade of general without vacating his permanent grade.
	[(c) Repealed. Pub. L. 104–106, div. A, title V, § 502(c), Feb. 10, 1996, 110 Stat. 293.]
	(d) Except as otherwise prescribed by law and subject to section 5013(f) of this title, the Commandant performs his duties under the authority, direction, and control of the Secretary of the Navy and is directly responsible to the Secretary.
	(e) Subject to the authority, direction, and control of the Secretary of the Navy, the Commandant shall—
	(1) preside over the Headquarters, Marine Corps;
	(2) transmit the plans and recommendations of the Headquarters, Marine Corps, to the Secretary and advise the Secretary with regard to such plans and recommendations;
	(3) after approval of the plans or recommendations of the Headquarters, Marine Corps, by the Secretary, act as the agent of the Secretary in carrying them into effect;
	(4) exercise supervision, consistent with the authority assigned to commanders of unified or specified combatant commands under chapter 6 of this title, over such of the members and organizations of the Marine Corps and the Navy as the Secretary determines;
	(5) perform the duties prescribed for him by sections 171 and 2547 of this title and other provisions of law; and
	(6) perform such other military duties, not otherwise assigned by law, as are assigned to him by the President, the Secretary of Defense, or the Secretary of the Navy.
	(f)(1) The Commandant shall also perform the duties prescribed for him as a member of the Joint Chiefs of Staff under section 151 of this title.
	(2) To the extent that such action does not impair the independence of the Commandant in the performance of his duties as a member of the Joint Chiefs of Staff, the Commandant shall inform the Secretary regarding military advice rendered by members of the Joint Chiefs of Staff on matters affecting the Department of the Navy.
	(3) Subject to the authority, direction, and control of the Secretary of Defense, the Commandant shall keep the Secretary of the Navy fully informed of significant military operations affecting the duties and responsibilities of the Secretary.
Assistant Commandant of the Marine Corps *Section 5044*	(a) There is an Assistant Commandant of the Marine Corps, appointed by the President, by and with the advice and consent of the Senate, from officers on the active-duty list of the Marine Corps not restricted in the performance of duty.
	(b) The Assistant Commandant of the Marine Corps, while so serving, has the grade of general without vacating his permanent grade.
	(c) The Assistant Commandant has such authority and duties with respect to the Marine Corps as the Commandant, with the approval of the Secretary of the Navy, may delegate to or prescribe for him. Orders issued by the Assistant Commandant in performing such duties have the same effect as those issued by the Commandant.
	(d) When there is a vacancy in the office of Commandant of the Marine Corps, or during the absence or disability of the Commandant—
	(1) the Assistant Commandant of the Marine Corps shall perform the duties of the Commandant until a successor is appointed or the absence or disability ceases; or
	(2) if there is a vacancy in the office of the Assistant Commandant of the Marine Corps or the Assistant Commandant is absent or disabled, unless the President directs otherwise, the most senior officer of the Marine Corps in the Headquarters, Marine Corps, who is not absent or disabled and who is not restricted in performance of duty shall perform the duties of the Commandant until a successor to the Commandant or the Assistant Commandant is appointed or until the absence or disability of the Commandant or Assistant Commandant ceases, whichever occurs first.

Table C.2—Continued

Position and Section*	Text
Commander, Marine Forces Reserve *Section 5144*	(a) Establishment of Office; Commander, Marine Forces Reserve.— There is in the executive part of the Department of the Navy an Office of the Marine Forces Reserve, which is headed by the Commander, Marine Forces Reserve. The Commander, Marine Forces Reserve, is the principal adviser to the Commandant on Marine Forces Reserve matters. (b) Appointment.— (1) The President, by and with the advice and consent of the Senate, shall appoint the Commander, Marine Forces Reserve, from general officers of the Marine Corps (as defined in section 5001(2)) who have had at least 10 years of commissioned service. (2) The Secretary of Defense may not recommend an officer to the President for appointment as Commander, Marine Forces Reserve, unless the officer— (A) is recommended by the Secretary of the Navy; and (B) is determined by the Chairman of the Joint Chiefs of Staff, in accordance with criteria and as a result of a process established by the Chairman, to have significant joint duty experience. (3) An officer on active duty for service as the Commander, Marine Forces Reserve, shall be counted for purposes of the grade limitations under sections 525 and 526 of this title. (4) Until December 31, 2006, the Secretary of Defense may waive subparagraph (B) of paragraph (2) with respect to the appointment of an officer as Commander, Marine Forces Reserve, if the Secretary of the Navy requests the waiver and, in the judgment of the Secretary of Defense— (A) the officer is qualified for service in the position; and (B) the waiver is necessary for the good of the service. Any such waiver shall be made on a case-by-case basis. (c) Term; Reappointment.— The Commander, Marine Forces Reserve, is appointed for a term determined by the Commandant of the Marine Corps, normally four years, but may be removed for cause at any time. An officer serving as Commander, Marine Forces Reserve, may be reappointed for one additional term of up to four years. (d) Annual Report.— (1) The Commander, Marine Forces Reserve, shall submit to the Secretary of Defense, through the Secretary of the Navy, an annual report on the state of the Marine Corps Reserve and the ability of the Marine Corps Reserve to meet its missions. The report shall be prepared in conjunction with the Commandant of the Marine Corps and may be submitted in classified and unclassified versions. (2) The Secretary of Defense shall transmit the annual report of the Commander, Marine Forces Reserve, under paragraph (1) to Congress, together with such comments on the report as the Secretary considers appropriate. The report shall be transmitted at the same time each year that the annual report of the Secretary under section 113 of this title is submitted to Congress.
Chief of Staff of the Air Force *Section 8033*	(a)(1) There is a Chief of Staff of the Air Force, appointed for a period of four years by the President, by and with the advice and consent of the Senate, from the general officers of the Air Force. He serves at the pleasure of the President. In time of war or during a national emergency declared by Congress, he may be reappointed for a term of not more than four years. (2) The President may appoint an officer as Chief of Staff only if— (A) the officer has had significant experience in joint duty assignments; and (B) such experience includes at least one full tour of duty in a joint duty assignment (as defined in section 664(f) [1] of this title) as a general officer. (3) The President may waive paragraph (2) in the case of an officer if the President determines such action is necessary in the national interest. (b) The Chief of Staff, while so serving, has the grade of general without vacating his permanent grade.

Table C.2—Continued

Position and Section*	Text
	(c) Except as otherwise prescribed by law and subject to section 8013(f) of this title, the Chief of Staff performs his duties under the authority, direction, and control of the Secretary of the Air Force and is directly responsible to the Secretary. (d) Subject to the authority, direction, and control of the Secretary of the Air Force, the Chief of Staff shall— (1) preside over the Air Staff; (2) transmit the plans and recommendations of the Air Staff to the Secretary and advise the Secretary with regard to such plans and recommendations; (3) after approval of the plans or recommendations of the Air Staff by the Secretary, act as the agent of the Secretary in carrying them into effect; (4) exercise supervision, consistent with the authority assigned to commanders of unified or specified combatant commands under chapter 6 of this title, over such of the members and organizations of the Air Force as the Secretary determines; (5) perform the duties prescribed for him by sections 171 and 2547 of this title and other provisions of law, including pursuant to section 8040 of this title; and (6) perform such other military duties, not otherwise assigned by law, as are assigned to him by the President, the Secretary of Defense, or the Secretary of the Air Force. (e) (1) The Chief of Staff shall also perform the duties prescribed for him as a member of the Joint Chiefs of Staff under section 151 of this title. (2) To the extent that such action does not impair the independence of the Chief of Staff in the performance of his duties as a member of the Joint Chiefs of Staff, the Chief of Staff shall inform the Secretary regarding military advice rendered by members of the Joint Chiefs of Staff on matters affecting the Department of the Air Force. (3) Subject to the authority, direction, and control of the Secretary of Defense, the Chief of Staff shall keep the Secretary of the Air Force fully informed of significant military operations affecting the duties and responsibilities of the Secretary.
Vice Chief of Staff of the Air Force *Section 8034*	(a) There is a Vice Chief of Staff of the Air Force, appointed by the President, by and with the advice and consent of the Senate, from the general officers of the Air Force. (b) The Vice Chief of Staff of the Air Force, while so serving, has the grade of general without vacating his permanent grade. (c) The Vice Chief of Staff has such authority and duties with respect to the Department of the Air Force as the Chief of Staff, with the approval of the Secretary of the Air Force, may delegate to or prescribe for him. Orders issued by the Vice Chief of Staff in performing such duties have the same effect as those issued by the Chief of Staff. (d) When there is a vacancy in the office of Chief of Staff or during the absence or disability of the Chief of Staff— (1) the Vice Chief of Staff shall perform the duties of the Chief of Staff until a successor is appointed or the absence or disability ceases; or (2) if there is a vacancy in the office of the Vice Chief of Staff or the Vice Chief of Staff is absent or disabled, unless the President directs otherwise, the most senior officer of the Air Force in the Air Staff who is not absent or disabled and who is not restricted in performance of duty shall perform the duties of the Chief of Staff until a successor to the Chief of Staff or the Vice Chief of Staff is appointed or until the absence or disability of the Chief of Staff or Vice Chief of Staff ceases, whichever occurs first.
Deputy Chiefs of Staff and Assistant Chiefs of Staff of the Air Force *Section 8035*	(a) The Deputy Chiefs of Staff and the Assistant Chiefs of Staff shall be general officers detailed to those positions. (b) The Secretary of the Air Force shall prescribe the number of Deputy Chiefs of Staff and Assistant Chiefs of Staff, for a total of not more than eight positions.

Table C.2—Continued

Position and Section*	Text
Chief of Air Force Reserve *Section 8038*	(a) There is in the executive part of the Department of the Air Force an Office of Air Force Reserve which is headed by a chief who is the adviser to the Chief of Staff on Air Force Reserve matters. (b) Appointment.— (1) The President, by and with the advice and consent of the Senate, shall appoint the Chief of Air Force Reserve from general officers of the Air Force Reserve who have had at least 10 years of commissioned service in the Air Force. (2) The Secretary of Defense may not recommend an officer to the President for appointment as Chief of Air Force Reserve unless the officer— (A) is recommended by the Secretary of the Air Force; and (B) is determined by the Chairman of the Joint Chiefs of Staff, in accordance with criteria and as a result of a process established by the Chairman, to have significant joint duty experience. (3) An officer on active duty for service as the Chief of Air Force Reserve shall be counted for purposes of the grade limitations under sections 525 and 526 of this title. (4) Until December 31, 2006, the Secretary of Defense may waive subparagraph (B) of paragraph (2) with respect to the appointment of an officer as Chief of Air Force Reserve if the Secretary of the Air Force requests the waiver and, in the judgment of the Secretary of Defense— (A) the officer is qualified for service in the position; and (B) the waiver is necessary for the good of the service. Any such waiver shall be made on a case-by-case basis. (c) Term; Reappointment.— The Chief of Air Force Reserve is appointed for a period of four years, but may be removed for cause at any time. An officer serving as Chief of Air Force Reserve may be reappointed for one additional four-year period. (d) Budget.— The Chief of Air Force Reserve is the official within the executive part of the Department of the Air Force who, subject to the authority, direction, and control of the Secretary of the Air Force and the Chief of Staff, is responsible for preparation, justification, and execution of the personnel, operation and maintenance, and construction budgets for the Air Force Reserve. As such, the Chief of Air Force Reserve is the director and functional manager of appropriations made for the Air Force Reserve in those areas. (e) Full Time Support Program.— The Chief of Air Force Reserve manages, with respect to the Air Force Reserve, the personnel program of the Department of Defense known as the Full Time Support Program. (f) Annual Report.— (1) The Chief of Air Force Reserve shall submit to the Secretary of Defense, through the Secretary of the Air Force, an annual report on the state of the Air Force Reserve and the ability of the Air Force Reserve to meet its missions. The report shall be prepared in conjunction with the Chief of Staff of the Air Force and may be submitted in classified and unclassified versions. (2) The Secretary of Defense shall transmit the annual report of the Chief of Air Force Reserve under paragraph (1) to Congress, together with such comments on the report as the Secretary considers appropriate. The report shall be transmitted at the same time each year that the annual report of the Secretary under section 113 of this title is submitted to Congress.
Chief of the National Guard Bureau *Section 10502*	(a) Appointment.—There is a Chief of the National Guard Bureau, who is responsible for the organization and operations of the National Guard Bureau. The Chief of the National Guard Bureau is appointed by the President, by and with the advice and consent of the Senate. Such appointment shall be made from officers of the Army National Guard of the United States or the Air National Guard of the United States who— (1) are recommended for such appointment by their respective Governors or, in the case of the District of Columbia, the commanding general of the District of Columbia National Guard;

Table C.2—Continued

Position and Section*	Text
	(2) are recommended for such appointment by the Secretary of the Army or the Secretary of the Air Force; (3) have had at least 10 years of federally recognized commissioned service in an active status in the National Guard; (4) are in a grade above the grade of brigadier general; (5) are determined by the Chairman of the Joint Chiefs of Staff, in accordance with criteria and as a result of a process established by the Chairman, to have significant joint duty experience; (6) are determined by the Secretary of Defense to have successfully completed such other assignments and experiences so as to possess a detailed understanding of the status and capabilities of National Guard forces and the missions of the National Guard Bureau as set forth in section 10503 of this title; (7) have a level of operational experience in a position of significant responsibility, professional military education, and demonstrated expertise in national defense and homeland defense matters that are commensurate with the advisory role of the Chief of the National Guard Bureau; and (8) possess such other qualifications as the Secretary of Defense shall prescribe for purposes of this section. (b) Term of Office.— (1) An officer appointed as Chief of the National Guard Bureau serves at the pleasure of the President for a term of four years. An officer may be reappointed as Chief of the National Guard Bureau. (2) Except as provided in section 14508(d) of this title, while holding the office of Chief of the National Guard Bureau, the Chief of the National Guard Bureau may not be removed from the reserve active-status list, or from an active status, under any provision of law that otherwise would require such removal due to completion of a specified number of years of service or a specified number of years of service in grade. (c) Advisor on National Guard Matters.—The Chief of the National Guard Bureau is— (1) a principal advisor to the Secretary of Defense, through the Chairman of the Joint Chiefs of Staff, on matters involving nonfederalized National Guard forces and on other matters as determined by the Secretary of Defense; and (2) the principal adviser to the Secretary of the Army and the Chief of Staff of the Army, and to the Secretary of the Air Force and the Chief of Staff of the Air Force, on matters relating to the National Guard, the Army National Guard of the United States, and the Air National Guard of the United States. (d) Member of Joint Chiefs of Staff.—As a member of the Joint Chiefs of Staff, the Chief of the National Guard Bureau has the specific responsibility of addressing matters involving nonfederalized National Guard forces in support of homeland defense and civil support missions. (e) Grade and Exclusion from General and Flag Officer Authorized Strength.— (1) The Chief of the National Guard Bureau shall be appointed to serve in the grade of general. (2) The Secretary of Defense shall designate, pursuant to subsection (b) of section 526 of this title, the position of Chief of the National Guard Bureau as one of the general officer and flag officer positions to be excluded from the limitations in subsection (a) of such section. (f) Succession. (1) When there is a vacancy in the office of the Chief of the National Guard Bureau or in the absence or disability of the Chief, the Vice Chief of the National Guard Bureau acts as Chief and performs the duties of the Chief until a successor is appointed or the absence or disability ceases. (2) When there is a vacancy in the offices of both the Chief and the Vice Chief of the National Guard Bureau or in the absence or disability of both the Chief and the Vice Chief of the National Guard Bureau, or when there is a vacancy in one such office and in the absence or disability of the officer holding the other, the senior officer of the Army National Guard of the United States or the Air National Guard of the United States on duty with the National Guard Bureau shall perform the duties of the Chief until a successor to the Chief or Vice Chief is appointed or the absence or disability of the Chief or Vice Chief ceases, as the case may be.

Table C.2—Continued

Position and Section*	Text
Three- and four-star positions *Section 601*	(a) The President may designate positions of importance and responsibility to carry the grade of general or admiral or lieutenant general or vice admiral. The President may assign to any such position an officer of the Army, Navy, Air Force, or Marine Corps who is serving on active duty in any grade above colonel or, in the case of an officer of the Navy, any grade above captain. An officer assigned to any such position has the grade specified for that position if he is appointed to that grade by the President, by and with the advice and consent of the Senate. Except as provided in subsection (b), the appointment of an officer to a grade under this section for service in a position of importance and responsibility ends on the date of the termination of the assignment of the officer to that position. (b) An officer who is appointed to the grade of general, admiral, lieutenant general, or vice admiral for service in a position designated under subsection (a) or by law to carry that grade shall continue to hold that grade— (1) while serving in that position; (2) while under orders transferring him to another position designated under subsection (a) or by law to carry one of those grades, beginning on the day his assignment to the first position is terminated and ending on the day before the day on which he assumes the second position; (3) while hospitalized, beginning on the day of the hospitalization and ending on the day he is discharged from the hospital, but not for more than 180 days; (4) at the discretion of the Secretary of Defense, while the officer is awaiting orders after being relieved from the position designated under subsection (a) or by law to carry one of those grades, but not for more than 60 days beginning on the day the officer is relieved from the position, unless, during such period, the officer is placed under orders to another position designated under subsection (a) or by law to carry one of those grades, in which case paragraph (2) will also apply to the officer; and (5) while awaiting retirement, beginning on the day he is relieved from the position designated under subsection (a) or by law to carry one of those grades and ending on the day before his retirement, but not for more than 60 days. (c)(1) An appointment of an officer under subsection (a) does not vacate the permanent grade held by the officer. (2) An officer serving in a grade above major general or rear admiral who holds the permanent grade of brigadier general or rear admiral (lower half) shall be considered for promotion to the permanent grade of major general or rear admiral, as appropriate, as if he were serving in his permanent grade. (d)(1) When an officer is recommended to the President for an initial appointment to the grade of lieutenant general or vice admiral, or for an initial appointment to the grade of general or admiral, the Chairman of the Joint Chiefs of Staff shall submit to the Secretary of Defense the Chairman's evaluation of the performance of that officer as a member of the Joint Staff and in other joint duty assignments. The Secretary of Defense shall submit the Chairman's evaluation to the President at the same time the recommendation for the appointment is submitted to the President. (2) Whenever a vacancy occurs in a position within the Department of Defense that the President has designated as a position of importance and responsibility to carry the grade of general or admiral or lieutenant general or vice admiral or in an office that is designated by law to carry such a grade, the Secretary of Defense shall inform the President of the qualifications needed by an officer serving in that position or office to carry out effectively the duties and responsibilities of that position or office.
Joint Requirements Oversight Council *Section 181*	(a) In General.—There is a Joint Requirements Oversight Council in the Department of Defense. (b) Mission.—In addition to other matters assigned to it by the President or Secretary of Defense, the Joint Requirements Oversight Council shall assist the Chairman of the Joint Chiefs of Staff in— (1) assessing joint military capabilities, and identifying, approving, and prioritizing gaps in such capabilities, to meet applicable requirements in the national defense strategy under section 118 1 of this title;

Table C.2—Continued

Position and Section*	Text
	(2) reviewing and validating whether a capability proposed by an armed force, Defense Agency, or other entity of the Department of Defense fulfills a gap in joint military capabilities; (3) developing recommendations, in consultation with the advisors to the Council under subsection (d), for program cost and fielding targets pursuant to section 2448a of this title that— (A) require a level of resources that is consistent with the level of priority assigned to the associated capability gap; and (B) have an estimated period of time for the delivery of an initial operational capability that is consistent with the urgency of the associated capability gap; (4) establishing and approving joint performance requirements that— (A) ensure interoperability, where appropriate, between and among joint military capabilities; and (B) are necessary, as designated by the Chairman of the Joint Chiefs of Staff, to fulfill capability gaps of more than one armed force, Defense Agency, or other entity of the Department; (5) reviewing performance requirements for any existing or proposed capability that the Chairman of the Joint Chiefs of Staff determines should be reviewed by the Council; (6) identifying new joint military capabilities based on advances in technology and concepts of operation; and (7) identifying alternatives to any acquisition program that meets approved joint military capability requirements for the purposes of sections 2366a(b), 2366b(a)(4), and 2433(e)(2) of this title. (c) Composition.— (1) In general.—The Joint Requirements Oversight Council is composed of the following: (A) The Vice Chairman of the Joint Chiefs of Staff, who is the Chair of the Council and is the principal adviser to the Chairman of the Joint Chiefs of Staff for making recommendations about joint military capabilities or joint performance requirements. (B) An Army officer in the grade of general. (C) A Navy officer in the grade of admiral. (D) An Air Force officer in the grade of general. (E) A Marine Corps officer in the grade of general. (2) Selection of members.—Members of the Council under subparagraphs (B), (C), (D), and (E) of paragraph (1) shall be selected by the Chairman of the Joint Chiefs of Staff, after consultation with the Secretary of Defense, from officers in the grade of general or admiral, as the case may be, who are recommended for selection by the Secretary of the military department concerned. (3) Recommendations.—In making any recommendation to the Chairman of the Joint Chiefs of Staff as described in paragraph (1)(A), the Vice Chairman of the Joint Chiefs of Staff shall provide the Chairman any dissenting view of members of the Council under paragraph (1) with respect to such recommendation. (d) Advisors.— (1) In general.—The following officials of the Department of Defense shall serve as advisors to the Joint Requirements Oversight Council on matters within their authority and expertise: (A) The Under Secretary of Defense for Policy. (B) The Under Secretary of Defense for Intelligence. (C) The Under Secretary of Defense for Acquisition, Technology, and Logistics. (D) The Under Secretary of Defense (Comptroller). (E) The Director of Cost Assessment and Program Evaluation. (F) The Director of Operational Test and Evaluation. (G) The commander of a combatant command when matters related to the area of responsibility or functions of that command are under consideration by the Council. (2) Input from combatant commands.—The Council shall seek and consider input from the commanders of the combatant commands in carrying out its mission under paragraphs (1) and (2) of subsection (b).

Table C.2—Continued

Position and Section*	Text
	(3) Input from chiefs of staff.—The Council shall seek, and strongly consider, the views of the Chiefs of Staff of the armed forces, in their roles as customers of the acquisition system, on matters pertaining to a capability proposed by an armed force, Defense Agency, or other entity of the Department of Defense under subsection (b)(2) and joint performance requirements pursuant to subsection (b)(3). (e) Performance Requirements as Responsibility of Armed Forces.—The Chief of Staff of an armed force is responsible for all performance requirements for that armed force and, except for performance requirements specified in subsections (b)(4) and (b)(5), such performance requirements do not need to be validated by the Joint Requirements Oversight Council. (f) Analytic Support.—The Secretary of Defense shall ensure that analytical organizations within the Department of Defense, such as the Office of Cost Assessment and Program Evaluation, provide resources and expertise in operations research, systems analysis, and cost estimation to the Joint Requirements Oversight Council to assist the Council in performing the mission in subsection (b). (g) Availability of Oversight Information to Congressional Defense Committees.— The Secretary of Defense shall ensure that, in the case of a recommendation by the Chairman of the Joint Chiefs of Staff to the Secretary that is approved by the Secretary, oversight information with respect to such recommendation that is produced as a result of the activities of the Joint Requirements Oversight Council is made available in a timely fashion to the congressional defense committees. (h) Definitions.—In this section: (1) The term "joint military capabilities" means the collective capabilities across the joint force, including both joint and force-specific capabilities, that are available to conduct military operations. (2) The term "performance requirement" means a performance attribute of a particular system considered critical or essential to the development of an effective military capability. (3) The term "joint performance requirement" means a performance requirement that is critical or essential to ensure interoperability or fulfill a capability gap of more than one armed force, Defense Agency, or other entity of the Department of Defense, or impacts the joint force in other ways such as logistics. (4) The term "oversight information" means information and materials comprising analysis and justification that are prepared to support a recommendation that is made to, and approved by, the Secretary of Defense.
Director of the National Geospatial-Intelligence Agency (if held by an officer of the armed forces) *Section 441*	(a) Establishment.—The National Geospatial-Intelligence Agency is a combat support agency of the Department of Defense and has significant national missions. (b) Director.— (1) The Director of the National Geospatial-Intelligence Agency is the head of the agency. (2) Upon a vacancy in the position of Director, the Secretary of Defense shall recommend to the President an individual for appointment to the position. (3) If an officer of the armed forces on active duty is appointed to the position of Director, the position shall be treated as having been designated by the President as a position of importance and responsibility for purposes of section 601 of this title and shall carry the grade of lieutenant general, or, in the case of an officer of the Navy, vice admiral. (c) Director of National Intelligence Collection Tasking Authority.—Unless otherwise directed by the President, the Director of National Intelligence shall have authority (except as otherwise agreed by the Director and the Secretary of Defense) to— (1) approve collection requirements levied on national imagery collection assets; (2) determine priorities for such requirements; and (3) resolve conflicts in such priorities. (d) Availability and Continued Improvement of Imagery Intelligence Support to All-Source Analysis and Production Function.—The Secretary of Defense, in consultation with the Director of National Intelligence, shall take all necessary steps to ensure the full availability and continued improvement of imagery intelligence support for all-source analysis and production.

Table C.2—Continued

Position and Section*	Text
Dean of the Academic Board of the United States Military Academy *Section 4335*	(a) The Dean of the Academic Board shall be appointed as an additional permanent professor from the permanent professors who have served as heads of departments of instruction at the Academy. (b) The Dean of the Academic Board shall perform such duties as the Superintendent of the Academy may prescribe with the approval of the Secretary of the Army. (c) While serving as Dean of the Academic Board, an officer of the Army who holds a grade lower than brigadier general shall hold the grade of brigadier general, if appointed to that grade by the President, by and with the advice and consent of the Senate. The retirement age of an officer so appointed is that of a permanent professor of the Academy. An officer so appointed is counted for purposes of the limitation in section 526(a) of this title on general officers of the Army on active duty.
Communications Security Review and Advisory Board *Section 189*	(a) Establishment.—There shall be in the Department of Defense a Communications Security Review and Advisory Board (in this section referred to as the "Board") to review and assess the communications security, cryptographic modernization, and related key management activities of the Department and provide advice to the Secretary with respect to such activities. (b) Members.— (1) The Secretary shall determine the number of members of the Board. (2) The Chief Information Officer of the Department of Defense shall serve as chairman of the Board. (3) The Secretary shall appoint officers in the grade of general or admiral and civilian employees of the Department of Defense in the Senior Executive Service to serve as members of the Board. (c) Responsibilities.— The Board shall— (1) monitor the overall communications security, cryptographic modernization, and key management efforts of the Department, including activities under major defense acquisition programs (as defined in section 2430(a) of this title), by— (A) requiring each Chief Information Officer of each military department to report the communications security activities of the military department to the Board; (B) tracking compliance of each military department with respect to communications security modernization efforts; (C) validating lifecycle communications security modernization plans for major defense acquisition programs; (2) validate the need to replace cryptographic equipment based on the expiration dates of the equipment and evaluate the risks of continuing to use cryptographic equipment after such expiration dates; (3) convene in-depth program reviews for specific cryptographic modernization developments with respect to validating requirements and identifying programmatic risks; (4) develop a long-term roadmap for communications security to identify potential issues and ensure synchronization with major planning documents; and (5) advise the Secretary on the cryptographic posture of the Department, including budgetary recommendations. (d) Exclusion of Certain Programs.-The Board shall not include the consideration of programs funded under the National Intelligence Program (as defined in section 3(6) of the National Security Act of 1947 (50 U.S.C. 3003(6))) in carrying out this section.
Judge Advocates General (Army, Navy, Air Force) and Staff Judge Advocate (Marine Corps)	previous requirement repealed by Pub. L. 114–328
Surgeons General of the Army, Navy, Air Force	previous requirement repealed by Pub. L. 114–328

Table C.2—Continued

Position and Section*	Text
Legislative Assistant to the Commandant	previous requirement repealed by Pub. L. 114–328
Chief of Legislative Liaison in the Department of the Army	previous requirement repealed by Pub. L. 114–328
Director of Expeditionary Warfare within the office of the Deputy Chief of Naval Operations	previous requirement repealed by Pub. L. 114–328
Assistant Surgeon General for Dental Services in the Air Force	previous requirement repealed by Pub. L. 114–328
Chief of the Dental Corps of the Navy	previous requirement repealed by Pub. L. 114–328
Chief of the Dental Corps of the Army	previous requirement repealed by Pub. L. 114–328
Legal Counsel to the Chairman of the Joint Chiefs of Staff	previous requirement repealed by Pub. L. 114–328
Director of the Department of Defense Test Resource Management Center	previous requirement repealed by Pub. L. 114–328
Senior members of the Military Staff Committee of the United Nations	previous requirement repealed by Pub. L. 114–328
Dean of the Faculty of the Air Force Academy	previous requirement repealed by Pub. L. 114–328

* Sections indicated in this column are within Title 10 unless otherwise specified.

Detailed Findings from the Structure and Organizational Assessments

This appendix contains detailed discussion of the findings from the structure and organizational approach. It covers each of the groups evaluated in this analysis, as listed in Chapter Three. The appendix begins with an overview of a generic staff organization, which is pertinent to the individual group discussions that follow. The discussion of each group contains a definition of the group (i.e., which organizations and G/FOs are included), an explanation of additional organization principles that apply to this group and why, an explanation of exceptions from the broader principles that may apply to this group and why, and a summary of the findings from the structure and organization evaluation. As a reminder, the analysis is based on the G/FO requirements provided to RAND by the services and joint community as of March 2017.

Overview of a Generic Staff Organization

Understanding the so called "command staff" (or "Napoleonic staff" or "J-code" staff) structure is essential to understanding how these principles apply to military staffs and concepts related to that structure are implicit in our findings. Thus, we include a brief overview of the command staff structure as used by the U.S. military.

In the headquarters of a military organization led by a G/FO, it has become customary for the organization to create a hierarchical division of labor. Led by a commander, who is also the highest-ranking G/FO in the organization, the organization works together to meet its mission as well as to meet the demands of the next level above in the organizational structure.

In a typical high-ranking general staff, the commander has a deputy commander who may fill in for the commander, lead the day-to-day activities of the organization, or assist as needed. Also, a commander may have a chief of staff who coordinates actions, as well as special assistants or military assistants to provide additional advice and perspective as requested from the commander.

The organization is broken down into directorates, each led by a director who may also have a deputy director and a chief of staff as well as a staff below. This J-code, or general staff structure, promotes unity of command, speeds hierarchical information flow, and ensures clear accountability and authority lines. This basic structure provides the commander with effective and efficient control, accountability, and administration characteristics less evident in other types of organizations. The typical J-code structure looks approximately as follows:

- J1: Manpower or Personnel
- J2: Intelligence
- J3: Operations
- J4: Logistics
- J5: Strategy, Policy, and Plans; or Plans and Requirements
- J6: Communications
- J7: Training and Education
- J8: Resource Management and Finance
- J9: Civil Affairs.

This J-code structure has proven to be effective for the military, and we see this model repeated at many levels throughout the Department of Defense, particularly in headquarters organizations. It is used in the services, Joint Staff, and combatant commands, and variants of the structure are seen even in the civilian parts of the department. Positions directly subordinate to the position filling a "one-digit" J-code (J1, J2, J3, etc.) are usually designated by two-digit codes (J31, J32, J33, etc.). Their subordinate positions are, in turn, designated by 3-digit codes (J321, J322, etc.).

The services also employ this same organizational model, with the difference that they replace the "J" with a service-specific letter. Positions in Army staffs are commonly designated by "G" codes (G1, G2, G3, etc.); Navy staff positions by "N" codes (N1, N2, N3, etc.); Marine Corps staff positions by "S" codes (S1, S2, S3, etc.), and Air Force staff positions by "A" codes (A1, A2, A3, etc.). For simplicity, we often refer to all these positions as J-codes. Not all the codes are relevant to all staffs, so codes are at times omitted or adapted. Similarly, staffs sometimes have functions that do not align neatly within the categories above, so J-codes may be repurposed for such organizations. This often happens most commonly with the J9, and to a lesser extent with the J7. Some staffs also extend the J-code structure with additional elements. An example illustrating both of these kinds of changes is the Air Force Air Staff, where repurposed and added J-codes are:

- A7: Installations and Mission Support
- A9: Analysis, Assessments and Lessons Learned
- A10: Strategic Deterrence and Nuclear Integration Office
- A11: Space Operations.

Joint Staff

The Joint Staff group includes the Chairman and the Vice Chairman of the Joint Chiefs of Staff as well as all the G/FO positions within the Joint Staff, for a total of 44 G/FO positions. The Chairman of the Joint Chiefs of Staff (CJCS) is the senior ranking member of the armed forces and, as such, is the principal military adviser to the President. The Joint Staff assists the Chairman in accomplishing the Chairman's advisory responsibilities for the "unified strategic direction of the armed forces, their operation under unified command, and for their integration into an efficient team of land, naval, and air forces."[1] The breakdown of authorized positions by grade is shown in Table D.1.

Additional Principles
The Joint Staff organizes itself under conventional staff lines and, therefore, can be compared to combatant commands and the military services. Because the role of the Joint Staff is to support the Chairman to develop the strategic direction of the armed forces and to provide the National Military Strategy, certain staff functions within the Joint Staff assume greater responsibilities, such as the J3, J5, and J8.

Relevant Subgroups
There are no relevant subgroups within the overall group of Joint Staff G/FO positions.

Exceptions
There are no relevant exceptions for the Joint Staff G/FO group.

Findings
The Joint Staff is responsible for providing a significant amount of information on a wide range of important topics and has a robust G/FO staff to lead its work. However, we identified some positions that did not meet the criteria used in our evaluation. Our findings, shown in Table D.2, are that seven G/FO positions on the Joint Staff do not meet criteria for a G/FO requirement.

Table D.1
Joint Staff G/FO Positions by Grade

O-7	O-8	O-9	O-10	Total
23	11	8	2	44

---

[1] 50 USC Section 3002.

Table D.2
Findings for Joint Staff

Finding	O-7	O-8	O-9	O-10	Total
Does not meet criteria for G/FO requirement	2	5	0	0	7

Based on our assessment, most directors meet the criteria for a G/FO at the current grade of O-9, but G/FOs in vice director positions do not meet the criteria for a G/FO. The primary function of the vice director is to act in place of and on behalf of the director, often managing the day-to-day business of a major organization or division. Whenever the director is not available, any one of the director's subordinate G/FOs can perform this function. If the director needs support in the administration and management of their J-code directorate, an individual in a non-G/FO position can provide such support. For similar reasons, all G/FO chiefs of staff working in the J-code directorates did not meet criteria for a G/FO requirement.

Our evaluation suggests that the J1 G/FO position does not meet the criteria of a G/FO because of the very narrow scope of the Joint Staff J1 function (to oversee filling of joint positions) compared to those in the service organizations, which have responsibility for a broader range of personnel management (including promotions, assignments, separations and retirements, etc.); for some of the services, this includes responsibility for policies on force development and training.

In our judgment, the department should conduct a thorough review of the overall structure of the Joint Staff and its use of G/FOs in managing the organization. This review should include the role of civilians, and of the senior executive service in particular, to see how the mission of the Joint Staff can still be met while using fewer G/FOs. It should also consider the role of reserve component Chairman's Reserve Positions (CRP) and G/FOs in individual mobilization augmentee (IMA) positions, the future of which is uncertain. For example, the data provided to RAND includes eight G/FO positions within the J5; however, we identified four other G/FO positions that are binned as either CRP or IMA. These CRP/IMA positions hold a significant amount of responsibility for requirements that are likely to remain for the foreseeable future, and the J5, in particular, may experience significant impacts as these G/FOs are eliminated. CRP and IMA positions are discussed further in the following section on combatant commands.

Combatant Commands

Overview

In our Combatant Command group, we consider all the combatant commands (CCMD) as well as the joint commands they lead. A combatant command is a military command that has a broad, continuing mission and is led by a single commander, ensuring a single strategic direction and unity of effort. Combatant commands are established and designated by the President, and they can be a unified or specified command. Both unified and specified commands are led by a combatant commander and are composed of significant forces; however, the forces for a unified command generally come from two or more military departments, while a specified command's forces come from a single military department.[2] The combatant commanders are responsible for the development and production of joint plans and orders, and they have operational command and control of the military forces under them. The unified combatant commands are either geographic or functional in scope, depending on whether the commander's area of responsibility is based on physical space or on the subject scope of the combatant command. The nine unified combatant commands are generally referred to in two groups: geographic commands and functional commands. The six geographic commands are:

- U.S. Africa Command (USAFRICOM)
- U.S. Central Command (USCENTCOM)
- U.S. European Command (USEUCOM)
- U.S. Northern Command (USNORTHCOM)
- U.S. Pacific Command (USPACOM)
- U.S. Southern Command (USSOUTHCOM).

The three functional commands are:

- U.S. Special Operations Command (USSOCOM)
- U.S. Strategic Command (USSTRATCOM)
- U.S. Transportation Command (USTRANSCOM).

Currently, no specified combatant commands are designated. The commander of a specified command has the same authority and responsibilities as the commander of a unified combatant command, except that she or he does not have the authority to establish subordinate unified commands.[3]

A unified combatant commander can set up subordinate unified commands, also known as subunified commands, on a geographical or functional basis.[4] While the subunified commander exercises authority similar to the unified commander, the unified commander maintains command authority over any of these subordinate unified commands as well as service component commands and any of the designated

---

[2] JP-1, "Doctrine for the Armed Forces of the United States," March 25, 2013, and 10 USC Section 161.

[3] JP-1, 2013, p. IV-9.

[4] JP-1, 2013, p. IV-9.

Figure D.1
Unified Combatant Command Organizational Options

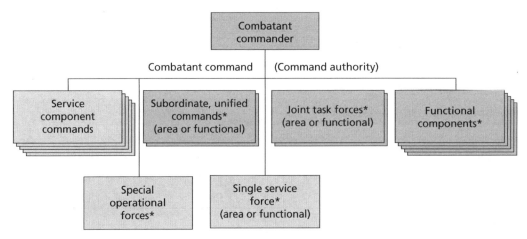

SOURCE: JP-1, Figure IV-2, p. IV-6.
*Optional
RAND *RR2384OSD-D.1*

single service forces, specific operational forces, joint task forces, and functional components.[5] Figure D.1 reflects these relationships.

Table D.3 shows the subordinate unified combatant commands established by its respective unified combatant command. The commanders of subordinate unified commands have functions and responsibilities similar to those of the commanders of unified combatant commands and exercise operational control of assigned commands and forces.[6]

Table D.3
Subordinate Unified Combatant Command

Subordinate Unified Combatant Command	Unified Combatant Command
Alaskan Command (ALCOM)	USNORTHCOM
U.S. Forces Korea (USFK)	USPACOM
U.S. Forces Japan (USFJ)	USPACOM
U.S. Cyber Command (USCYBERCOM)[a]	USSTRATCOM

[a] The process to elevate USCYBERCOM from a subunified command to a unified combatant command was initiated by the President on August 18, 2017, but at the time of writing this report, USCYBERCOM remains a subunified command.

---

[5] JP-1, 2013, p. IV-6 and chart.

[6] JP-1, 2013, p. IV-10.

In this Combatant Command group, we included only G/FO positions that are part of the joint pool; service G/FO positions (including service component G/FOs) are discussed in their respective service group. Two combatant command G/FO positions are also considered in the Contingency group—the Director of the USCENTCOM Forward Operational Contract Support Integration Cell and the Director of Central Command Deployment and Distribution Operations Center (CDDOC) in USCENTCOM—since they are included as OCO positions. Table D.4 shows the distribution of the 126 G/FO positions that we considered in the Combatant Command group:

Table D.4
Combatant Commands G/FO Positions by Grade

Command	O-7	O-8	O-9	O-10	Total
Total	53	46	16	11	126
Geographic					
USAFRICOM	4	3	1	1	9
USCENTCOM	9	6	1	1	17
USEUCOM	5	3	1	1	10
USNORTHCOM	4	3	1	1	9
USPACOM	4	5	1	1	11
USSOUTHCOM	2	2	1	1	6
Functional					
USSOCOM	4	4	1	1	10
USSTRATCOM	4	3	1	1	9
USTRANSCOM	1	2	1	1	5
Subunified Commands (subordinate to)					
ALCOM (USNORTHCOM)	0	0	1	0	1
USCYBERCOM (USSTRATCOM)	4	3	1	1	9
USFJ (USPACOM)	0	1	1	0	2
USFK (USPACOM)	2	3	1	1	7

Table D.4—Continued

Command	O-7	O-8	O-9	O-10	Total
Joint Commands					
Cyber National Mission Force (CNMF) (USCYBERCOM)	0	1	0	0	1
Joint Enabling Capabilities Command (JECC) (USTRANSCOM)	1	0	0	0	1
Joint Functional Component Commands (JFCCs) (USSTRATCOM)	2	1	0	0	3
JFHQ-DODIN (USCYBERCOM)	1	1	0	0	2
Joint Task Forces (JTFs) (various)	5	2	0	0	7

Additional Principles

The unified combatant commands as well as their subordinate unified commands are structurally very similar, following the traditional J-code structure of the general staff. However, each combatant command tailors its staff to meet the specific needs and missions of the command, and different combatant commands may have larger staffs or higher-ranking G/FOs to lead their organization. In general, the directors of J3 (operations) and J5 (planning and policy) are high priorities for placing military leadership within the combatant commands, and the J2 (intelligence) is a higher priority for the combatant commands than for the services.

Many combatant commands have a unique feature in their J-code structure: USEUCOM combines their J5/8, USAFRICOM uses a J1/8, and USTRANSCOM has a J4/5. USSOCOM uses more G/FOs than other combatant commands, since it also performs service-like functions and has military department-like responsibilities and authorities.[7] USSOCOM's unique attributes are further discussed later in this section. Furthermore, combatant commands use civilians and non-G/FOs in parts of the organization that require less military expertise or less seniority. Nearly all combatant commands use a senior executive service employee to lead their J8 (resources). Since their structures are so similar, we compared unified and subunified commands together, although, except for the case of United States Forces Korea, subunified commands do not have many joint G/FO positions.

In addition to the traditional J-code structure, each combatant command maintains other G/FO positions, which are used to further tailor the combatant command's

---

[7] Joint Publication JP3-05, *Special Operations*, Joint Chiefs of Staff, July 16, 2014, p. ix.

leadership to meet its unique needs and missions. These additional positions are more difficult to compare across combatant commands, because they are so different.

Relevant Subgroups

United States Special Operations Command and joint commands stand out as unique subgroups within the overall group of Combatant Commands G/FO positions.

United States Special Operations Command

United States Special Operations Command, or USSOCOM, presents a unique case among all CCMDs. As a functional command, it is responsible for the execution of special operations globally and for synchronizing certain missions across geographic CCMD boundaries, such as counterterrorism and countering weapons of mass destruction. Although the command operates in support of relevant geographic CCMDs in most cases, USSOCOM retains substantial responsibility despite its relatively narrow focus. Within the USSOCOM chain of command are several G/FO OCO positions and task forces that are relevant for today's combat operations and, in many cases, appear to require G/FO positions. The centrality of USSOCOM leadership and focus in some of DoD's key priority missions, such as its counter-Islamic State mission, and the command's anticipated responsibilities in shaping combat operations into the future, tend to justify G/FO authorizations for certain positions even when individuals in those positions are one of two deputies or oversee relatively smaller budgets or number of personnel.

In concert with its functional combatant command role, part of USSOCOM's unique charter is to execute significant "organize, train and equip" responsibilities. This service-like role requires USSOCOM representation on par with the other services, particularly in resourcing, force structure, and manpower issues. For example, the O-9 Vice Commander of USSOCOM serves as the command's chief representative for these service-like roles, and is strategically co-located in Washington, D.C. with equivalent representatives from the services. In other circumstances where a command has two deputy or deputy-like positions, we generally determined that at least one of these positions did not meet the criteria for a G/FO requirement. USSOCOM also has an O-9 deputy commander, located in Tampa, Florida, who performs oversight of USSOCOM's combatant command responsibilities. In USSOCOM's unique case, however, we found that its substantial service-like responsibilities and combatant command responsibilities demand two dedicated representatives at the O-9 grade.

Each theater special operations command (TSOC) was reviewed through the USSOCOM chain of command and through each of TSOC's respective geographic CCMD chains of command. Rank of TSOC commanders vary: TSOCs with greater operational tempo and responsibility for combat operations, such as United States Special Operations Command Central (SOCCENT), or very large areas of responsibility, such as United States Special Operations Command Pacific (SOCPAC), are authorized at the grade of O-8, whereas commands more limited in scope or current operations, such as Special Operations Command South (SOCSOUTH) are commanded by O-7s. These command positions satisfy criteria for a G/FO requirement.

Joint Commands

This small subgroup of 14 G/FO positions represents a diverse collection of organizations. Like their superior unified combatant commands, these Joint Commands are, indeed, joint, and the G/FOs are a part of the joint pool. Five of these G/FO positions are considered OCO positions and are discussed further as a part of the Contingency group. These OCO G/FO positions include the Commander and Deputy Commander of Joint Task Force-Horn of Africa, the Commander and Deputy Commander for Special Operations Joint Task Force-Afghanistan (SOJTF-A), and the Commander-Joint Task Force-Guantanamo. Although the Deputy Commander-Joint Task Force-Guantanamo is not considered an OCO position, we also consider it within the Contingency, since the Commander is included as well.

The organizational structure of these joint commands does not mirror the standard J-code structure, and each organization only has one or two G/FO positions. This subgroup includes:

- Cyber National Mission Force (CNMF), USCYBERCOM
- Joint Enabling Capabilities Command (JECC), USTRANSCOM
- Joint Force Headquarters Department of Defense Information Networks (JFHQ-DODIN), USCYBERCOM
- Joint Functional Component Commands (JFCC), USSTRATCOM, for:
  - Global Strike
  - Intelligence Surveillance and Reconnaissance[8]
  - Space
- Joint Task Forces
  - Joint Interagency Task Force (JIATF) South, USSOUTHCOM
  - Joint Task Force-Guantanamo, USSOUTHCOM
  - Combined Joint Task Force-Horn of Africa, USAFRICOM (see the Contingency group for more discussion)
  - Special Operations Joint Task Force-Afghanistan (SOJTF-A).

While there are many more task forces, these four are the only ones led by G/FOs in the joint pool. The Track Four Efficiency Initiatives decisions from March 14, 2011, directed the Department of Defense to transform ten joint task forces and two JIATFs into a total of six JIATFs. We recommend that the department again review not only the use of JTFs and the G/FO positions that support them but also the role of all the other joint commands listed above.

---

8   The Joint Functional Component Command-Intelligence Surveillance & Reconnaissance is in the process of moving from USSTRATCOM to the Joint Staff J-3.

Exceptions

United States Forces Korea (USFK) is a subordinate unified combatant command under USPACOM. The commander of USFK reports to the USPACOM commander. However, because the commander of USFK is also the United Nations Command Commander as well as the Combined Forces Command Commander, this same commander also reports directly to the Secretary of Defense and to the Chairman of the Joint Chiefs of Staff. With these reporting relationships, the USFK commander can bypass the USPACOM commander, and in many instances, USPACOM allows USFK to operate very autonomously.

Since many other G/FOs within USFK also serve in multi-hatted roles in these international commands, it is difficult to separate out and evaluate the job responsibilities for each role. In addition, as the responsibilities increase, the need for additional G/FOs as well as for additional chiefs of staff and assistants also increases.

In many ways, USFK is more comparable to other unified combatant commands than to its fellow subordinates, including its USPACOM "sister" subunified command, United States Forces Japan, which has only two joint G/FO positions. The same can be said for Alaskan Command; even though it is comparable to USFK in that its commander is dual-hatted with an international organization, North American Aerospace Defense (NORAD) (as well as to the 11th Air Force commander), it only has one joint G/FO position. This special relationship between USFK and the United Nations Command and the Combined Forces Command is discussed further in the International group.

Findings

Within our Combatant Command group, we analyzed 126 G/FO positions, with 112 serving directly in the unified or subunified combatant commands and 14 in the joint commands under the unified combatant command. Our findings are reported in Table D.5. Of the 126 G/FO positions, seven positions do not meet criteria for G/FO

Table D.5
Findings for Combatant Commands

Finding	O-7	O-8	O-9	O-10	Total
Meets criteria for a G/FO at a lower grade (downgrade)	0	3	1	0	4
Does not meet criteria for a G/FO (convert to civilian)	1	0	0	0	1
Does not meet criteria for a G/FO	5	1	0	0	6
Further review	9	2	0	0	11
Total	15	6	1	0	22

requirements and four positions meet criteria for a G/FO requirement at a lower grade. Additional research into the overall composition of the joint commands is needed to arrive at specific findings for 11 additional positions.

These findings generally bring the combatant commands more into line with each other. Because the combatant commands are structured in a similar manner, using the J-code general staff, we can compare the authorized grades of the directors and deputy directors of the J-code staff. When doing so, we identified cases where a G/FO position does not align with the other combatant commands. Sometimes these variances are due to the unique missions of the combatant command, but other times there is no apparent reason for the difference.

In the instances where the differences cannot be explained, our findings are to align the leadership structure across the combatant commands. Most often the differences are in the authorized rank, but sometimes it is also the use of a civilian instead of a G/FO in a leadership position. For example, the J8 directors vary from an O-7 in USCYBERCOM, to an O-8 in USSOCOM, to a civilian in all other combatant commands. As discussed previously, there is a defensible reason that USSOCOM uses an O-8 as the J8 director, since it has many attributes and requirements similar to a military service; USCYBERCOM's J8 G/FO director stands out as an anomaly. Alternatively, USEUCOM has opted to combine the J5 and J8 directorates into one: J5/8 Policy, Strategy, Partnering and Capabilities. By combining these two directorates, USEUCOM is able to reduce the number of G/FO positions in its organization.

We also identified a few occurrences in which a combatant command employs more G/FOs compared to their cohorts, such as more than one J5 (plans and policy) deputy director. In this case, both positions do not meet the criteria for a G/FO requirement (eliminate or combine the matching positions). Similar to the Joint Staff, combatant commands make great use of CRP and IMA G/FOs, and, as explained in the Joint Staff section, the positions filled by the CRP and IMA G/FOs are enduring requirements. The CRP positions are scheduled for elimination in 2022.[9] This adds urgency to our recommendation that the department conduct a zero-based review of G/FO requirements at combatant commands and all joint commands to both understand the overall requirements for joint G/FO leadership and address how that leadership will be provided via a mix of active and reserve component G/FOs.

Finally, we suggest that some historical vestiges, such as ALCOM, be reviewed for potential restructure, transformation, or elimination; such organizational changes could reduce G/FO requirements.

For any position that rotates to the United States Coast Guard or to a foreign military, even more so if the position has been vacant, an option is to withdraw from the rotation and use the authorized strength for a G/FO elsewhere within the Depart-

---

[9]   10 U.S. Code § 526a no longer contains a provision for Chairman's Reserve Positions. See Chapter Two for additional details.

ment of Defense. See the International group for more discussion on the topic of rotational G/FO positions.

As previously mentioned, in our judgment, the department should review G/FO requirements in all joint commands, not only JTFs.

Positions in International Organizations

Overview

The International group includes G/FO positions assigned to a collection of international organizations with whom the U.S. government and the U.S. military participate and support, such as intergovernmental military alliances between a group of countries, binational organizations, combined staffs, and unified command structures for multinational military forces. These international organizations include:

- NATO (North Atlantic Treaty Organization, the political and military alliance between member countries, including the United States)
- NORAD (North American Aerospace Defense Command, the binational organization between the United States and Canada)
- UNC (United Nations Command, the multinational command supporting the Republic of Korea)
- CFC (Combined Forces Command, the combined warfighting headquarters for the United States and the Republic of Korea)

Among these organizations are 49 G/FO positions, as shown in Table D.6. For our purposes, we include only G/FO positions that are a part of the joint pool, although there is ample opportunity for the military services to interact within these international organizations. Many of the international G/FO positions are multi-hatted with a similar G/FO position in the U.S. military command structure, such as the Commander, United Nations Command is also the Commander, Combined Forces

Table D.6
International G/FO Positions by Grade

	O-7	O-8	O-9	O-10	Total
NATO	13	5	7	3	30
NORAD	3	2	2	1	8
UNC	2	3	1	1	7
CFC	2	2	1	1	6
Total	20	12	11	6	49

Command as well as the Commander, United States Forces Korea. It is, indeed, a challenge to consider these different hats separately. In this section, we omitted G/FO positions considered in the Contingency group.

Additional Principles

When examining the international G/FO positions, we focused on the value of the international organization to the United States. Since many of these positions are multi-hatted with G/FO positions in the U.S. military structure, we also analyzed the incremental work created by the multi-hatting role. In all cases, the international organization carries strong value to the United States, and the relationships between the United States and the various foreign countries is of vital strategic interest; no relationship was deemed less significant than another.

Due to the multi-hatting of G/FO positions between combatant commands and their international counterparts, these multi-hatted positions are also considered within the context of the respective combatant command. This comparison is only intended to provide perspective on the relevance of the G/FO position and is not a final recommendation within the context of the International group. From the data provided to us from the Department of Defense, all G/FO positions in NORAD, United Nations Command, and Combined Forces Command are multi-hatted with another G/FO position within the U.S. military command structure. In NATO, this multi-hatting exists only for nine of the 30 G/FO positions.

Relevant Subgroups

Each of the four international organizations was treated as a subgroup of the International group. In addition, there is much similarity between the United Nations Command and the Combined Forces Command since they are both in support of the Republic of Korea.

Exceptions

There are no relevant exceptions for the International G/FO group.

Findings

In general, the international positions reviewed meet the criteria for a G/FO requirement. It is likely that if the United States were to pursue either a grade change or a change in country assigned to a G/FO position, the result might require renegotiations with the member parties, which we expect would be a cumbersome process and full of potential diplomatic pitfalls. More important, such a change could result in a loss of influence within the international organization or might result in the position being filled by a G/FO from another nation. Having a foreign G/FO in that position may or may not be acceptable to the United States, and the process to make changes may be laborious and politically hazardous.

Of the 30 G/FO positions within NATO, six G/FO positions rotate between the United States and other member countries. If the position is eligible to be filled by an international G/FO, an option is to exit the rotation, to free up a U.S. G/FO for an internal Department of Defense requirement. If the U.S. prioritizes filling its internal G/FO positions above those serving international roles or roles that can be filled by another entity, then the United States could choose to end its turn in these rotational G/FO positions or send a non-G/FO to serve in the role—and all the more reason to do so if the G/FO position has been sitting vacant for a long while. Before considering this alternative, however, the department needs to answer these questions: What are the advantages to the United States of remaining in the rotation? If the United States does not fill the G/FO position, what will happen if no one else fills the role? What will happen if the United States no longer takes a turn serving in the position?

In NORAD, the Commander, Alaskan North American Aerospace Defense Region is triple-hatted with the Commander, Alaskan Command, United States Northern Command and the Commander, Eleventh Air Force, Pacific Air Forces. Both these positions meet the criteria for a G/FO requirement, but at a lower grade. Thus, the NORAD position, which also meets the criteria for a G/FO requirement, must also be (1) downgraded, (2) the "hat" must be shifted to another O-9 to fulfill the position's responsibilities, or (3) the dual-hatting maintained and the other positions filled at a higher than necessary grade.

Similarly, the majority of the international G/FO positions are triple-hatted between the United Nations Command, Combined Forces Command, and United States Forces Korea. Of the 13 total G/FO positions in the United Nations Command and the Combined Forces Command, two Deputy Assistant Chief of Staff positions do not meet the criteria for a G/FO requirement (downgrade from O-7 or convert to civilian) because it is unclear from the data why these G/FO-level deputies are necessary. This finding is consistent with our findings across the joint staffs that G/FO positions with a primary function to act in place of and on behalf of the one-digit J-code positions do not meet the criteria for a G/FO requirement.

Contingency Positions

Overview

Due to their emergent and nonpermanent nature, we reviewed 59 contingency G/FO positions as a group of their own. We define *contingency* in a broad sense. First, we include all 34 G/FO positions designated for overseas contingency operations (OCO). (Note that some of these positions are dual-hatted with each other, for a total of 27 OCO positions, which is under the cap of 30 G/FO OCO positions in the joint pool as mandated by Congress.)[10] These organizations include:

---

[10] NDAA of 2017, Sec. 501(a)(3)

- United States Forces-Afghanistan
- Operation Resolute Support (NATO-led)
- Combined Security Transition Command-Afghanistan
- USCENTCOM positions in Afghanistan, Iraq, and Qatar
- Combined Joint Task Force-Horn of Africa
- Joint Task Force-Guantanamo
- Kosovo Forces NATO
- NATO Headquarters, Sarajevo.

Second, we incorporate many G/FO positions not officially considered OCO positions but with responsibilities focused on ongoing contingency operations. Defined by law, the term *contingency operation* means a military operation that is designated by the Secretary of Defense as an operation in which members of the armed forces are or may become involved in military actions, operations, or hostilities against an enemy of the United States or against an opposing military force; or under certain provisions of law during a war or during a national emergency declared by the President or Congress.[11] Most of these G/FO positions are part of the joint pool, although eight are from the Air Force in support of these contingency operations. We considered non-OCO G/FO positions from the following organizations:

- United States Forces-Afghanistan
- Operation Resolute Support (NATO-led)
- Headquarters, International Security Assistance Force (ISAF) (NATO-led)
- USCENTCOM positions in Afghanistan
- U.S. Department of State (Military Deputy to the Special Representative for Afghanistan/Pakistan)
- Combined Joint Task Force-Operation Inherent Resolve
- Office of Security Cooperation-Iraq
- Joint Task Force-Guantanamo.

The breakdown of authorized positions by grade is shown in Table D.7.

Table D.7
Contingency G/FO Positions by Grade

	O-7	O-8	O-9	O-10	Total
OCO	20	13	0	1	34
Non-OCO	12	13	0	0	24
Total	32	26	0	1	59

---

[11] 10 USC Sec. 101(a)(13)

Additional Principles

In analyzing the Contingency G/FO positions, we focused on the question: Will these job responsibilities continue indefinitely into the future? In most cases, we expect that contingency operations will shift with time, and therefore, the need for G/FO positions will also change.

Relevant Subgroups

There are no relevant subgroups within the overall group of Contingency G/FO positions.

Exceptions

When considering the Contingency G/FO group, potential exceptions include:

- *Positions that are not a direct part of large-scale military operations.* Both the Commander/Senior Military Representative for NATO Headquarters Sarajevo (O-7) as well as the Chief of Staff for Headquarters Kosovo Forces (O-7) are identified as temporary NATO positions in the Blue Book. In the International group, we discuss additional considerations for positions that are a part of international organizations.
- *Positions within organizations where the OCO designation is not equally applied.* The Commander (O-7) for Joint Task Force-Guantanamo is considered OCO while the Deputy Commander (O-7) for the same organization is not designated as an OCO position. There is additional discussion of joint task forces in the Joint Command group.
- *Positions within organizations that have a broad, ongoing mission, in particular for a combatant command.* With USAFRICOM's dearth of assigned military forces, the combatant command relies heavily on the Combined Joint Task Force-Horn of Africa (CJTF-HOA) to meet its mission to "build defense capabilities, respond to crisis, and deter and defeat transnational threats in order to advance U.S. national interests and promote regional security, stability, and prosperity."[12] Since CJTF-HOA's supporting mission and widespread geographic reach covering about 21 countries is likely to be enduring, the Commander (O-8) and the Deputy Commander (O-7) for CJTF-HOA could change from a designation of OCO. See also the Combatant Command and Joint Command groups for further consideration of these G/FO positions.

Findings

We recommend that all Contingency G/FO positions be referred to the Department of Defense for further review to determine whether the requirement for these positions

---

[12] United States Africa Command, "What We Do," webpage, undated.

still exists. Such a review should occur at regular periodic intervals since contingency operations evolve. Several of these positions have already been slated for elimination as part of the Track Four efficiencies. In addition, at least three (more if the positions are dual-hatted) of the non-OCO positions could be designated as OCO to make full use of the congressional cap of 30 G/FO OCO-designated positions. By fully using the OCO cap, there is additional authorized strength for non-OCO G/FO positions.

G/FO Positions in the Office of the Secretary of Defense and the Department of State

Overview

G/FO positions within the Office of the Secretary of Defense and the Department of State include the military assistants to the Secretary and Deputy Secretary, positions in the Principal Staff Assistants (PSAs), as well as the Joint Strike Fighter Program, the Defense Innovation Unit Experimental (DIUx), and the Office of Military Commissions. The specific organizations within the Office of the Secretary of Defense that contain G/FO positions are:

- Immediate Offices of the Secretary and Deputy Secretary
- Under Secretary of Defense, Policy (USD [P])
- Under Secretary of Defense, Acquisition, Technology, and Logistics (USD [AT&L])
- Defense Innovation Unit Experimental (DIUx)
- Under Secretary of Defense, Intelligence (USD [I])
- Cost Assessment and Program Evaluation (CAPE)
- Chief Information Officer (CIO)
- Office of Military Commissions
- National Guard Bureau (National Guard Bureau has been grouped with the OSD organizations because it reports to the Secretary of Defense and does not logically fit with any other group).

The Department of State positions include a military deputy, a security coordinator, and a role in the Bureau of Political-Military Affairs. This section excludes Defense Agencies and DoD Field Activities (DAFA) subordinate to the OSD PSAs, which are reviewed in other sections of this appendix. The organizations at the Department of State with G/FO positions are:

- Military Deputy to the Special Representative for Afghanistan/Pakistan
- Deputy Assistant Secretary for Plans, Programs and Operations, Bureau of Political-Military Affairs
- United States Security Coordinator, Israel-Palestinian Authority.

Table D.8
OSD and State G/FO Positions by Grade

O-7	O-8	O-9	O-10	Total
9	5	6	1	21

Within these OSD and State organizations, our database contained 21 authorized G/FO positions, ranging from O-7 to O-10, all of which are considered joint positions, as shown in Table D.8.

Additional Principles

Our analysis of the OSD and State G/FO positions focused on the question: Why does the position specifically require a military person as opposed to a civilian? This is a particularly important question for OSD, given that OSD exists to provide civilian guidance and oversight of the military—and civilian control of the military is one of the United States' fundamental constitutional principles. Similarly, the State Department exercises its power and influence through diplomacy, done with a civilian workforce and through the Secretary of State and ambassadors, which are political appointees.

Relevant Subgroups

There are no relevant subgroups within the overall group of OSD and State Department G/FO positions.

Exceptions

The roles of the military assistants to Secretary and Deputy Secretary are unique within the Department of Defense, not only bringing military advice to the Secretary and Deputy but also serving as channel for discreet communications between Secretary and Deputy and the uniformed military at very senior levels. For this reason, we judge that these two positions meet the criteria for a G/FO requirement even though the usual organizational considerations (very limited scope and scale of formal responsibilities, lack of subordinates, etc.) would have suggested that these positions do not meet the criteria for a G/FO. We did not extend this exception to the other military assistant positions within OSD.

Similarly, the Military Deputy to the Special Representative for Afghanistan/Pakistan serves as a senior military advisor but not to a leader as senior as the Secretary of Defense. However, this role should be phasing out because the Special Representative is being eliminated. We also considered this position in our Contingency group.

Findings

Of the 18 G/FO positions in OSD organizations, six positions meet the criteria for a G/FO requirement at the current grade, and three positions do not meet the criteria for a G/FO requirement (eliminate or convert to civilian). For the remaining nine OSD G/FO positions and the three State Department G/FO positions, we were unable to reach a decision based on organizational principles and existing departmental guidance. The fundamental issue is a policy question for the DoD to answer: What is the appropriate role of G/FO positions within the Office of the Secretary of Defense and for civilian organizations outside of the Department of Defense?

All 11 positions in question have roles and responsibilities commensurate with a senior official such as a G/FO and would benefit from the experience and perspectives of a G/FO. But, in our assessment all nine of the OSD positions could be performed by appropriately experienced and qualified civilians. The question is whether the benefits justify the opportunity cost of using a G/FO for these positions. We assess the pros of such assignments to be:

- Brings senior military experience and perspectives to a civilian organization
- Provides valuable experience and understanding of OSD and the State Department to G/FOs who may go on to even more senior positions within the Department of Defense
- Serves as a liaison between OSD, the State Department, and the uniformed military.

The cons of such assignments include:

- May bypass OSD's formal and official mechanisms for reaching out to the Joint Staff, the services, or any of the combatant commands to obtain military advice and perspectives
- Places a senior military G/FO in the command chain of the State Department
- Puts a senior military person in OSD, an organization that provides civilian guidance to and oversight over the military
- More junior military personnel within OSD (especially O-6s) can provide informal military advice and perspectives to OSD and State Department staffs
- Puts a senior military person in a civilian government agency (the Department of State) outside of the Department of Defense.
- Uses a G/FO resource that could be employed elsewhere in positions that cannot be filled by a civilian.

In our judgment, neither the pros nor the cons are entirely compelling. We recommend the Department of Defense conduct a review of these G/FO positions to accomplish the following:

- Provide overarching guidance on the appropriate uses of G/FO positions within OSD.
- Review the existing G/FO positions within OSD to identify those that are consistent with said guidance and meet the criteria for a G/FO, and transition to civilian positions those that are not.

- Review, in conjunction with the Department of State, the appropriateness and necessity of G/FO positions assigned to the Department of State.

Defense Agencies and DoD Field Activities G/FO Positions

Overview

Defense agencies and DoD field activities (collectively, DAFA) are entities that perform "a supply or service activity that is common to more than one military department by a single agency of the Department of Defense."[13] By law, the Secretary of Defense must determine that the creation of a DAFA would produce "effective, economical, or efficient" benefits.[14]

Whether an entity is designated as a defense agency or a DoD field activity is largely arbitrary and based on which title is sought in the designation process; their legal definitions are identical.[15] Further, in practice, defense agencies and DoD field activities are not fundamentally different. Accordingly, defense agencies and DoD field activities were treated as interchangeable entities for the purposes of this analysis.

Each DAFA organization falls within the Secretary of Defense's chain of command and reports through the relevant Under Secretary of Defense or other OSD component. By the nature of the mission of these organizations, which span the military services, each of the positions is joint.

Twenty defense agencies and eight DoD field activities compose the DAFA subgroup, as shown in Table D.9. Of the defense agencies, nine are designated as Combat Support Agencies (CSAs), which are those defense agencies whose missions are recognized as providing direct support to the warfighter. We excluded both DHA and all intelligence-related DAFA positions from this group. While consequential members of the DAFA subgroup, our analysis of these positions is more effectively summarized in the Health and Intelligence groups, respectively.

Within the DAFA group (excluding the DHA and intelligence positions), we analyzed 26 G/FO positions, ranging from O-7 to O-9 (Table D.10). No O-10 positions are authorized in this group.

Additional Principles

We considered several additional factors specific to DAFA organizations.

- Each DAFA tends to have global responsibilities, so we looked closely at whether the scope of responsibilities of G/FOs in these organizations included global responsibilities.

---

[13] 10 USC 191.

[14] 10 USC 191.

[15] Interview with DCMO representative, March 7, 2017.

Table D.9
Defense Agencies and DoD Field Activities

Defense Agencies (Noncombat Support)	• Defense Advanced Research Projects Agency (DARPA) • Missile Defense Agency (MDA) • Defense Security Cooperation Agency (DSCA) • DoD POW/MIA Accounting Agency • Defense Contract Audit Agency (DCAA) • Defense Finance and Accounting Service (DFAS) • Defense Legal Services Agency (DLSA) • Defense Commissary Agency (DCA) • Defense Security Service (DSS) • National Reconnaissance Office (NRO) • Pentagon Force Protection Agency (PFPA)
Defense Agencies (Combat Support Agencies)	• Defense Contract Management Agency (DCMA) • Defense Logistics Agency (DLA) • Defense Threat Reduction Agency (DTRA) • Joint Improvised-Threat Defeat Agency (JIDA)[a] • Defense Information Systems Agency (DISA) • Defense Health Agency (DHA) • Defense Intelligence Agency (DIA) • National Geospatial-Intelligence Agency (NGIA) • National Security Agency/Central Security Service (NSA/CSS)
DoD Field Activities	• Defense Technical Information Center (DTIC) • DoD Test Resource Management Center (TRMC) • Office of Economic Adjustment (OEA) • Defense Technology Security Administration (DTSA) • DoD Education Activity (DoDEA) • DoD Human Resources Activity (DoDHRA) • Washington Headquarters Services (WHS) • Defense Media Activity (DMA)

[a] JIDA was designated a defense agency between 2015 and 2016, and we have included it in this group for purposes of G/FO analysis.

SOURCE: Department of Defense Deputy Chief Management Officer, webpage.

Table D.10
DAFA G/FO Positions by Grade

O-7	O-8	O-9	O-10	Total
11	9	6	0	26

- Given OSD oversight of each DAFA and the inherently civilian missions of many of the DAFAs, we focused closely on whether positions required military expertise or whether civilian leadership could suffice.

Overall, these additional principles affected our findings for seven of the 26 total DAFA positions analyzed in this section.

Relevant Subgroups

We applied general criteria to the combat support agencies, but also more heavily weighed the need for military expertise in certain G/FO roles, depending on the agency's function.

Exceptions

For positions that require senior responsibility for DoD actions and will likely garner intense DoD, congressional, and public scrutiny at least into the near future, we made an exception to some of our broad analytic principles. These positions may not oversee substantial budgets or any G/FO or SES positions, but were still considered to merit G/FOs. An example of such a position is the director of the Sexual Assault and Prevention Response (SAPRO) office (O-8) within DHRA. In this case, we determined that the position meets the criteria for a G/FO requirement at the current grade, while other positions with similar personnel oversight responsibilities may not have.

Findings

For the 26 positions in the DAFA group, our findings are:

- Ten positions meet the criteria for a G/FO requirement at current grade.
- Eight positions meet the criteria for a G/FO at a lower grade.
- Six positions do not meet the criteria for a G/FO (convert to civilian).
- Two positions do not meet the criteria for a G/FO at their current grade (O-8), but we could not determine whether they meet the criteria for a G/FO at a reduced grade (O-7).

Of the 17 positions in combat support agencies, six meet the criteria for a G/FO requirement at current grade. Five positions meet the criteria for a G/FO at a lower grade, five positions do not meet the criteria for a G/FO (some or all could be converted to civilian positions), and one position does not meet the criteria for a G/FO at its current grade (O-8), but we could not determine whether it meets the criteria for a G/FO at a reduced grade (O-7). Four O-9 positions are currently authorized within the combat support agency subgroup. Of these four, our assessment shows that two meet the criteria for a G/FO at the O-9 grade, one does not meet criteria for a G/FO requirement (convert to civilian), and one meets the criteria for a G/FO at a lower grade.

For the nine positions in noncombat support agencies and DoD field activities, our findings are that four positions meet the criteria for G/FO requirements at current grade because of their enhanced global responsibilities; three of these positions also required military expertise. Four positions meet the criteria for a G/FO requirement at a lower grade, one does not meet the criteria for a G/FO requirement, and one does not meet the criteria for a G/FO at its current grade (O-8), but we could not determine whether it meets the criteria for a G/FO at a reduced grade (O-7).

We also observed that although the overall supply and service support mission is at the core of each DAFA mission, we discovered little utility in comparing positions across DAFAs given each organizational entity's different scope and responsibilities. Accordingly, each DAFA was analyzed individually without comparison to the other DAFA.

Intelligence-Related G/FO Positions Within the Services, Combatant Commands, and Agencies

Overview

The group of intelligence-related G/FO positions encompasses service-specific and joint positions focused on intelligence collection, analysis, and dissemination and positions with responsibility for management, guidance, and oversight of intelligence activities. The majority of the positions, which are in the joint community, are particularly diverse, including positions within the Joint Staff, combatant commands, and U.S. Forces Afghanistan (USFOR-A); positions at the DNI, CIA, NSA, NRO, NGA, and DIA; and various DATT, OSD, and NATO positions. In the services, intelligence G/FO positions are found in the service chief's immediate headquarters staff, leading service intelligence centers, and/or service intelligence schools and centers of excellence. Table D.11 lists joint and service organizations containing intelligence G/FO positions.

Intelligence G/FO positions in the Joint Staff J2 directorate are formally positions assigned to DIA. While these positions serve to connect the Chairman and the entire Joint Staff to information and expertise available within the entirety of DIA, on a day-to-day basis the intelligence G/FO positions within the Joint Staff J2 function as members of the Joint Staff and are, therefore, treated as part of the Joint Staff (and not DIA) in this analysis.

We analyzed 52 authorized G/FO positions in the Intelligence group, ranging from O-7 to O-10, as shown by grade in Table D.12.

Table D.11
Organizations Containing Intelligence G/FO Positions

Joint	• Director of National Intelligence • Central Intelligence Agency (CIA) • National Security Agency/Central Security Service (NSA/CSS) • National Geospatial-Intelligence Agency (NGA) • Defense Intelligence Agency (DIA) • Office of the Secretary of Defense (OSD) • Joint Staff[a] • Combatant Commands (Unified and Sub-Unified) • USFOR-A • NATO Headquarters (International Military Staff)
Service	• Headquarters of the Department of the Army (HQDA G2) • Office of the Chief of Naval Operations (OPNAV N2) • Headquarters Marine Corps (HQMC S2) • U.S. Air Force Air Staff (Air Staff A2) • U.S. Army Intelligence and Security Command (INSCOM) • Office of Naval Intelligence/National Maritime Intelligence-Integration Office (ONI/NMIO) • Air Combat Command (ACC) • U.S. Army Intelligence Center of Excellence (USAICoE)

[a] Joint Staff intelligence G/FO positions are formally assigned to DIA, but function as part of the Joint Staff and for that reason are treated as part of the Joint Staff in this analysis.

Table D.12
Intelligence G/FO Positions by Grade

Service/Joint	O-7	O-8	O-9	O-10	Total
Air Force	3	1	1	0	5
Army	0	2	1	0	3
Joint	20	15	5	1	41
Marine Corps	1	0	0	0	1
Navy	0	1	1	0	2
Total	24	19	8	1	52

Additional Principles

We considered additional factors specific to intelligence organizations. When considering positions within the civilian intelligence agencies, we looked closely at whether the roles and responsibilities of the position made clear why a military (as opposed to civilian) person was required; and (if so) why a G/FO was required. We applied this lens to all intelligence agencies, but with particular emphasis on the agencies traditionally considered civilian intelligence activities: CIA, NRO, and NGA. While these agencies have different missions, reflected in the broad variation in their internal organization, we did find a degree of consistency in how they employed G/FOs. These agencies assigned G/FOs in roles that put them either at the center point of interactions between these agencies and the military or in charge of functions that inherently have significant military aspects.

The services, in contrast, have very parallel roles in their intelligence organizations, which are focused on the organizing, training, and equipping of that service's intelligence forces and generating the necessary intelligence to support service-specific requirements (especially with regard to supporting the development and acquisition processes for service capabilities). This translated to similar organizational structures, with all services having top-level headquarters staff (Air Staff A2, HQDA G2, etc.), an organization dedicated to generating service-specific intelligence (e.g., Office of Naval Intelligence [ONI], National Ground Intelligence Center [NGIC], Marine Corps Intelligence Activity [MCIA], Naval Air Systems Command [NASC], etc.), and one or more organizations dedicated to training intelligence personnel. This parallelism in structure provided a basis for comparing and contrasting how the services employed G/FOs within these organizations. Exploring why these organizational elements are commanded by G/FOs in some services but by O-6s in others provided useful insights to our assessment.

Additionally, some intelligence organizations perform functions that are parallel to functions performed by organizations outside the intelligence community. In these cases, we compared intelligence organizations to similar organizations outside the intelligence community. For example, we compared intelligence schools and/or training commands to similar nonintelligence schools and training commands (e.g., we compared the Army's Intelligence Center of Excellence to other Army Centers of Excellence). Similarly, we compared Joint Functional Component Command for Intelligence, Surveillance and Reconnaissance (JFCC-ISR), whose primary function is the allocation of intelligence, surveillance, and reconnaissance (ISR) capabilities to ISR requirements, to nonintelligence joint organizations whose primary function is the allocation of capabilities and/or forces to requirements.

Finally, for reasons of classification, position descriptions for G/FO positions within the intelligence community may not always accurately reflect the full spectrum of duties and responsibilities. In fact, detailed organization charts for some organizations are classified. To ensure we did not overlook important factors or considerations, we complement the unclassified data we received by reviewing classified documents describing roles and functions made available by the various agencies in classified channels.

Relevant Subgroups

As indicated, we considered the intelligence agencies and the service intelligence organizations as two different subgroups. For the agencies, we put emphasis on the question of whether positions required a G/FO or could be filled by an appropriately qualified civilian. For the service intelligence organizations, we put emphasis on whether the number and grade of the G/FOs were commensurate with the scope and nature of functions performed.

Exceptions

Within the agencies, we found G/FO positions that interacted at a very senior level across the civilian intelligence community and the military but did not formally have responsibility for major portfolios or substantial resources within their organizational structures, nor did they have numerous senior subordinates. Given the nature and importance of these interactions, we gave deference to the existing grades of these positions, even when other factors might have suggested a downgrade.

Findings

Our findings are as follows:

- 24 positions meet the criteria for a G/FO requirement.
- Four positions meet the criteria for a G/FO requirement at a lower grade (downgrade).
- Seven positions did not meet the criteria of a G/FO (at least two, if not more, could be converted to civilian).

- One position does not meet the criteria for a G/FO at their current grade (O-8), but we could not determine whether they meet the criteria for a G/FO at a reduced grade (O-7) or converted to civilian.
- 16 positions should be reviewed further by the department for the following reasons:
  - One intelligence G/FO position with OSD (Director for Defense Intelligence [Warfighter Support]) should be reviewed as part of a larger departmental review of the role, value, appropriateness, and opportunity cost of G/FO positions within OSD. This issue is discussed in greater detail in the section on OSD G/FO positions.
  - Five intelligence G/FO positions are associated with contingency operations and should be included in the previously recommended review of contingency-related G/FO positions
  - For ten DATT G/FO positions,[16] it was not evident to us why these positions are staffed with G/FOs and not others even though the countries to which these individuals are assigned are clearly important to the United States (China, Egypt, India, Israel, Kuwait, Mexico, Russia, Turkey, United Arab Emirates, and United Kingdom). We lacked sufficient subject matter expertise and time to assess why these positions merited a G/FO of the rank specified as compared to other DATT positions around the world, the criteria for determining the appropriate grade of a G/FO DATT, and/or how many of the available G/FO resources should be dedicated to DATT missions. We recommend DoD conduct a review of all DATT G/FO positions to determine, based on systematic criteria, when G/FOs are needed in DATT positions, the countries that should be assigned G/FO DATTs, and the appropriate grades for these positions.

Three of the positions that meet the criteria for a G/FO at a lower grade (downgrade) are in the joint community. This finding was driven by grade levels inconsistent with peers or inconsistent with the grade levels of the leaders of nonintelligence organizations performing equivalent functions. The two positions with the finding of convert to civilian were in the joint community as well.

The findings associated with the other positions in service intelligence organizations were driven primarily by comparison with peer organizations outside of the intelligence community.

The one O-10 position (Director NSA/CSS) met criteria for a G/FO at the current grade, although if USCYBERCOM and NSA/CSS are separated, the Secretary and the DNI should consider whether a civilian could be assigned as the Director of NSA/CSS.

---

[16] We received data for 10 DATT G/FO positions; the DATT G/FO positions vary over time, both in number and location.

We scrutinized 13 military positions within the intelligence agencies to ensure a military person was required. As mentioned, these agencies almost always assigned G/FOs in roles that put them either at the center point of interactions between these agencies and the military or in charge of functions that inherently have significant military aspects. For this reason, we found that only two of these 13 positions did not meet the criteria for a G/FO requirement (convert to civilian).

As mentioned, the very parallel structure of the service intelligence organizations allowed fairly direct comparison across the services. Our most significant observation is that the Air Force has five G/FO positions within its service intelligence organizations and major commands, while no other service has more than three such G/FO positions. While the Air Force manages a significant airborne ISR enterprise, the other services (apart from the Marine Corps) also manage significant service-specific collection programs and capabilities (e.g., human intelligence for the Army, undersea collection programs for the Navy) but do so with fewer G/FOs. Our findings suggest reductions in the Air Force intelligence G/FO positions, but we also recommend that the Air Force conduct a zero-based review of its intelligence G/FO positions.

Legal Positions

Overview

Legal services within the Department of Defense and the service branches are provided by two complementary components: one civilian, one military. The general counsel of DoD is a civilian appointed by the President, who serves as the chief legal officer of the department.[17] Likewise, within the service branches, there is a civilian general counsel who serves as the principal legal advisor to the Secretary of the branch. In parallel to this, each service also has a corresponding G/FO, The Judge Advocate General (TJAG), who, in conjunction with their staff of military judge advocates, is responsible for providing advice to the Secretary of the service as they carry out their Title 10 responsibilities.[18]

The Judge Advocates General provide a wide range of legal advice to the Secretaries of their service, ranging from military law, to law of war, administrative and environmental law, and contracting. Their roles typically encompass a wide range of responsibilities, ranging from advocate to judge, counselor, and "the conscience."[19] The Judge Advocates are also responsible for military courts martial; operational responsibility for this function is typically managed by the Deputy Judge Advocate General (DJAG).

---

[17] Joint Publication 1-04, "Legal Support for Military Operations," Washington, D.C., Joint Chiefs of Staff, August 2, 2016, p. I-1.

[18] Joint Publication 1-04, especially Chapter One.

[19] Matthew E. Winter, "Finding the Law—The Values, Identity, and Function of the International Law Adviser," *Military Law Review*, Vol. 128, 1990, pp. 1–13, 14.

As the legal complexity of military operations has increased in recent years, moving from formally declared wars against state armies to counterterror operations against nonstate actors, the demands placed on TJAGs have become more complex, as have the political demands on the position.[20] In recognition of this, and in light of the disputes with civilian legal advisors to the Secretary of Defense discussed later, the 2008 NDAA promoted the TJAGs to O-9s and their deputies to O-8s to guarantee them higher-level access in Pentagon decisionmaking.[21] In addition to the TJAGs and DJAGs, the Marine Corps has its own Staff Judge Advocate, and the Chairman of the Joint Chiefs of Staff has a G/FO Legal Counsel drawn on a rotating basis from each of the services.

In addition to these legal advisory positions, the Army and Air Force each operate legal centers and agencies and criminal investigations divisions, each headed by a G/FO. At one time, the Navy operated its own military criminal investigations division, but in the wake of the Tailhook scandal[22] these functions were transferred to civilian command.

In total, we analyzed 14 G/FO legal organizations as part of this review, as shown in Table D.13, of which seven were Judge Advocates, Deputy Judge Advocates, or Staff Judge Advocates.

Table D.13
Organizations Containing Legal Positions

Service/Joint	Position
Army	• Judge Advocate General • Deputy Judge Advocate General • Assistant Judge Advocate General for Military Law and Operations • Commanding General, Criminal Investigation Command • Commanding General/Commandant, Legal Center and School • Dual-hatted as the Provost Marshal General (PMG) • Commanding General, Legal Services Agency/Chief Judge, Court of Criminal Appeals
Navy	• Judge Advocate General • Deputy Judge Advocate General
Air Force	• Judge Advocate General • Deputy Judge Advocate General • Commander, Air Force Legal Operations Agency
Marine Corps	• Staff Judge Advocate
Joint	• Legal Counsel to the Chairman of the Joint Chiefs of Staff

---

[20] Lisa L. Turner, "The Detainee Interrogation Debate and the Legal-Policy Process," *Joint Force Quarterly*, Vol. 53, 2009, pp. 40–47.

[21] Scott Horton, "Jim Haynes's Long Twilight Struggle," *Harper's Magazine: Browsings, The Harper's Blog*, February 8, 2008.

[22] Tailhook is the name given to the incident in 1991 at the Las Vegas Hilton in which many Navy and Marine Corps aviators were alleged to have been involved in a multitude of sexual assault incidents. These assaults occurred when the Navy and Marine Corps personnel involved were attending the annual 35th Annual Tailhook Association Symposium.

Table D.14
Legal Positions by Service and Grade

Service/Joint	O-7	O-8	O-9	O-10	Total
Army	3	3	1	0	7
Navy	0	1	1	0	2
Air Force	4	1	1	0	6
Marine Corps	0	1	0	0	1
Joint	1	0	0	0	1
Total	8	6	3	0	17

Within the Legal group, we evaluated 17 positions, as shown by service and grade in Table D.14.

Relevant Subgroups

Within the services, legal positions fall into two broad categories: (1) the G/FO Judge Advocates (which provide legal counsel to the senior military leadership) and (2) the legal centers and agencies, criminal investigations commands, and associated legal staff functions (which provide for the operation and provision of legal services within each service branch).

Exceptions

Though technically G/FO positions, three Air Force O-7 positions have already been identified as Track Four candidates and are currently staffed by O-6s. In addition, several joint and agency positions were determined to be outside the scope of this portion of the organizational analysis. The Director, Rule of Law serves with United States Forces-Afghanistan and is not part of the core legal function of the military services. Likewise, the Chief Prosecutor of Military Commissions and the Chief Defense Counsel, Office of Military Commissions were excluded from this analysis.

Additional Principles

Though the parallel military and civilian legal structures within the DoD might seem like an inefficiency that could be addressed by consolidating the general counsels and the JAG corps, the Congress expressly considered but rejected this option while providing guidance to reorganize and streamline DoD in 1986.[23] Accordingly, we have not pursued this option in our analysis.

---

[23] The rationale was summarized by then Secretary of the Army Marsh as he testified in Senate Hearings in 1986: "I . . . disagree with having the general counsel directly supervise the Judge Advocate General. The general

Findings

Our findings for the 17 positions in the legal group are as follows:

- Seven positions meet the criteria for a G/FO requirement at the current grade.
- Two positions meet the criteria for a G/FO requirement at a lower grade (downgrade).
- Seven positions do not meet the criteria for a G/FO.
- One position we were unable to make a conclusive assessment.

Our analysis considered reducing the rank of TJAG and DJAG positions from O-9 and O-8, to O-8 and O-7, respectively, which was the rank of these positions prior to 2008. We rejected this option, however, after reviewing the historical circumstances that led to their promotion. During the debates about the permissibility of "enhanced interrogation" and other issues related to the global war on terror, the general counsel of the DoD attempted to sideline the JAG corps from decisionmaking; politicize the positions by taking control of the promotion process; subordinate JAGs to civilian general counsels; transfer staff away from the JAG corps to the general counsels' office; and otherwise attempted to undermine the autonomy and integrity of the position.[24]

Congress responded in two ways. Statutory language was added to protect the JAG corps from interference and, in the 2008 NDAA, the rank of the TJAG and DJAG positions were increased to guarantee the lawyers higher-level access to Pentagon decisionmaking.[25] Understanding that the JAG positions exist in balance with their civilian counterparts within both the DoD and the services, and recognizing the explicit steps Congress took to reestablish balance within this ecosystem, our findings did not extend to altering the current ranks of these positions.

In addition to the JAG corps, a number of G/FO legal positions are responsible for the operations of legal agencies, schools, and administrative infrastructure within the services. Review of these positions identified several areas in which the grades and number of G/FO positions did not meet our criteria. Management of legal agencies did not meet the criteria for a G/FO requirement, particularly in light of the fact that the Navy has operated without a flag officer in these roles since the early 1990s. Likewise, criminal investigations positions did not meet the criteria for a G/FO requirement. Of note is that control of the Navy's criminal investigation division was taken from the military chain of command and placed under civilian control. While other services

---

counsel is my senior legal advisor on matters concerned with civilian oversight while the Judge Advocate General advises the Chief of Staff and through him, myself on legal matters of the military to include administration of military justice. It is important that those two posts remain separate." Quoted in Kurt A. Johnson, "Military Department General Counsel as Chief Legal Officers: Impact on Delivery of Impartial Legal Advice at Headquarters and in the Field," *Military Legal Review*, Vol. 82, 1993, pp. 1–81, 41.

[24] Horton, 2008.

[25] Horton, 2008.

have retained military control of their criminal investigation division functions and have placed them under the command of a general officer, the precedent of the Navy's case indicates these functions can be performed by civilians.

Medical Positions (MEDCOM, Command Surgeons, Veterinary Corps)

Overview

The DoD operates one of the largest and most complex health care organizations in the nation. In 2013, military treatment facilities (MTFs) included 56 hospitals, 361 ambulatory care clinics, and 249 dental clinics operating worldwide, employing 60,389 civilians and 86,051 military personnel.[26] As a 2014 report to the Secretary of Defense describes, Military Health Services is responsible for a "continuum of health services from austere operational environments through remote, fixed medical treatment facilities to major tertiary care medical centers distributed across the United States."[27] As of 2017, these MTFs are variously managed by the Army, Navy, Air Force, or directly by DHA. Moreover, in addition to maintaining a substantial medical corps charged both with providing deployable medical facilities and care to support military operations, the services are also responsible for managing and staffing medical facilities that deliver care to the military personnel, dependents, and veterans enrolled in the military TRICARE system.

The 2017 NDAA mandated a substantial reorganization of the existing system, however, primarily by centralizing control of medical treatment facilities under the reorganized DHA.[28] At the core of this reorganization was the intent to "eliminate duplicative activities carried out by elements of the Defense Health Agency and the military departments" based on the model that there should be "a single agency responsible for the administration of all MTFs."[29] We considered the reorganized health system in our assessment.

Currently, the organizational structure that enables the delivery of medical care differs among the services. The Army, Navy, and Air Force operate independent medical departments that are each established under Title 10, with the Navy providing the structure used by the Marine Corps. The Army and Navy each have a medical command headed by a Surgeon General who manages the medical treatment facilities and other responsibilities through a regional command structure. In the Army, this was accomplished with a parallel hierarchy of dual-hatted positions, in which the

---

[26] U.S. Department of Defense, *Military Health System Review, Final Report to the Secretary of Defense*, Washington, D.C., August 2014, p. 19.

[27] U.S. Department of Defense, 2014, p. 19.

[28] 10 USC 1073c.

[29] U.S. Department of Defense, *Plan to Implement Section 1073c of Title 10, United States Code, Report to the Armed Services Committees of the Senate and House of Representatives,* Second Interim Report, Washington, D.C., June 30, 2017, pp. 1–2.

Commanding General, United States Army Medical Command is responsible for the command of the geographic medical commands. Within the Air Force, the Surgeon General is responsible for medical facilities that are organized and commanded under the air wings rather than geographically.

In each of the services, the multiple responsibilities of the military health service are reflected in complex organizational and chain of command structures that address the dual concerns of command of medical personnel and the operation of MTFs. The impact of the 2017 NDAA will be to rationalize these organizational structures to some extent, placing the MTFs under DHA control, while leaving the services with medical systems commanded by the Surgeons General and responsible for fulfilling their obligations to recruit, organize, train, and equip.

We analyzed 49 medical positions, 27 O-7s, 18 O-8s, and four O-9s, as shown in Table D.15. There are no medical positions at the grade of O-10.

Relevant Subgroups

Medical positions within the services are broadly divided into two categories, often associated with separate command hierarchies. The first group is comprised of the surgeons general, who, together with their deputies and staffs are responsible for all health care matters within the service. The bulk of the positions fall into a second category focused on management and provision of medical care. These positions, which include hospital, service, and market managers, are the focus of the reorganization that places responsibility for these functions under DHA.

Exceptions

None.

Additional Principles

In addition to applying the general principles outlined in the introduction, our analysis of medical positions was guided by the current plans for the implementation of the health care restructuring guidance in the 2017 NDAA.

Table D.15
Medical Positions by Service and Grade

Service/Joint	O-7	O-8	O-9	O-10	Total
Army	15	10	1	0	26
Navy	5	2	1	0	8
Air Force	5	3	1	0	9
Joint	2	3	1	0	6
Total	27	18	4	0	49

Findings

Within the Medical group, our findings are as follows:

- 12 positions meet the criteria for a G/FO requirement at the current grade.
- Four positions meet the criteria for a G/FO requirement at a lower grade.
- 33 positions do not meet the criteria for a G/FO requirement.

The mechanism for this reorganization will be to select a single agency, the DHA, to administer all MTFs. Under this new management model, "The DHA will be responsible for the administration of each MTF, including budgetary matters, information technology, health care administration and management, administrative policy and procedure, military medical construction, and other appropriate matters."[30] The scope and intent of this provision is clear. As the second interim report on the act's implementation states,

> The MHS [medical health system] currently operates the MTFs through multiple agency and command structures, including Service Medical Departments, multiple Regional Commands (Army and Navy), the Air Force Medical Operations Agency, five enhanced Multi-Service markets (eMSMs), and the National Capital Region Medical Directorate. As the Department rationalizes and consolidates MTF administration and management, the Department will work to streamline and eliminate unwarranted duplicative activities carried out within these management structures.[31]

While these sections dramatically impact the need for G/FO positions to manage the delivery of care through MTFs, section 702 explicitly references the roles of the Surgeons General as "chief medical advisor[s] . . . to the Director of the Defense Health Agency on matters pertaining to military health readiness requirements and safety of members of the [service branch]." Likewise, the guidance that the director of the Defense Health Agency "shall coordinate with the Joint Staff Surgeon to ensure that the Director most effectively carries out the responsibilities of the Defense Health Agency as a combat support agency" ensures that these positions will be retained, though no new guidance is given regarding their rank. Finally, while the position of the Director of the DHA is referenced without specifying a new rank or selection criteria, the deputy directors of the DHA are identified as non-G/FO, civilian positions.

Following this guidance, our finding is that the Joint Staff Surgeon and Surgeons General of each service and their deputies meet the criteria for a G/FO requirement at the current grade. In addition to being referenced in section 702 of the NDAA, these

[30] 10 USC 1073c.; Second Interim Report, June 30, 2017, p. 3.

[31] Second Interim Report, June 30, 2017, p. 4.

positions serve the necessary function of providing medical leadership and oversight within each of the services.

Our rationale for the 33 positions that do not meet the criteria for a G/FO is as follows. Many of these positions are responsible for the management of the "service Medical Departments, multiple Regional Commands (Army and Navy), the Air Force Medical Operations Agency, five enhanced Multi-Service markets (eMSMs)" referenced in the legislation as areas that will be consolidated under DHA control. Eighteen of these positions are in the Army, and include five commanding generals of regional health commands or medical centers, and an additional four deputy commanders of similar health delivery regions. Six positions are in the Air Force, including the commanders of the 59th Medical Wing and the medical operations agency. An additional five positions are in the Navy, including the Commanders of the Navy Medicine regional commands. An additional four joint positions do not meet the criteria for a G/FO since, despite the increasing role of the DHA, the structuring of the agency represents a shift away from G/FO managers to Senior Executive Service (SES) positions with medical management experience. With management and budgetary authority under the control of DHA, there is little justification for retaining these positions at the G/FO level.

There is some uncertainty in this analysis, however, because additional language in the second interim report suggests that:

> The DHA together with the Military Departments will establish three Component Commands—one aligned with each military department to serve as the integration point for healthcare delivery and military personnel readiness missions at each MTF. Each of these has two roles—one as a component of the DHA responsible to the DHA director for MTF healthcare operations and the other as a military command under the command and control chain under the Secretary of the Military Department concerned.[32]

The organization of these dual-hatted component commanders and their rank and function within each of the services is still being analyzed as part of the NDAA implementation process. It is likely, however, that these functions will meet the criteria for G/FO requirements and will be drawn from the 33 positions that currently do not appear to meet the criteria for a G/FO. Sixteen of these positions are directly related to management of MTFs, and the remaining 17 serve more general management and coordination functions. While the final implementation of the NDAA guidance is still being negotiated and the G/FO positions involved in the transition have yet to be identified, it seems reasonable to assume that at least half of the 33 positions will represent opportunities for reductions in the G/FO force.

---

[32] Second Interim Report, June 30, 2017, p. 4.

Chaplain Positions

Overview

Chaplain Services is a formal group within each service branch established to "accommodate religious needs, to provide religious and pastoral care, and to advise commanders on the complexities of religion with regard to its personnel and mission, as appropriate."[33] Due to the religious nature of their work, chaplains have rank without command authority; service regulations prohibit chaplains from bearing arms and classify chaplains as noncombatants.[34] They function in the dual roles of religious leader and staff officer.

Currently there are three Chiefs of Chaplains at the O-8 rank and three Assistant Chiefs of Chaplains at the O-7 rank. These officers serve in the Army, Navy, and Air Force. The Navy directs its Chaplain Corps to provide chaplains for the Marine Corps, the Coast Guard, and the Merchant Marine. The distribution of the six chaplain positions of G/FO rank across the services is shown in Table D.16.

Additional Principles

Two additional factors were important to the organizational analysis for the chaplain group. Because they have rank without command, chaplains exist outside the main military hierarchy. They have no other alternatives for advancement aside from the ranks of the chaplain corps. Because chaplains must have an academic degree at an appropriate level and an ecclesiastical endorsement by a religious group prior to their entry into the military, they typically enter at the rank of captain (O-3). As a special group, eligible only for promotion within their professional track, we chose to retain a chaplain G/FO position in each service to provide a career progression pathway that would otherwise be limited to an already saturated pool of O-6s.

Table D.16
Chaplain Positions by Service and Grade

Service/Joint	O-7	O-8	O-9	O-10	Total
Army	1	1	0	0	2
Navy	1	1	0	0	2
Air Force	1	1	0	0	2
Marine Corps	0	0	0	0	0
Joint	0	0	0	0	0
Total	3	3	0	0	6

---

[33] JP 1-05, p. vii.

[34] Title 10, USC, Sections 3581, and 8581; JP 1-05, p. vii.

Findings

Among the six positions in this group, our findings are as follows:

- The three Chief of Chaplains in each service meet the criteria for a G/FO requirement at a lower grade (downgrade to O-7).
- The three Assistant Chief of Chaplains do not meet the criteria for a G/FO requirement (reduce to O-6).

In keeping with the principle just articulated, this retains one G/FO chaplain position in each service to accord the profession formal stature within each of the services and to provide a G/FO apex of the profession's career pyramid. Given the special position of the chaplains and their limited command authority, the duties of the Chief can be performed by a G/FO in a lower grade (O-7). However, the duties of the Assistant Chiefs do not meet the criteria for a G/FO because their ability to perform the functions of their position does not rely on their rank.

Program Executive Officers and Gansler 5 Positions

Overview

A subset of DoD acquisition positions, PEOs are primarily responsible for one or several related acquisition programs. We included positions specifically identified as PEO or deputy PEO positions by their organizations in the data provided by the services and joint community. In addition to PEO positions, we also include the Gansler Five Acquisition Positions as designated in the November 2016 Blue Book. The Gansler 5 positions stem from the recommendations in the 2007 report of the Commission on Army Acquisition and Program Management in Expeditionary Operations, *Urgent Reform Required: Army Expeditionary Contracting*.[35] While many other acquisition-related and research and development programs exist within DoD, this group includes only the PEO and Gansler 5 positions.

Table D.17 shows the distribution of the 33 joint and service PEO positions we analyzed. Of these, 24 are service positions and nine are joint. The majority of positions are at the O-7 and O-8 grade, with three at O-9.

Additional Principles

We applied two additional principles to the PEO and Gansler 5 positions. First, we looked closely at parity across the services, determining that program administration

---

[35] This commission is commonly called the Gansler Commission for commission chair Dr. Jacques Gansler, former Under Secretary of Defense for Acquisition, Technology and Logistics. Commission on Army Acquisition and Program Management in Expeditionary Operations, *Urgent Reform Required, Army Expeditionary Contracting*, October 31, 2007.

Table D.17
Acquisition Positions by Sponsor and Grade

Service/Joint	O-7	O-8	O-9	O-10	Total
Army	4	4	0	0	8
Navy	4	5	0	0	9
Air Force	3	2	1	0	6
Marine Corps	0	1	0	0	1
Joint	4	3	2	0	9
Total	15	15	3	0	33

and execution generally required the same rank of G/FO. Second, we examined intra-service program parity—looking at parity across ranks of G/FOs administering acquisition programs within a service.

Relevant Subgroups

We divided this group into two subgroups: (1) the PEO positions, which served as a natural subgroup for this analysis and facilitated comparison across services and types of programs; and (2) the Gansler 5 positions, which were each analyzed independent of the others due to their varied roles and responsibilities.

Exceptions

In a few cases, we determined that the G/FO role for certain PEO positions required substantial responsibility—due to program size and significance and level of public and congressional scrutiny—that a higher rank relative to other acquisition programs was merited. The Joint Strike Fighter program is one example.

Findings

Our findings for the 33 positions in the PEO/Gansler 5 group are as follows:

- Eight positions meet the criteria for a G/FO requirement at the current grade.
- 11 positions meet the criteria for a G/FO requirement at a lower grade (downgrade).
- 11 positions do not meet the criteria for a G/FO requirement.
- Three positions we could not reach a conclusive determination.

The 28 positions in the PEO subgroup included the eight positions that meet criteria for a G/FO at current grade, ten positions that meet the requirement for a G/FO at a lower grade, one position to convert to civilian, six positions to reduce to O-6, and three positions for which our assessment was inconclusive.

Among the Gansler 5 positions, all of which are joint positions, one position meets the criteria for a G/FO at a lower grade (downgrade) and four do not meet the criteria for a G/FO requirement. For the four that do not meet G/FO criteria, the findings were to convert two positions to civilian and reduce two positions to O-6.

Looking at the findings by grade:

- Of the three O-9 positions, one meets the criteria for a G/FO at the current grade, one meets the criteria for a G/FO at a lower grade (downgrade), and one does not meet the criteria for a G/FO (convert to civilian).
- Of the 15 O-8 positions, ten meet the criteria for a G/FO at a lower grade (downgrade) and two do not (convert to civilian), and for three our analysis was inconclusive.
- Of the 15 O-7 positions, seven meet the criteria for a G/FO at the current grade, and eight do not (at least three could be converted to civilian).

These findings are distributed across the services as follows. For the Army, two positions meet criteria for a G/FO at the current grade, four meet the criteria at a lower grade (downgrade), and two do not meet the criteria (reduce to O-6). For the Navy, four requirements meet the criteria for a G/FO at the current grade and five meet the criteria at a lower grade (downgrade). In the Air Force, three meet the criteria for a G/FO at the current grade and three meet the criteria at a lower grade (downgrade). The Marine Corps position meets the criteria for a G/FO at a lower grade (downgrade), and among the joint positions, one meets criteria for a G/FO at the current grade, two meet the criteria for a G/FO at a lower grade (downgrade), and six do not (three reduce to O-6 and three convert to civilian). Overall, we observed what appeared to be inflated ranks across the services and joint positions, with no particular service or subgroup harboring significantly more positions than others.

Education Positions

Overview

Education positions are an unofficial group defined by positions, both service and joint, that are affiliated with the provision or oversight of education at military institutes of higher learning. This group excludes DoD Education Activity positions and training-specific positions.

The education positions in this group span degree-granting institutions at the undergraduate and graduate level, intermediate-level PME institutions, senior service colleges (e.g., war colleges), joint professional military education (JPME) schools, and education oversight positions. Some institutions are currently authorized multiple G/FO positions, while others have only one. The specific institutions with G/FO positions included in this analysis are listed in Table D.18.

Table D.18
Organizations Containing Education Positions

Army	• United States Army Command and General Staff College • United States Military Academy • United States Army War College • Army University
Navy	• Naval War College • United States Naval Academy • Naval Education and Training Command
Air Force	• Air War College • Air Force Institute of Technology • United States Air Force Academy • Air University
Marine Corps	• Marine Corps University
Joint	• National Defense University • Joint Forces Staff College • Dwight D. Eisenhower School for National Security and Resource School • Inter-American Defense College

Table D.19
Education Positions by Sponsor and Grade

Service/Joint	O-7	O-8	O-9	O-10	Total
Army	2	2	2	0	6
Navy	0	2	1	0	3
Air Force	4	1	2	0	7
Marine Corps	0	1	0	0	1
Joint	3	2	0	0	5
Total	9	8	5	0	22

Of the 22 education positions we analyzed, five were joint and 17 were service positions, as shown in Table D.19.

Additional Principles

Overall, we applied general criteria identified in the introduction of this chapter uniformly: span of control, grade and number of subordinates, and necessity for military personnel in a senior level position. All were critical principles in this analysis. However, we also applied additional principles to the education group. First, an additional consideration not applicable to other groups was the rank of the students each relevant position oversees. Second, we also looked carefully at service parity across similar positions in this analysis, as the fundamental purpose and responsibilities of most of the positions were roughly equal. However, while service parity was an important factor in our analysis, in some cases we determined that this principle should not necessarily outweigh other common principles.

Relevant Subgroups

The education group was divided into three subgroups: service academies (United States Military Academy, United States Naval Academy, and United States Air Force Academy); midcareer and senior service colleges (Army War College, United States Army Command and General Staff College, Naval War College, Air War College, Air Force Institute of Technology, Marine Corps University, National War College, Dwight D. Eisenhower School for National Security and Resource School, Joint Forces Staff College, and Inter-American Defense College); and education oversight positions (Army University, United States Army Combined Arms Center, Naval Training and Education Command, Air University, Marine Corps Education Command, Headquarters Air Education and Training Command, and National Defense University).

These subgroups were analyzed separately from each other because the positions require different ranks primarily due to the predominant grade of students attending the pertinent institution. These particular subgroups facilitated cross-service comparisons in many cases: for example, the functions and G/FO responsibilities at a military academy are largely similar (although not redundant) across services. In cases that facilitated cross-service comparisons, we directly compared like positions within like institutions (e.g., superintendents, commandants, commanding generals). Not all positions fit within these three subgroups and some, such as President, Marine Corps University (MCU)/Commanding General, Education Command, qualify under both. For positions that were not members of a particular subgroup, we analyzed the positions on a case-by-case basis and compared them to any applicable cross-service corollaries.

Exceptions

Certain education positions at centers of higher learning were also combined or dual-hatted with headquarters-level education positions, such as Commander and President, Air University/Director of Education, Headquarters Air Education and Training Command. In these cases, we considered both roles of the position and compared those responsibilities to analogs in the other services, even if the comparison position was not included in the education group due to that position's primary responsibilities.

Findings

Among the 22 positions in this group our findings are as follows:

- Eight positions meet the criteria for a G/FO requirement at the current grade.
- Nine positions meet the criteria for a G/FO at a lower grade (downgrade).
- Four positions do not meet the criteria for a G/FO (two reduce to O-6 and two convert to civilian).
- One position was inconclusive due to its multiple roles.

Certain G/FOs in this group held roles and responsibilities beyond their education position, whether in a dual-hat or combined-role scenario. One such example is the Deputy Commandant, United States Army Command and General, Staff College/Deputy Commanding General-Education, United States Army Combined Arms Center. In these cases, we further reviewed the position from the lens of the other role's relevant group (and even then, in one case it was inconclusive).

In the service academy subgroup of seven positions, our findings are that three positions meet criteria for a G/FO at a lower grade (downgrade) and that four positions do not meet the criteria for a G/FO (two reduce to O-6 and two convert to civilian). In most cases, these findings were the result of service parity considerations and of rank and number of subordinates. Of the ten midcareer and senior service college positions, seven positions meet the criteria for a G/FO at current rank, two meet the criteria at a lower rank (downgrade) and one resulted in a conflicting finding. Among the three education oversight positions, one position meets the criteria for a G/FO at current grade and two positions meet the criteria at a lower grade (downgrade). The two positions that spanned the oversight and midcareer/senior service subgroups meet the criteria for a G/FO at a lower grade (downgrade). We applied both additional principles in our analysis of the senior service college positions. One education oversight position was analyzed as part of its parent service major command due to the position's broader responsibilities.

Our findings by grade are as follows:

- All five O-9 positions, the senior-most rank in the education group, meet the criteria for a G/FO requirement at a lower grade (downgrade).
- Among the eight O-8 positions, three positions meet the criteria for a G/FO at current grade, four meet the criteria at a lower grade (downgrade), and one position was indeterminate.
- Of the nine O-7 positions, five meet criteria for a G/FO position at the current grade and, based on service parity considerations, four do not (two reduced to O-6 and two converted to civilian). Overall, position grades appeared to be inflated most at the service superintendent and president positions, where those positions tended not to oversee G/FOs at the rank directly below.

By service, our findings are summarized as follows. Among the six Army positions, four positions meet the criteria for a G/FO requirement at a lower grade (downgrade), and two positions did not meet the criteria for a G/FO (one reduce to O-6 and one convert to civilian). Of the three Navy positions, which was the service with the fewest G/FOs in education positions, one position meets the criteria for a G/FO at the current grade and two meet the criteria at a lower grade (downgrade). The Air Force, with the largest number of education positions at seven, two positions meet the criteria for a G/FO at the current grade, three meet the criteria at a lower grade), and two did not meet the criteria for a G/FO requirement (one reduce to O-6 and one convert to civilian). Our findings for the sole G/FO education position in the Marine Corps is that this position meets the criteria for a G/FO at a lower grade (downgrade) on the basis of service parity. All five joint education positions meet the criteria for a G/FO at the current grade.

Military Service Major Command and Subordinate Command Positions

Overview
The following sections detail our analysis of each of the four services' major command and subordinate command positions. While not every position is reviewed within each service, the majority of those commands led by four-star G/FOs and the commands directly subordinate to those four-star commands are included in our review.

These service-focused analyses considered a position's responsibilities within that specific command and, where relevant compared those responsibilities (and grades) across similar intraservice and interservice organizations. In many cases, the service major command and subordinate command reviews analyzed positions that were also part of other subgroup analyses. As a result, in some instances (such as with the Legal subgroup), the service major command analysis for a specific position resulted in a different recommendation than that of another subgroup analysis, such as education or chaplains.

Each service command/subordinate command analysis required an individually tailored approach because none of the services are organized into major commands in the same way, and each of the services has its own mission that its commands support. However, each of the service analyses adhered to the analytic process and principles outlined in Chapter Three.

Generally, the G/FO positions recommended for downgrades or determined to not meet the criteria for a G/FO fall into one or more of the following categories:

- The positions function as G/FO-level "assistants" and these functions can be provided by non-G/FO personnel (military or in some cases civilian).
- The positions had functions that did not reflect a clear requirement for a military person and could, therefore, be filled by a civilian person.
- The positions were in nonwarfighting functions that had low-risk, low-consequences of downgrading to O-6s or converting to civilian.
- The positions did not oversee personnel at the O-6/GS-15 level and did not otherwise require a G/FO position.

Principles

Within the service major command and subordinate analyses, several principles were of particular importance in determining our recommendations.

- *Parity.* In analyzing the service headquarters organizations, we considered the principle of parity across services to be important so as to create an even playing field for all the services. For example, given the critical role they play in resource allocation discussions and debates, it would be inappropriate for the "8s" of the services (e.g., the A8, G8, and N8—and, for that matter, the Joint Staff J8) to be of unequal grade. For this reason, the review of each service headquarters staff was cross-referenced with reviews of the other service headquarters staffs. Parity could not be applied mechanically due to differences between the service staffs, and the Marine Corps in particular, but it was one of the key considerations during the review of each service's headquarters staffs.
- *Ability for civilians to execute responsibilities.* We particularly examined G/FO positions in nonwarfighting communities and/or functions (chaplains, medical, education, research and development, etc.) for positions that did not meet the criteria for a G/FO requirement and could be converted to civilian or positions that met the criteria for a G/FO requirement but at a lower grade (downgrade). Recall that in this review we did not consider whether these G/FO positions were important for the "health" of these communities but, rather, whether the service command in question needed to have a G/FO in that particular position for the organization to function effectively.
- *Grade inflation.* Applicable to many positions in this analysis was whether the grades of all positions within a chain of command might be inflated. While we used the principle of grade and number of subordinates throughout this analysis, we found that, in some groups, this principle might inaccurately influence the analysis if all grades that give a particular position context are higher than they need to be. Accordingly, there are several instances in which large portions of certain chains of command from O-7 up to O-9 or O-10 did not met the criteria for G/FO at their current grade.

Exceptions

One type of position of particular interest is each service's intelligence staff director, or the service "2s." A service "2" generally is responsible for the organization, training, and equipping of that service's intelligence personnel. While there is also a function in each service to provide intelligence support to the development and acquisition functions of that service, this latter function is generally performed by other service intelligence organizations at a lower level (and in doing so, these organizations perform their intelligence support functions as part of the overall federated national-level intelligence construct). Of note, no other professional community within the services (e.g., the Air

Force's tactical aviators) has an O-9 on the service staff to oversee and advocate the organization, training, and equipping of that community.

Given this disparity, an extreme position would be that the organization, equipping, and training of intelligence personnel and functions within a service staff should be carried out no differently than any other subcommunity in a service; this would imply managing the intelligence community through the other directorates of the service staff and the various major commands, potentially even dis-establishing a service's "2" directorate. That would be a major reorganization, the pros and cons of which are beyond the scope of this study (nor do we advocate such an extreme position). Nevertheless, the disproportionate seniority of the service staff position charged with the organization, training, and equipping of intelligence personnel relative to other service professional communities led us to a finding that the Air Force and Army "2" positions meet the criteria for a G/FO at a lower grade. The Marine Corps' equivalent position, the Director of Intelligence, is an O-7 that we found met the criteria for G/FO at its current or higher grade, indicating our consideration of service-wide parity in this position. The Navy presented a different case, because its intelligence chief is actually the N2/N6—reflecting its communications staff oversight responsibilities—and, further, is dual-hatted as the Navy's Chief Information Officer, another senior-level position. Due to these additional responsibilities, we found that the N2/N6 meets the criteria for G/FO at its current grade.

Selected U.S. Army Major Command and Subordinate Command Positions

Overview

In this section, we describe our analysis of the Army G/FO positions that report directly to one of the six Army headquarters or major commands or to one of those entities' subordinate commands. We define Army major commands as each of the Army's traditional four-star commands: United States Army Forces Command (FORSCOM); United States Army Training and Doctrine Command (TRADOC); Army Materiel Command (AMC); and United States Army Pacific (USARPAC). We define headquarters elements as those reporting to the Chief of Staff of the Army and the Secretary of the Army. This delineation differs somewhat from the Army's definition of Headquarters of the Department of the Army. While we did not analyze every Army G/FO position in this section, we did review 227 of 290 total Army positions, or 78.3 percent. Further, we also included one dual-role joint position, Commanding General, Eighth Army/Chief of Staff, Combined Forces Command, as it is an Army command position. In total, we reviewed 228 positions in this section.

The analysis in this section does not include organizations assigned to: United States Army Corps of Engineers, United States Army Medical Command, United States Army Installation Management Command, positions at the United States Military Academy, United States Army Criminal Investigation Command, Combat

Readiness Center/Army Safety, United States Army Intelligence and Security Command, the Office of the Assistant Chief of Staff for Installation Management, and Program Executive Officer positions. Other sections cover many of the Army G/FO positions in these organizations.

The positions in this group span the ranks of O-7 to O-10 and range from command surgeons to staff officers to corps and numbered army commanders to personnel managers. Some commands include several G/FOs in their headquarters alone, while others have one G/FO representative in their organization. The diversity and specific purposes among commands prevented direct comparisons across each major command and headquarters element, but certain types of commands, such as corps and divisions within the combat arms, facilitated intracommand or even intercommand comparison in some cases. These subgroups are explained in detail later in this section.

The subordinate commands we analyzed are organized by major command and headquarters elements positions as detailed in Table D.20.

Table D.20
Army Major Commands and Direct Subordinate Units Reviewed

Chief of Staff of the Army	• Director of the Army Staff
	  – Military District of Washington-Joint Force Headquarters—National Capital Region
	  – Test and Evaluation Command
	    ▪ Operational Test Command
	    ▪ White Sands Missile Range
	    ▪ Army War College
	• Chaplains
	• G1
	  – Human Resources Command
	  – Army Physical Disability Agency
	• G2
	• G3/5/7
	• G4
	• G8
	• Judge Advocate General
	  – JAG Legal Service and School
	  – Army Legal Services Agency/Court of Criminal Appeals
	• Chief of Army Reserve
	• Director, Army National Guard
	• Third Army/United States Army Central
	  – 1st Sustainment Command
	• 5th Army/United States Army North
	• Space and Missile Defense Command/Army Strategic Forces Command
	• Army Cyber Command
	  – Army Network Enterprise
	  – 7th Signal Command
	• 7th Army/United States Army Europe
	  – 10th Army Air and Missile Defense Command
	  – 21st Theater Sustainment Command
	  – 7th Army Training Command
	  – 5th Signal Command
	• United States Army Africa
	• United States Army South
	• United States Army Special Operations Command
	  – Army Special Operations Aviation Command
	  – John F. Kennedy Special Warfare Center and School
	  – 1st Special Forces Command

Table D.20—Continued

Secretary of the Army	• Military Postal Service Agency
	• Chief Information Officer/G6
	• Inspector General
	• Legislative Liaison
	• Public Affairs
	• Under Secretary of the Army
	  – Assistant Secretary of the Army for Acquisition, Logistics and Technology
	  – Assistant Secretary of the Army for Financial Management and Comptroller
	    ▪ Army Financial Management Command
	    ▪ Office of Business Transformation

FORSCOM	• 20th Chemical, Biological, Radiological, Nuclear, Explosives Command
	• XVII Airborne Corps and Fort Bragg
	  – 82nd Airborne Division
	  – 3rd Infantry Division
	  – 101st Airborne Division
	  – 10th Mountain Division
	  – 3rd Sustainment X
	• III Corps and Fort Hood
	  – 1st Cavalry Division
	  – 4th Infantry Division
	  – 13th Sustainment X
	  – 1st Armored Division
	  – 1st Infantry Division
	• I Corps and Joint Base Lewis-McChord
	  – 593d Sustainment Command (Expeditionary)
	  – 7th Infantry Division
	• First Army
	  – First Army Division East
	  – First Army Division West
	• National Training Center and Fort Irwin
	• Joint Readiness Training Center and Fort Polk
	• 32d Army and Air Missile Defense Command
	• United States Army Reserve Command

TRADOC	• Combined Arms Center/Fort Leavenworth
	  – Maneuver Center of Excellence
	    ▪ Infantry School
	    ▪ Armor School
	  – Mission Command Center of Excellence
	  – Fires Center of Excellence
	    ▪ Air Defense Artillery School
	    ▪ Army Field Artillery School
	  – Maneuver Support Center of Excellence
	    ▪ Army Engineer School
	    ▪ Army Military Police School
	    ▪ Chemical, Biological, Radiological, Nuclear School
	  – Army Aviation Center of Excellence
	  – Cyber Center of Excellence
	    ▪ Army Signal School
	    ▪ Army Cyber School
	  – Army Intelligence Center of Excellence/Fort Huachuca
	• Army Center for IMT
	  – Army Training Center/Fort Jackson
	• Army Recruiting Command
	• Combined Arms Support Command/Sustainment Center of Excellence/Fort Lee
	  – Transportation School
	  – Ordnance School
	  – Soldier Support Institute
	  – Quartermaster School
	• Army Cadet Command
	• United States Army Capabilities Integration Center
	  – Brigade Modernization Command

Table D.20—Continued

AMC	• Army Contracting Command
	  – Army Expeditionary Contracting Command
	  – Army Mission and Installation Contracting Command
	• Army Aviation and Missile Command, Life Cycle Management Command
	• Army Communications-Electronics Command
	• Tank-Automotive and Armaments Command Life Cycle Management Command
	• Army Research, Development and Engineering Command
	• Army Security Assistance Command
	• Army Sustainment Command
	  – Joint Munitions Command
	• Military Surface Deployment and Distribution Command

USARPAC	• 94th Army Air Missile Defense Command • 8th Theater Sustainment Command • 311th Theater Signal Command • 25th Infantry Division • Alaska/Alaskan Command • Japan/I Corps Forward • 8th Army/Combined Forces Command • 19th Sustainment Command • 2d Infantry Division

The 228 positions analyzed in this group include six O-10s, 32 O-9s, 77 O-8s, and 113 O-7s, as shown in Table D.21. The number of G/FOs, and distribution by rank, within each major command and headquarters element varied greatly due to substantial differences in size of command, responsibilities, number of subordinate commands, and other factors. Accordingly, the number of G/FOs in each major command/organization included in Table D.21 is displayed for descriptive purposes, but was not necessarily used in a comparative analysis.

Table D.21
Army Headquarters Element and Major Command G/FO Positions by Grade and Organization

	O-7	O-8	O-9	O-10	Total
Chief of Staff of the Army	34	26	15[a]	2	77
Secretary of the Army	7	7	5	0	19
FORSCOM	32	16	5	1	54
TRADOC	23	11	4	1	39
AMC	8	8	2	1	19
USARPAC	9	9	1	1	20
Total	113	77	32	6	228

[a] The Chief of Army Reserve/Commanding General/United States Army Reserve Command position is counted here rather than under FORSCOM.

Additional Principles

The Army major command/headquarters element group was too large and diverse to apply many meaningful specific additional principles across all positions. However, several additional principles were applied depending on the major command, subordinate command, type of position, or subgroup (discussed later).

For specific command or deputy command positions in combat arms units, we considered military necessity more than in other analyses, as those positions are often responsible for leading soldiers in combat-centric military operations.

Among certain comparable commands, such as TRADOC's Centers of Excellence, the Chief of Staff of the Army's regionally focused service component commands and numbered armies, in headquarters staff at each of the major commands, the Chief of Staff of the Army's and the Secretary of the Army's front offices, the Army Staff, and combat arms and direct support to combat arms units, we weighed parity across like entities while keeping in mind differences in geography, size, and relative responsibility.

While this was an analysis of Army-only positions and one joint position with Army command duties, some positions or subgroups, such as the Army Staff and USARPAC, merited comparison to similar positions in other services.

Relevant Subgroups

Aside from the major commands and headquarters elements themselves, relevant subgroups among the reviewed Army positions include combat and direct combat-support positions; service component commands; Centers of Excellence and training schools; and the Army staff. Each of these constitute a separate subgroup because their unique characteristics distinguished them from other Army positions and required additional organizational considerations and internal comparisons that provided key insight into our analysis and findings.

For analyses that benefited from cross-unit or even cross-service comparisons, we directly compared similar positions and took into consideration necessary differences between those units or positions. For example, while we concluded that infantry divisions across the Army could all be treated equally in determining G/FO requirements, we found that training organizations could be structured differently than in other services.

Exceptions

In other group analyses, deputy chief of staff positions were scrutinized as potentially redundant or unnecessary. However, in the Army Staff structure, that same title is used for positions of great responsibility and oversight, such as the Deputy Chief of Staff, G3/5/7.

Findings

Of the 228 positions reviewed, our findings, shown in Table D.22, are as follows:

- 158 positions meet the criteria for a G/FO requirement at the current grade (69 percent).
- 37 positions meet the criteria for a G/FO at a lower grade (downgrade) (16 percent).
- 28 positions do not meet the criteria for a G/FO requirement (12 percent).
- Five positions resulted in mixed findings (2 percent).[36]

The high number of positions in FORSCOM that met the criteria for a G/FO at the current grade relative to the other major commands points to the concentration of combat and direct combat support units overseen by FORSCOM. Similarly, many positions reporting to the Chief of Staff of the Army met the criteria for a G/FO at the current grade for similar reasons: G/FO requirements to execute fundamental organize, train and equip, or planning functions. The majority of Army staff positions meet the criteria for a G/FO requirement at the current grade, except those deputy or deputy-like positions that appeared redundant in nature. Positions that did not meet the criteria for a G/FO requirement were largely O-7 positions that we determined could be fulfilled by O-6s. The highest proportion of these positions was in Secretary of the Army and AMC organizations.

Our overall findings by grade are shown in Tables D.23. At the O-10 grade, three positions meet criteria for a G/FO requirement at the current grade and another three positions meet criteria for a G/FO at a lower grade (AMC, USARPAC, and TRADOC). In the case of USARPAC, in addition to USARPAC oversight responsibilities, we considered parity with other Army service component commands as well

Table D.22
Findings by Army Major Command/Headquarters Element

	CSA	SecArmy	FORSCOM	TRADOC	AMC	USARPAC	Total
Meets criteria for G/FO at current grade	59	9	49	25	1	15	158
Meets criteria for G/FO at a lower grade (downgrade)	6	5	0	13	9	4	37
Does not meet criteria for a G/FO	9	5	5	1	7	1	28
Inconclusive	3				2		5
Total	77	19	54	39	19	20	228

---

[36] These numbers may not add to 100 percent due to rounding.

as parity across other services USPACOM-supporting component commands. For AMC, we also looked at the grade structure and distribution of other services' corollary commands and identified potential grade inflation throughout the entire chain of command. Finally, for TRADOC, we compared its role and responsibilities to similar organizations in the other services in addition to our standard principles and identified a few cases of high-level leadership ranks that could be downgraded without harming the command. Further, while our findings indicate that several of TRADOC's training school commandants meet the criteria for a G/FO requirement at the current grade of O-7, other similar positions could be downgraded from O-8 to O-7. We did not identify clear requirements for some training schools to be led by an O-8 while others are led by O-7s.

The rest of our findings are summarized by major command or headquarters element in Tables D.24 to D.29.

Table D.23
Findings by Grade: Total

	O-7	O-8	O-9	O-10	Total
Meets criteria for G/FO at current grade	84	50	21	3	158
Meets criteria for G/FO at a lower grade (downgrade)	0	23	11	3	37
Does not meet criteria for a G/FO	28	0	0	0	28
Inconclusive	1	4	0	0	5
Total	113	77	32	6	228

Table D.24
Chief of Staff of the Army Findings by Grade

	O-7	O-8	O-9	O-10	Total
Meets criteria for G/FO at current grade	24	20	13	2	59
Meets criteria for G/FO at a lower grade (downgrade)	0	4	2	0	6
Does not meet criteria for a G/FO	9	0	0	0	9
Inconclusive	1	2	0	0	3
Total	34	26	15	2	77

Table D.25
Secretary of the Army Findings by Grade

	O-7	O-8	O-9	O-10	Total
Meets criteria for G/FO at current grade	2	5	2	0	9
Meets criteria for G/FO at a lower grade (downgrade)	0	2	3	0	5
Does not meet criteria for a G/FO	5	0	0	0	4
Inconclusive	0	0	0	0	0
Total	7	7	5	0	19

Table D.26
FORSCOM Findings by Grade

	O-7	O-8	O-9	O-10	Total
Meets criteria for G/FO at current grade	27	16	5	1	49
Meets criteria for G/FO at a lower grade (downgrade)	0	0	0	0	0
Does not meet criteria for a G/FO	5	0	0	0	5
Inconclusive	0	0	0	0	0
Total	32	16	5	1	54

Table D.27
TRADOC Findings by Grade

	O-7	O-8	O-9	O-10	Total
Meets criteria for G/FO at current grade	22	3	0	0	25
Meets criteria for G/FO at a lower grade (downgrade)	0	8	4	1	13
Does not meet criteria for a G/FO	1	0	0	0	1
Total	23	11	4	1	39

Table D.28
AMC Findings by Grade

	O-7	O-8	O-9	O-10	Total
Meets criteria for G/FO at current grade	1	0	0	0	1
Meets criteria for G/FO at a lower grade (downgrade)	0	6	2	1	9
Does not meet criteria for a G/FO	7	0	0	0	7
Inconclusive	0	2	0	0	2
Total	8	8	2	1	19

Table D.29
USARPAC Findings by Grade

	O-7	O-8	O-9	O-10	Total
Meets criteria for G/FO at current grade	8	6	1	0	15
Meets criteria for G/FO at a lower grade (downgrade)	0	3	0	1	4
Does not meet criteria for a G/FO	1	0	0	0	1
Mixed	0	0	0	0	0
Total	9	9	1	1	20

Selected U.S. Navy Major Command and Subordinate Command Positions

Overview

This section describes our analysis of the Navy G/FO positions that report directly to one of the headquarters or major commands or to one of those entities' subordinate commands. We define the Navy's major commands as each of the Navy's organizations overseen by a four-star: the Secretariat, Naval Operations (OPNAV), Pacific Fleet (PACFLT), Fleet Forces (FLTFOR), Sixth Fleet/Europe (NAVEUR), and Naval Reactors, as well as the Navy's three-star Systems Commands (SYSCOMs). Because there is just one G/FO position in the Naval Reactors major command, we included that position in the OPNAV summary statistics. Further, we combined several operational commands under an "Other" major command category. Excluded from our analysis were the Navy Installations Command, Facilities Engineering, and Reserve Forces Commands as well as several smaller groups. The full list appears in Table D.30.

Table D.30
Navy Major Commands and Direct Subordinate Units Reviewed

Major Command	Direct Subordinate Unit

Secretariat	• Assistant Secretary of the Navy (Research, Development and Acquisition)
	  – Program Executive Officer, Submarines
	  – Director, Columbia Class Program
	  – Program Executive Officer, Aircraft Carriers
	  – Program Executive Officer for Unmanned Aviation and Strike Weapons
	  – Program Executive Officer, PEO Command, Control, Computers, Communications and Intelligence and PEO Space Systems, Space and Naval Warfare Systems Command
	• Navy International Programs Office
	• Assistant Secretary of the Navy (Financial Management and Comptroller) Fiscal Management Division
	• Judge Advocate General of the Navy
	• Chief of Information (CHINFO), Navy Staff
	• Chief of Legislative Affairs, Navy Staff
	• Chief of Naval Research
	• Naval Inspector General

Naval Operations (OPNAV)	• Chief of Naval Operations, Chief of Naval Operations
	• Director, Navy Staff
	• N1 (Manpower, Personnel, Training, and Education)
	  – Military Personnel Plans and Policy (N13)
	  – 21st Century Sailor Office (N17)
	  – Naval Personnel Command
	  – Naval Education and Training Command
	    ▪ Naval Service Training Command
	• N2/N6 Information Warfare
	• N3/N5 Operations, Plans, and Strategy, N3/N5
	• N4, Fleet Readiness and Logistics
	• N8, Integration of Capabilities and Resources
	• N9, Warfare Systems

Other Commands	• Naval Special Warfare Command • U.S. Naval Forces Central Command • U.S. Naval Forces, Southern Command • U.S. Fleet Cyber Command/U.S. Tenth Fleet

Systems Commands	• Naval Air Systems Command
	  – Fleet Readiness Centers
	  – Naval Air Warfare Center Aircraft Division
	  – Naval Air Warfare Center, Weapons Division
	  – Naval Undersea Warfare Center
	• Naval Sea Systems Command
	  – Naval Surface Warfare Center
	  – Regional Maintenance Center/Surface Warfare
	• Naval Supply Systems Command
	  – NAVSUP Global Logistics Support Command
	  – Naval Supply Systems Command, Weapons Systems Support
	• Space and Naval Warfare Systems Command

Fleet Forces	• Commander, U.S. Fleet Forces Command
	  – Naval Air Force, U.S. Atlantic Fleet
	    ▪ Patrol and Reconnaissance Group/Pacific
	  – Navy Recruiting Command
	  – Deputy Commander, U.S. Fleet Forces Command
	    ▪ Fleet Ordnance and Supply
	    ▪ Fleet Maintenance

Table D.30—Continued

Major Command	Direct Subordinate Unit
	■ Maritime Operations (N3/N5/N2/N7), U.S. Fleet Forces Command
	Director, Joint and Fleet Operations (N3)
	Carrier Strike Group TWO
	Carrier Strike Group FOUR
	Carrier Strike Group EIGHT
	Carrier Strike Group TEN
	Carrier Strike Group TWELVE
	Expeditionary Strike Group TWO
	■ Fleet and Joint Training, N7
	– Board of Inspection and Survey
	– Military Sealift Command
	– Naval Information Forces
	– Navy Warfare Development Command
	– Naval Submarine Forces
	■ Submarine Group EIGHT, Director, CNE-CNA (N3)
	■ Submarine Group TEN
	■ Undersea Warfighting Development Center
	– Naval Surface Force, U.S. Atlantic Fleet
	– Naval Surface and Mine Warfighting Development Center
Pacific Fleet	• Commander, U.S. Pacific Fleet
	– Maritime Headquarters, U.S. Pacific Fleet
	■ Fleet Maintenance, U.S. Pacific Fleet
	■ Logistics, Fleet Supply and Ordnance (N4), U.S. Pacific Fleet
	■ Facilities and Environmental/Fleet Civil Engineer
	– Naval Air Forces, U.S. Pacific Fleet
	■ Patrol and Reconnaissance Group/Pacific
	■ Naval Aviation Warfighting Development Center
	– U.S. THIRD Fleet
	■ Submarine Force, U.S. Pacific Fleet
	Submarine Group NINE
	■ Carrier Strike Group ONE
	■ Carrier Strike Group THREE
	■ Carrier Strike Group NINE
	■ Carrier Strike Group ELEVEN
	■ Carrier Strike Group FIFTEEN
	■ Expeditionary Strike Group THREE
	■ Naval Support Group, MIDPAC
	– U.S. SEVENTH Fleet
	■ Carrier Strike Group FIVE
	■ Submarine Group SEVEN
	■ Expeditionary Strike Group SEVEN
	■ U.S. Naval Forces, Korea
	■ Logistics Group, Western Pacific
	■ Naval Support Group, MIDPAC
	– Navy Expeditionary Combat Command
	– Naval Region Japan
	– Navy Region Hawaii
	– Navy Region Korea
	– Navy Region Singapore
	– Joint Region Marianas
	– Naval Surface Force, U. S. Pacific Fleet
	• Naval Facilities Engineering Command Pacific
Sixth Fleet/Europe	• Commander, U.S. Naval Forces Europe/U.S. Naval Forces Africa/U.S. SIXTH Fleet
	– U.S. SIXTH Fleet/Task Force SIX/Striking and Support Forces NATO
	■ Strategy, Resources, and Plans (N5)
	■ Submarine Group EIGHT, Director, CNE-CNA (N3)
	– Commander, Navy Region Europe, Africa, Southwest Asia
Naval Reactors, Naval Nuclear Propulsion Program	• Director, Naval Reactors, Naval Nuclear Propulsion Program

While our analysis did not include every flag officer in the Navy, 142 of 171 positions, or 83 percent, of Navy flag officers were reviewed as part of this group, with many of the remaining positions analyzed separately as part of other groups. The Navy positions not covered in any of the structure and organizational reviews, 15 in total, account for 8.8 percent of the Navy's requirements.

The 124 positions analyzed in this group included six O-10s, 17 O-9s, 29 O-8s, and 72 O-7s. The number of G/FOs, and distribution by grade, within each major command and headquarters element varied considerably, as shown in Table D.31. However, given the substantial differences in size, responsibilities, and number of subordinate commands, the number of G/FOs in each command should not necessarily be used in a direct comparative analysis.

Additional Principles

One important consideration within the Navy is the division between unrestricted line officers who can assume any type of command, and restricted line officers—typically professional officers such as doctors, dentists, or lawyers—who are limited in the positions they can assume. The positions we analyzed here were all filled by unrestricted line officers, and because they were reviewed separately from the professional positions, the restricted/unrestricted line officer division was not relevant to this analysis.

Relevant Subgroups

The major commands included in this group serve very different functions within the service. Of the seven command groupings analyzed, four are headquarters commands and three are operational force providers. The Secretariat denotes those positions that directly report to the Secretary of the Navy or one of the Secretary's direct subordinates (such as assistant secretaries). OPNAV represents the headquarters staff for the Chief

Table D.31
Navy Headquarters Element and Major Commands G/FO Positions by Grade and Organization

	O-7	O-8	O-9	O-10	Total
Secretariat	4	7	3	0	14
OPNAV	15	11	6	3	35
Other	3	2	2	0	7
SYSCOMs	17	6	2	0	25
FLTFOR	15	7	2	1	25
PACFLT	22	4	4	1	31
NAVEUR	2	1	1	1	5
Total	78	38	20	6	142

of Naval Operations (CNO) and includes the support staff that report directly to the CNO and deputy CNO. The Director, Naval Reactors, Naval Nuclear Propulsion Program is responsible for the design, operation, and maintenance of all naval reactors. Though the position has no G/FO subordinates, the grade of O-10 gives the position wide authority to ensure the safety and performance of the reactor program.

SYSCOMs are a group of several commands responsible for management of the commands involved in design, construction, and maintenance of the ships, aircraft, and weapons systems used by operational units. FLTFOR is one of the Navy's primary force providers and also the Navy service component command to USNORTHCOM and USSTRATCOM. Originally formed as the Atlantic Fleet, the command evolved and was renamed U.S. Fleet Forces in 2006. Its counterpart in the Pacific is PACFLT, which is the Navy's other primary force provider and the Navy service component command to U.S. Pacific Command (USPACOM). NAVEUR is the component commander to USEUCOM and, dual-hatted as U.S. Naval Forces Africa (NAVAF), also the service component command to USAFRICOM.

Exceptions

In other sections of our structural analyses, deputy chief and deputy commander positions were scrutinized as potentially redundant or unnecessary. However, in the Navy command structure, this title is used for positions of great responsibility and oversight, such as the Deputy Commander, U.S. Fleet Forces Command. Accordingly, we judged these positions met the criteria for a G/FO requirement in light of their significant responsibilities and despite the use of deputy in the title.

Findings

Our findings for the 142 positions in the Navy major and subordinate commands group are as follows:

- 104 positions meet the criteria for a G/FO requirement at the current grade (73.2 percent).
- 14 positions meet the criteria for a G/FO at a lower grade (downgrade) (9.6 percent).
- 21 positions do not meet the criteria for a G/FO requirement (14.8 percent).
- Three positions resulted in an inconclusive finding (2.4 percent).

While the majority of our findings affected only O-8 and O-7 grades, one finding affects an O-10 position. We noted that there were structural parallels and redundancies between the organization and responsibilities of the Pacific Fleet and Fleet Forces commands. Accordingly, Pacific Fleet could be restructured as a service component to USPACOM with the responsibility for fleet organization and maintenance transferring to Fleet Forces, making it the single primary Navy force provider. In doing so, the O-10 Commander, Pacific Fleet could be downgraded to an O-9 and the positions that duplicate tasks performed by Fleet Forces eliminated. In addition, the OPNAV N4 is authorized as an O-8, but could be upgraded to an O-9 to maintain parity with the other services.

More generally, deputy directors of several divisions do not meet the criteria for a G/FO requirement and could be converted to SES positions rather than their authorized O-7 positions. Many of these positions are currently occupied by nonmilitary SES occupants, and by formalizing this practice these positions would provide institutional memory and stability to complement the O-8 Director positions to whom they report.

The distribution of our findings across major commands and headquarters elements is depicted in Table D.32, and by grade across all major commands and headquarters elements in Table D.33. By grade, the rest of our findings are summarized by major command or headquarters element in Tables D.34 to D.40.

Table D.32
Findings by Navy Major Command/Headquarters Element: Total

	Secretariat	OPNAV	Other	SYSCOMs	FLTFOR	PACFLT	NAVEUR	Total
Meets criteria for G/FO at current grade	7	20	7	15	24	26	5	104
Meets criteria for G/FO at a lower grade (downgrade)	6	6	0	1	0	1	0	14
Does not meet criteria for a G/FO	1	8	0	7	1	4	0	21
Inconclusive	0	1	0	2	0	0	0	3
Total	14	35	7	25	25	31	5	142

Table D.33
Navy Major Command/Headquarters Findings by Grade: Total

	O-7	O-8	O-9	O-10	Total
Meets criteria for G/FO at current grade	60	21	18	5	104
Meets criteria for G/FO at a lower grade (downgrade)	0	11	2	1	14
Does not meet criteria for a G/FO	18	3	0	0	21
Inconclusive	0	3	0	0	3
Total	78	38	20	6	142

Table D.34
Secretariat Findings by Grade

	O-7	O-8	O-9	O-10	Total
Meets criteria for G/FO at current grade	3	2	2	0	7
Meets criteria for G/FO at a lower grade (downgrade)	0	5	1	0	6
Does not meet criteria for a G/FO	1	0	0	0	1
Inconclusive	0	0	0	0	0
Total	4	7	3	0	14

Table D.35
OPNAV Findings by Grade

	O-7	O-8	O-9	O-10	Total
Meets criteria for G/FO at current grade	8	4	5	3	20
Meets criteria for G/FO at a lower grade (downgrade)	0	5	1	0	6
Does not meet criteria for a G/FO	7	1	0	0	8
Inconclusive	0	1	0	0	1
Total	15	11	6	3	35

Table D.36
Other Commands Findings by Grade

	O-7	O-8	O-9	O-10	Total
Meets criteria for G/FO at current grade	3	2	2	0	7
Meets criteria for G/FO at a lower grade (downgrade)	0	0	0	0	0
Does not meet criteria for a G/FO	0	0	0	0	0
Total	3	2	2	0	7

Table D.37
SYSCOMs Findings by Grade

	O-7	O-8	O-9	O-10	Total
Meets criteria for G/FO at current grade	11	2	2	0	15
Meets criteria for G/FO at a lower grade (downgrade)	0	1	0	0	1
Does not meet criteria for a G/FO	6	1	0	0	7
Inconclusive	0	2	0	0	2
Total	17	6	2	0	25

Table D.38
FLTFOR Findings by Grade

	O-7	O-8	O-9	O-10	Total
Meets criteria for G/FO at current grade	14	7	2	1	24
Meets criteria for G/FO at a lower grade (downgrade)	0	0	0	0	0
Does not meet criteria for a G/FO	1	0	0	0	1
Total	15	7	2	1	25

Table D.39
PACFLT Findings by Grade

	O-7	O-8	O-9	O-10	Total
Meets criteria for G/FO at current grade	19	3	4	0	26
Meets criteria for G/FO at a lower grade (downgrade)	0	0	0	1	1
Does not meet criteria for a G/FO	3	1	0	0	4
Total	22	4	4	1	31

Table D.40
NAVEUR Findings by Grade

	O-7	O-8	O-9	O-10	Total
Meets criteria for G/FO at current grade	2	1	1	1	5
Meets criteria for G/FO at a lower grade (downgrade)	0	0	0	0	0
Does not meet criteria for a G/FO	0	1	0	0	0
Total	2	1	1	1	5

U.S. Marine Corps Major Headquarters and Commands and Subordinate Command Positions

Overview

In the Marine Corps group, we reviewed all 88 G/FO positions within the United States Marine Corps (USMC). Our analysis of G/FO positions within USMC includes Marine G/FOs that report through the Navy command chain or are dual-hatted with a G/FO position in the Navy, as well as a few other Marine Corps positions that are solely within the Navy command chain. The G/FO positions examined fall into the parts of the organization listed in Table D.41 The breakdown of authorized positions by grade is shown in Table D.42.

In a conventional G/FO pyramid, the number of G/FOs decreases as the authorized grade increases; however, the Marine Corps does not model such a grade pyramid. While it has more authorized O-8 G/FO positions than O-7, the Marine Corps makes use of a lot of multi-hatting for its G/FO population, with one G/FO wearing four hats. Further, the Marine Corps generally operates a younger organization than the other services, and it is not uncommon for the senior positions to be filled by less senior G/FOs than in other services.[37] Because the Marine Corps is a part of the Department of Navy and is a smaller service compared to the others, its general staff does not have some of the same directorates as the other services.

Additional Principles

Due to the Marine Corps' unique position as a service under the Department of the Navy, its headquarters organizational structure departed from that of the other services. Accordingly, we emphasized service parity less in certain relevant cases at the headquarters level than throughout the rest of the analysis.

---

[37] Office of the Deputy Assistant Secretary of Defense for Military Community and Family Policy (ODASD [MC&FP]), "2015 Demographics: Profile of the Military Community," pp. 15, 16, 37.

Table D.41
Marine Corps Organizations with G/FO Positions Reviewed

Organization	Position
Headquarters, United States Marine Corps	• Commandant of the Marine Corps • Assistant Commandant of the Marine Corps • Staff Judge Advocate to the Commandant of the Marine Corps • Inspector General of the Marine Corps (reports through Navy) • Director, Marine Corps Staff Intelligence (DIRINT)[a] • Command, Control, Communications, and Computers (C4)[b] • Legislative Assistant to CMC (OLA) • Office of U.S. Marine Corps Communication (OMCC) • Manpower and Reserve Affairs • Installations and Logistics (I&L) • Plans, Policies, and Operations (PP&O) • Programs and Resources (P&R) • Aviation • Combat Development and Integration • Marine Corps Combat Development Command (MCCDC) • Marine Corps Systems Command (MCSC) • Marine Corps Recruiting Command (MCRC) • Headquarters, United States Marine Corps—Health Services and Medical Officer of the Marine Corps
Service Component Commands	• U.S. Marine Corps Forces Command (MARFORCOM) • U.S. Marine Corps Forces Pacific (MARFORPAC) • U.S. Marine Corps Forces Africa Command (MARFOR AFRICOM) • U.S. Marine Corps Forces European Command (MARFOR EUCOM) • U.S. Marine Corps Forces Central Command (MARFOR CENTCOM) • U.S. Marine Corps Forces Northern Command (MARFOR NORTHCOM) • U.S. Marine Corps Forces Southern Command (MARFOR SOUTHCOM) • U.S. Marine Corps Forces Strategic Command (MARFOR STRATCOM) • U.S. Marine Corps Forces Special Operations Command (MARFORSOC) • U.S. Marine Corps Forces Cyberspace Command (MARFOR CYBERCOM) • U.S. Marine Corps Forces, Korea (MARFORK) • U.S. Marine Corps Forces Reserve (MARFORRES)
Operating Forces	• I Marine Expeditionary Force (MEF) (Pendleton) • 1st Marine Division • 3d Marine Aircraft Wing • 1st Marine Logistics Group • 1st Marine Expeditionary Brigade • II MEF (Lejeune) • 2d Marine Division • 2d Marine Aircraft Wing • 2d Marine Logistics Group • 2d Marine Expeditionary Brigade • III MEF (Hawaii and Okinawa) • 3d Marine Division • 1st Marine Aircraft Wing • 3d Marine Logistics Group • 3d Marine Expeditionary Brigade • 5th Marine Expeditionary Brigade/Commander, Naval Amphibious Forces, CTF 51
Additional Navy Staff	• Deputy Department of the Navy Chief Information Officer (DDCIO[MC]) • Expeditionary Warfare Division (N95) • PEO, NAVAIR, Department of the Navy

[a] The FY 2017 NDAA created an O-9 position to lead the newly-formed Deputy Commandant for Information, and it will incorporate the current Director of Intelligence and the Director of Command, Control, Communications, and Computers (C4). This new position is not included in our data.
[b] The FY 2017 NDAA created an O-9 position to lead the newly-formed Deputy Commandant for Information, and it will incorporate the current Director of Intelligence and the Director of Command, Control, Communications, and Computers (C4). This new position is not included in our data.

Table D.42
Marine Corps G/FO Positions by Grade

	O-7	O-8	O-9	O-10	Total
Headquarters, United States Marine Corps	15	25	7[a]	2	50
Service Component Commands	2	7	4	0	13
Operating Forces	17	7	2	0	26
Additional Navy Staff	0	3	0	0	3
Total	34	39	13	2	88

[a] The Deputy Commandant, Combat Development and Integration multi-hatted as Commanding General, Marine Corps Combat Development Command and Commanding General, Marine Corps Strategic Command is counted here.

Relevant Subgroups

Relevant subgroups for the Marine Corps include Headquarters, United States Marine Corps, service component commands, and operating forces. Each of these subgroups' unique characteristics differentiates it from other Marine Corps positions and required additional organizational considerations and internal comparisons. When there were comparable organizations in other military services, we directly compared similar positions and considered necessary differences between those units or positions. In our analysis, we distinguish between service component commands that maintain operational force units and those that do not.

Exceptions

Since the Marine Corps frequently fills its senior positions with less senior G/FOs than other services, we see more "breaks" in the G/FO hierarchy. In our overall organizational guidelines, we generally flagged gaps in the hierarchy, such as an O-8 with no O-7 reports. However, in the case of the Marine Corps, these gaps did not necessarily indicate that the O-8 G/FO position did not meet the criteria at the current grade, but rather that the Marine Corps puts great trust and authority in their O-6 officers to sometimes fill more senior positions compared to the other services.[38] While we did not dismiss all these gaps in the G/FO hierarchy, we more carefully scrutinized these subordinate positions. In a few cases, we even recommended an upgrade of these O-6 positions to be filled by an O-7 G/FO.

[38] Department of Defense, Office of the Deputy Assistant Secretary of Defense for Military Community and Family Policy (ODASD [MC&FP]), "2015 Demographics: Profile of the Military Community," pp. 15, 16, 37.

Findings

Of 88 positions, our findings are as follows (summarized in Table D.43):

- 54 positions meet the criteria for a G/FO requirement at the current grade.
- 16 positions meet the criteria for a G/FO requirement at a lower grade.
- Ten positions do not meet the criteria for a G/FO requirement.
- Eight positions for which we could not make a definitive assessment.

The authorized grade of the G/FO positions in the Headquarters, United States Marine Corps (HQMC) should closely mirror the grade of their respective positions in the other military services. Consequently, our findings suggest that O-9s fill the deputy commandant positions, and the assistant deputy commandant positions should be filled by O-7s and O-8s, depending on the directorate, responsibilities, or multi-hats associated with the role. In addition, some HQMC positions did not meet the criteria for a G/FO requirement and could be converted to civilian positions, since the positions could be filled with a civilian who has appropriate knowledge and experience. Another option is to combine similar positions and organizations. If a position has been sitting vacant for a long period of time, it should either be eliminated or combined with another position.

Table D.44 summarizes our findings for Marine Corps Headquarters and Table D.45 summarizes our findings for Marine Corps service component commands. Within service component commands, our findings indicate downgrading G/FO positions if the highest level they supervise is primarily two or more grades below them.

Table D.46 contains our findings for the operational units. Operationally, the Marine expeditionary force (MEF) is the principal Marine Corps warfighting orga-

Table D.43
USMC Major Headquarters and Command G/FO Findings

	O-7	O-8	O-9	O-10	Total
Meets the criteria for a G/FO at current grade	25	16[a]	11	2	54
Meets the criteria for a G/FO at a lower grade (downgrade)	0	15	1	0	16
Does not meet the criteria for a G/FO requirement	9	0	1		10
Inconclusive	0	8	0	0	8
Total	34	39	13	2	88

[a] This includes one position, Commanding General–II MEF, which met the requirement for G/FO at a higher grade (O-9) than the position is currently authorized.

Table D.44
Findings Within Headquarters, United States Marine Corps

	O-7	O-8	O-9	O-10	Total
Meets criteria for a G/FO at current grade	12	5	6	2	25
Meets criteria for a G/FO at a lower grade (downgrade)	0	11		0	11
Does not meet criteria for a G/FO	3	0	1	0	4
Inconclusive	0	6	0	0	6
Total	15	22	7	2	46

Table D.45
Findings for Marine Corps Service Component Commands

	O-7	O-8	O-9	O-10	Total
Meets criteria for a G/FO at current grade	2	5	3	0	10
Meets criteria for a G/FO at a lower grade (downgrade)	0	2	1	0	3
Total	2	7	4	0	13

Table D.46
Findings for Marine Corps Operating Units

	O-7	O-8	O-9	O-10	Total
Meets criteria for a G/FO at current grade	11	6[a]	2	0	19
Meets criteria for a G/FO at a lower grade (downgrade)	0	1	0	0	1
Does not meet criteria for a G/FO	6	0	0	0	6
Total	17	7	2	0	26

[a] This includes one position, Commanding General–II MEF, which met the requirement for G/FO at a higher grade (O-9) than the position is currently authorized.

nization, and each standing MEF consists of a permanent command element (CE), a Marine division (MARDIV), a Marine aircraft wing (MAW), and a Marine logistics group (MLG). The MEF deputy commanding general also serves as the commanding general of the Marine expeditionary brigade (MEB), also known as the MEF Forward; in a combat deployment, the MEB commanding general takes the MEB forward with the expectation that the MEF normally follows. In a scenario where the MEF is not close behind the MEB, there would likely only be the MEB commanding general and no other G/FOs. Consequently, the MEF deputy commanding generals meet the criteria for a G/FO requirement.

When comparing the different parts of these operating forces, not all commanding generals are currently authorized at equal rank, and therefore our findings indicate an upgrade to two commanding general G/FO positions to match the others.

Conversely, all six assistant division commanders and assistant wing commanders are currently authorized as O-7s, yet in the judgment of the Marine Corps, they are filled by O-6s (perhaps selected for O-7). For these positions, our finding is that the position does not meet the criteria for a G/FO requirement and could continue to be filled at the grade of O-6. During peacetime, the Marine Corps has used these G/FO positions for joint nominations and other opportunities. However, there may be a need for G/FO assistant division and wing commanders in wartime. If a MEB is initially ground or aviation heavy, the assistant division or wing commander may deploy to lead the ground or aviation combat element, especially when the rest of the division or wing is to follow on quickly. When needed in wartime, these G/FO positions can be created through existing authorities to exceed G/FO caps.

For the three USMC G/FOs assigned to Navy headquarters positions, one meets the criteria for G/FO at a lower grade (downgrade), and our assessment for two was inconclusive. As noted, the FY2017 NDAA created an O-9 position to lead the newly-formed Deputy Commandant for Information, which will incorporate the current Director of Intelligence and the Director of Command, Control, Communications, and Computers (C4). This new position was not submitted in our data.

U.S. Air Force Major Headquarters and Commands Positions

Overview

We focused on the major headquarters and commands of the air forces, specifically looking at the Air Force Secretariat, the Air Force Air Staff, the Air Force Major Commands and subordinate commands of the Major Commands. We included all subordinates of the Major Commands that had G/FO positions, down to those commanded by O-6s. The specific list of organizations is shown in Table D.47.

In this group, we analyzed 206 authorized G/FO positions, ranging from O-7 to O-10. Of these positions, 17 were in the Air Force Secretariat, 40 in the Air Staff and 149 in the major commands. The breakdown of authorized positions by grade is shown in Table D.48.

Table D.47
Air Force Organizations with G/FO Positions Reviewed

Secretariat and Air Staff	• Air Force Secretariat
	• Air Force Air Staff
	  – All "A" code staff organizations
	  – Chief of Chaplains
	  – Judge Advocate General
	  – Chief of Air Force Reserve
	  – Safety
	  – Surgeon General

Major Commands	• Air Combat Command (ACC)
	  – Air Warfare Center
	  – First Air Force
	  – 9th Air Force
	  – 12th Air Force
	  – 25th Air Force
	  – Subordinate commands of the above commands down to those commanded by O-6s
	• Air Education and Training Command (AETC)
	  – 2nd Air Force
	  – 19th Air Force
	  – Air University
	  – Air Force Institute of Technology
	  – Recruiting Services
	  – 502nd Air Base Wing
	  – 59th Medical Wing
	  – Subordinate commands of the above commands down to those commanded by O-6s
	• Air Force Space Command (AFSPC)
	  – 14th Air Force
	  – 24th Air Force
	  – Space and Missile Systems Center (SMC)
	  – Subordinate commands of the above commands down to those commanded by O-6s
	• Air Force Global Strike Command (AFGSC)
	  – 8th Air Force
	  – 20th Air Force
	  – Subordinate commands of the above commands down to those commanded by O-6s
	• Air Force Materiel Command (AFMC)
	  – Air Force Installation and Mission Support Center
	  – Air Force Life Cycle Management Center
	  – Air Force Nuclear Weapons Center
	  – Air Force Research Laboratory
	  – Air Force Sustainment Center
	  – Air Force Test Center
	  – 96th Test Wing
	  – 412th Test Wing
	  – Subordinate commands of the above commands down to those commanded by O-6s
	• Air Force Reserve Command (AFRC)[a]
	• Air Force Special Operations Command (AFSOC)
	  – Subordinate commands of AFSOC down to those commanded by O-6s
	• Air Mobility Command
	  – 18th Air Force
	  – Air Force Expeditionary Center
	  – Subordinate commands of the above commands down to those commanded by O-6s

Table D.47—Continued

- Pacific Air Forces (PACAF)
  - 5th Air Force
  - 7th Air Force
  - 11th Air Force
  - Subordinate commands of the above commands down to those commanded by O-6s
- U.S. Air Forces Europe and Africa (USAFE-AFAFRICA)
  - 3rd Air Force
  - Subordinate commands of the above commands down to those commanded by O-6s
- U.S. Air Forces Central Command (CENTAF)
  - 9th Air Expeditionary Task Force
  - Subordinate commands of the above commands down to those commanded by O-6s

^a Three Air Force Reserve G/FO positions are counted as active-duty, but G/FO positions in subordinate Air Force Reserve organizations have no reserve G/FO positions counted as active duty.

Table D.48
USAF Major Headquarters and Command G/FO Positions by Grade

Service	O-7	O-8	O-9	O-10	Total
Secretariat	5	9	3	0	17
Air Staff	14	14	10	2	40
Major Commands	79	47	16	7	149
Total	98	70	29	9	206

Additional Principles

Within the Air Force, there were many occurrences of G/FO positions in organizations that were very similar in function, organization, scale, and scope (e.g., the numerous Air Force wings). Given the close similarities in positions and organizations, all within a single service, we put particular emphasis on parity for such organizations, looking for these similar G/FO positions to have similar grades in their leadership positions.

Relevant Subgroups

The G/FO positions in the Secretariat and the Air Staff are clearly different from each other and from the major commands. We, therefore, treated these as separate subgroups. The major commands are each unique in their own way, so our analysis focused on each command individually. However, at the echelons below we often found similar subordinate organizations (numbered air forces, wings, etc.), which lent themselves to comparisons with equivalent subordinates under other major commands. For this reason, all the G/FO positions within the major commands and subordinate organizations are reported in as a single subgroup.

Exceptions

Our findings do not make any exception for, or otherwise account for, outside pressures on the Department of Defense and the Department of the Air Force to change how the Air Force organizes space-related functions and operations. Thus, we do not consider the possible formation of a Space Service. We have dealt with these positions as they are today. (Chapter Nine discusses this topic in this context of future management challenges.)

Findings

For the 206 positions in the Air Force Headquarters and major commands, our findings are as follows (and summarized in Table D.49):

- 128 positions meet the criteria for a G/FO requirement at the current grade.
- 23 positions meet the criteria for a G/FO requirement at a lower grade.
- 48 positions do not meet the criteria for a G/FO requirement.
- Five positions should be subject to the previously discussed review of contingency-related G/FO positions.
- Two positions for which we could not make a definitive assessment.

For the 17 positions in the Air Force Secretariat subgroup our findings are summarized in Table D.50.

The downgrades of G/FOs in the Air Force Secretariat subgroup are driven by two factors. The first is the finding that an O-9 military deputy to the Assistant Secretary of the Air Force for Acquisition meets the criteria for a G/FO requirement at a lower grade (downgrade to an O-8). This led to a corresponding finding to downgrade

Table D.49
USAF Major Headquarters and Command G/FO Findings

	O-7	O-8	O-9	O-10	Total
Meets criteria for a G/FO at current grade	50	55	18	5	128
Meets criteria for a G/FO at a lower grade (downgrade)	0	9	10	4	23
Does not meet the criteria for a G/FO requirement	44	3	1	0	48
Further review (contingency-related positions)	4	1	0	0	5
Inconclusive	0	2	0	0	2
Total	98	70	29	9	206

Table D.50
USAF Secretariat G/FO Findings

	O-7	O-8	O-9	O-10	Total
Meets criteria for a G/FO at current grade	5	4	2	0	11
Meets criteria for a G/FO at a lower grade (downgrade)	0	5	1	0	6
Total	5	9	3	0	17

other G/FOs in that hierarchy. The second factor was to establish parity across positions with analogous responsibilities within the Air Force Secretariat, which led to a finding to downgrade O-8s to O-7s (including O-8s that were also indicated for downgrading by the first factor).

Our findings for the Air Force Air Staff subgroup are summarized in Table D.51. The two G/FO positions that meet criteria for a G/FO at a lower grade (downgrade) are either in groups that we systematically downgraded throughout the service Pentagon headquarters staffs (chaplains, judge advocates general) or reflected a disparity across the Air Staff.

Our findings for the remaining major headquarters and commands of the U.S. Air Force are summarized in Table D.52. Recall that for these commands (summarized in Table D.47) we include not only G/FO positions within the command headquarters itself but also within all commands subordinate to that organization. For example, for ACC we included the G/FOs at ACC, with the Air Force Warfare Center, within First, 9th, 12th, and 29th Air Forces, and within any of the various wings subordinate to the Warfare Center or these numbered air forces.

Table D.51
USAF Air Staff G/FO Findings

	O-7	O-8	O-9	O-10	Total
Meets criteria for a G/FO at current grade	9	10	8	2	29
Meets criteria for a G/FO at a lower grade (downgrade)	0	1	1	0	2
Does not meet criteria for a G/FO	5	2	1	0	8
Inconclusive	0	1	0	0	1
Total	14	14	10	2	40

Table D.52
USAF Major Command Staff and Subordinates G/FO Findings

	O-7	O-8	O-9	O-10	Total
Meets criteria for a G/FO at current grade	36	41	8	3	88
Meets criteria for a G/FO at a lower grade (downgrade)	0	3	8	4	15
Does not meet criteria for a G/FO	39	1	0	0	40
Further review (contingency-related positions)	4	1	0	0	5
Inconclusive	0	1	0	0	1
Total	79	47	16	7	149

The first finding is that the number of O-10 positions in Air Force major commands is both disproportionate with the other services and not commensurate with the scale and scope of responsibilities assigned. Furthermore, comparison with the other services did not help clarify why these Air Force positions required O-10s when other services are able to perform equivalent functions with officers of lower grades. Thus, our finding is that four of the O-10 positions meet the criteria for a G/FO requirement at a lower grade. Note that in some cases (e.g., materiel commands), we arrived at the same finding for equivalent positions across the services (not just the Air Force). Furthermore, in some of these O-10 commands chains, the only high-ranking G/FOs are on the immediate staff of the O-10; commanders of subordinate units are all O-8s or lower. In these cases we not only find that the O-10 positions meet the criteria for a G/FO at a lower grade but come to the same finding for G/FOs on the O-10's immediate staff.

The most salient feature and second most significant finding is that 39 O-7 positions do not meet the criteria for a G/FO requirement. Nearly two-thirds of these are 24 O-7 Wing Commanders that could be downgraded to O-6. This finding derives from the simple fact that the majority of wings in the Air Force (about 80 percent, or four of five) are commanded by O-6s. We could not find justification in the position descriptions or identify any patterns that could explain why a limited number of wings are commanded by O-7s. This is true even when squadrons are by all appearances very similar (same or similar aircraft types and numbers). Thus, we concluded that—in the Air Force's own judgment as made evident by assigning O-6s to the great majority of these positions—the positions did not meet the criteria for a G/FO and all Wing commanders could be filled at the grade of O-6.

The third finding is not evident in the table: that the Air Force needs to rationalize the grade and position of the commander of a numbered air force. Currently, numbered air forces vary both in the grade of the Commander (which can be either O-9 or O-8) and the grade of the Vice-Commander (which can be O-7 or O-6). Furthermore, the grade of the Commander and Vice-Commander are not correlated: Some O-9 Commanders have Vice-Commanders that are O-7s yet others have O-6s; similarly, O-8 Commanders may have either O-7 or O-6 Vice-Commanders. It is not evident from the type of numbered air force commanded, nor from the position description, why the Air Force has established the Commander and Vice-Commander positions at the given grades: positions that appear to us similar in scope, scale, and responsibilities have different grades.

Unlike the Air Force wings, however, it is clear that each numbered air force is to some extent unique, and comparisons cannot be made as easily and confidently as we did with the wings. For this reason, the principle we used is that commanders of numbered air forces should be no more than one grade higher that their subordinates (so in the case of an O-9 numbered air force commander whose subordinate commanders were all O-7s or below, our finding was that the commander met the criteria for a G/FO requirement at a lower grade of O-8). In applying this principle, we did not consider immediate staff of the O-9 (these could be downgraded with the commander) and considered subordinate commanders after applying any logic or factors that would result in downgrades for them. Regardless of our findings, we recommend that the Air Force review these positions, articulate clear principles as to what merits an O-9 or O-8 commander (and what merits an O-7 or O-6 Vice-Commander), apply them to these positions, and make corresponding adjustments in grade and position descriptions.

Pyramid Calculator

To quickly calculate size- and shape-related pyramid health metrics for a particular pyramid, we built a spreadsheet-based pyramid calculator that automatically generates both the desired output metrics and a visual representation of the pyramid. The pyramid calculator is designed to facilitate quick-turn analysis of a proposed set of changes to G/FO requirements (e.g., eliminating or downgrading a position) to identify potential pyramid health problem areas. The calculator includes the metrics of number of promotions, selectivity, and joint to in-service ratio, as described in Chapter Six, providing an assessment of aggregate pyramid size, vertical movement, and lateral movement. Pyramid calculations can be performed in aggregate across the whole force, for each individual service, or for a specific sub-pyramid category (either within a service or in aggregate). The calculator allows for quick before-and-after comparisons of pyramid health based on a user-specified set of position changes. This appendix describes the detailed inputs and outputs associated with the calculator and includes tables for each of the three metrics for the functional pyramids (by service and grade).

The pyramid calculator tool calculates pyramid metrics for a user-defined set of requirements. Requirements are input as a list of jobs with information about each position's service, sub-pyramid category, and grade. The tool also accounts for dual-hatted positions, allowing users to specify a flag identifying the primary hat for each individual. Users have the ability to change time-in-grade and time-in-job assumptions and select the service and sub-pyramid category for which results should be displayed. Additional logic outside the pyramid calculator aids in the creation of job lists to be fed into the pyramid calculator. This logic employs user-defined flags for potential downgrades and eliminations, and users can choose whether or not subordinate positions to a downgraded position should also be downgraded. A screen shot of the position list input page is provided in Figure E.1.

To perform pyramid calculations, the tool assumes that joint positions are "fairly shared" across services. Within each sub-pyramid category and grade, each service's share of the joint pool is based on the proportion of that service's in-service representation at that grade. While this is clearly an oversimplification of how joint assignments are managed, it intends to capture the likelihood that a given service would produce the "best person for the job" for a position in a given category. The tool does allow

Figure E.1
Pyramid Calculator Inputs

Enter information in yellow columns only

Basic Position Info					Pyramid and status			
RAND ID (optional)	Joint/ Service	Duty Title (optional)	Authorized grade	Pyramid category		Eliminate? (0 or 1)	Downgrade? (0 or 1)	Single or primary hat? (0 or 1)
⬇	⬇	⬇	⬇		⬇	⬇	⬇	⬇
_____	Army	X	O8	X		0	0	0
_____	Army	X	O8	X		0	0	1
_____	Army	X	O7	X		0	0	0
_____	Army	X	O7	X		1	0	1
_____	Army	X	O7	X		0	0	1
_____	Army	X	O9	X		0	0	1
_____	Army	X	O7	X		0	0	1
_____	Army	X	O7	X		1	0	1
_____	Army	X	O8	X		0	0	0
_____	Army	X	O8	X		0	0	0
_____	Army	X	O8	X		0	0	1
_____	Army	X	O7	X		0	0	0
_____	Army	X	O7	X		0	0	1

RAND RR2384OSD-E.1

fractional joint positions to be assigned to each service, conveying the average number of joint positions a service might expect to fill in a particular grade and sub-pyramid category over time.

The pyramid calculator provides outputs summarizing the number of officers in each service and grade for the sub-pyramid category of interest, as well as the pyramid metrics for the desired service and sub-pyramid category. Finally, it shows pictorial representations of the overall, in-service, and joint pyramid in the selected service and sub-pyramid category. A screenshot of the pyramid calculator's outputs is provided in Figure E.2.

Pyramid Health Metrics

Tables E.1 through E.3 contain the pyramid health metrics—promotions, selectivity, and joint to in-service ratio—for the functional pyramids used in our analysis.

Figure E.2
Pyramid Calculator Outputs

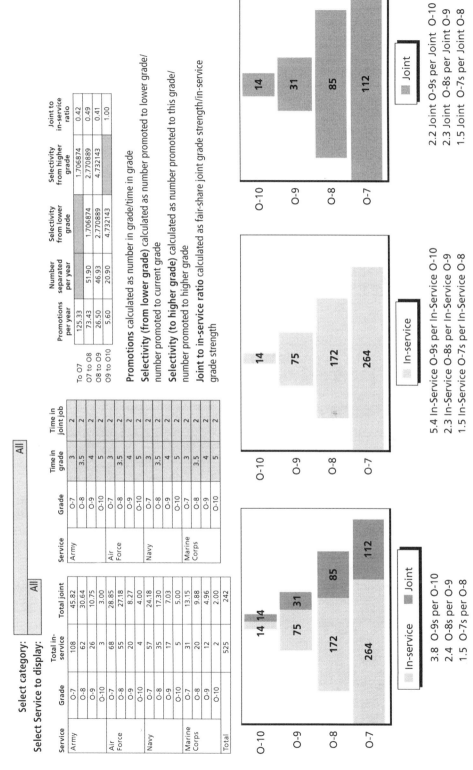

RAND RR2384OSD-E.2

Table E.1
Position Pyramid Health Metric: Promotions

Functional Sub-Pyramids	Army				Navy				Air Force				Marine Corps				Joint			
	O-10	O-9	O-8	O-7	O-10	O-9	O-8	O-7	O-10	O-9	O-8	O-7	O-10	O-9	O-8	O-7	O-10	O-9	O-8	O-7
Acquisition/Research and Development		0.43	3.28	5.18	0.20	1.29	3.28	4.78		1.29	3.28	4.38			0.73			3.00	10.57	14.33
C4I		0.31	0.86	1.44		0.63	0.43	2.17		0.31	0.43	0.72			0.86			1.25	2.57	4.33
Chaplain			0.29	0.33			0.29	0.33			0.29	0.33								
Engineer		0.25	2.29	1.33			0.29	1.00				0.33								
Intelligence		0.75	1.07				1.07			0.75	2.14	4.75				1.58		1.50	4.29	6.33
Legal		0.25	0.29	1.22		0.25	0.29			0.25	0.29	2.44			0.29					3.67
Manpower and Personnel		0.30	1.14	2.67		0.60	0.38	1.78		0.30	0.38	1.78		0.30	1.52	0.44		1.50	3.43	6.67
Materiel and Logistics	0.30	1.63	3.87	5.98		0.65	2.11	7.58	0.30	0.65	1.76	4.78	0.60	0.33	1.41	1.99		3.25	9.14	20.33
Medical		0.33	2.18	3.33		0.33	0.73	1.67		0.33	1.09	1.67						1.00	4.00	
Military Operations	1.70	7.79	22.02	36.78	1.70	4.45	8.64	21.58	2.72	7.05	17.71	26.48	0.68	3.71	8.21	8.83	6.80	23.00	56.57	93.67
Other special staff		0.25	0.86	1.54		0.25	0.29	0.77		0.25	1.14	1.92			0.29	0.77				5.00
Program Management/ Financial Management		0.50	0.96	1.45		0.25	0.96				0.64	2.18		0.25		0.36			2.57	4.00

NOTE: Cells that are blank have no positions in that category.

Table E.2
Position Pyramid Health Metric: Selectivity

Functional Sub-pyramids	Army				Navy				Air Force				Marine Corps				Joint			
	O-10	O-9	O-8	O-7	O-10	O-9	O-8	O-7	O-10	O-9	O-8	O-7	O-10	O-9	O-8	O-7	O-10	O-9	O-8	O-7
Acquisition/Research and Development		7.66	1.58		6.43	2.55	1.46			2.55	1.33				0.00			3.52	1.36	
C4I		2.74	1.69			0.69	5.06			1.37	1.69				0.00			2.06	1.69	
Chaplain			1.17				1.17				1.17									
Engineer		9.14	0.58				3.50													
Intelligence		1.43	0.00				0.00			2.86	2.22							2.86	1.48	
Legal		1.14	4.28			1.14	0.00			1.14	8.56				0.00					
Manpower and Personnel		3.81	2.33			0.63	4.67			1.27	4.67			5.08	0.29			2.29	1.94	
Materiel and Logistics	5.42	2.38	1.55		2.17	3.25	3.59			2.70	2.72			4.33	1.42		5.42	2.81	2.22	
Medical		6.55	1.53			2.18	2.29			3.27	1.53							4.00	1.67	
Military Operations	4.58	2.83	1.67		2.62	1.94	2.50		2.59	2.51	1.50		5.46	2.21	1.08		3.38	2.46	1.66	
Other special staff		3.43	1.79			1.14	2.69			4.57	1.68				2.69					
Program Management/ Financial Management		1.93	1.51			3.86	0.00				3.39			0.00					1.56	

NOTE: Cells that are blank in the O-8 to O-10 columns have no positions in that category. The O-7 columns are blank because we do not calculate selectivity to that grade from O-6.

Table E.3
Position Pyramid Health Metric: Joint to In-Service Ratio

Functional Sub-Pyramids	Army				Navy				Air Force				Marine Corps				Joint		
	O-10	O-9	O-8	O-7	O-10	O-9	O-8	O-7	O-10	O-9	O-8	O-7	O-10	O-9	O-8	O-7	O-9	O-8	O-7
Acquisition/Research and Development		0.71	0.28	0.19		0.71	0.28	0.19		0.71	0.28	0.19			0.28		0.71	0.28	0.19
C4I		0.25	0.50	1.17		0.25	0.50	1.17		0.25	0.50	1.17			0.50		0.25	0.50	1.17
Chaplain			0.00	0.00			0.00	0.00			0.00	0.00							
Engineer		0.00	0.00	0.00		0.00	0.00	0.00				0.00							
Intelligence		2.00	2.75	3.75			2.75			2.00	2.75	3.75				3.75	2.00	2.75	3.75
Legal		0.00	0.00	0.83		0.00	0.00	0.83		0.00	0.00	0.83			0.00				0.83
Manpower and Personnel		0.20	0.33	0.33		0.20	0.33	0.33		0.20	0.33	0.33		0.20	0.33	0.33	0.20	0.33	0.33
Materiel and Logistics	0.50	0.30	0.23	0.20	0.50	0.30	0.23	0.20	0.50	0.30	0.23	0.20	0.50	0.30	0.23	0.20	0.30	0.23	0.20
Medical		0.33	0.27	0.00		0.33	0.27	0.00		0.33	0.27	0.00					0.33	0.27	
Military Operations	0.70	0.48	0.51	0.47	0.70	0.48	0.51	0.47	0.70	0.48	0.51	0.47	0.70	0.48	0.51	0.47	0.48	0.51	0.47
Other special staff		0.00	0.00	0.15		0.00	0.00	0.15		0.00	0.00	0.15			0.00	0.15			0.15
Program Management/Financial Management		0.00	0.13	0.09		0.00	0.13	0.09			0.13	0.09		0.00		0.09		0.13	0.09

NOTE: Cells that are blank have no positions in that category.

Abbreviations

ACC	Air Combat Command
AETC	Air Education and Training Command
AETF	air expeditionary task force
AEW/CC	commander, air expeditionary wing
AF/DPG	Air Force General Officer Management Office
AFGSC	Air Force Global Strike Command
AFMC	Air Force Materiel Command
AFNORTH	Air Forces North
AFRC	Air Force Reserve Command
AFSOC	Air Force Special Operations Command
AFSPC	Air Force Space Command
ALCOM	Alaskan Command
AMC	Army Materiel Command
C4	command, control, communications, and computers
C4I	command, control, communications, computers, and intelligence
CAPE	Cost Assessment and Program Evaluation
CCMD	combatant command
CDDOC	CENTCOM Deployment and Distribution Operations Center
CE	command element

CENTAF	U.S. Air Forces Central Command
CENTCOM	U.S. Central Command
CFC	Combined Forces Command
CHINFO	Chief of Information
CIA	Central Intelligence Agency
CIO	Chief Information Officer
CJCS	Chairman of the Joint Chiefs of Staff
CJCSI	Chairman of the Joint Chiefs of Staff Instruction
CJTF-HOA	Combined Joint Task Force-Horn of Africa
CJTF-OIR	Combined Joint Task Force-Operation Inherent Resolve
CNMF	Cyber National Mission Force
CNO	Chief of Naval Operations
COMNAVAIRFOR	Commander, Naval Air Forces
CRP	Chairman's Reserve Position
DAFA	defense agencies and DoD field activities
DARPA	Defense Advanced Research Projects Agency
DATT	defense attaché
DCA	Defense Commissary Agency
DCAA	Defense Contract Audit Agency
DCMA	Defense Contract Management Agency
DFAS	Defense Finance and Accounting Service
DHA	Defense Health Agency
DIA	Defense Intelligence Agency
DISA	Defense Information Systems Agency
DIUx	Defense Innovation Unit Experimental
DJAG	Deputy Judge Advocate General
DLA	Defense Logistics Agency
DLSA	Defense Legal Services Agency

DMA	Defense Media Activity
DNA/CSS	Director of the National Security Agency/Central Security Service
DoD	Department of Defense
DoDEA	DoD Education Activity
DoDHRA	DoD Human Resources Activity
DOPMA	Defense Officer Personnel Management Act of 1980
DSCA	Defense Security Cooperation Agency
DSS	Defense Security Service
DTIC	Defense Technical Information Center
DTRA	Defense Threat Reduction Agency
DTSA	Defense Technology Security Administration
eMSMs	enhanced Multi-Service markets
FLTFOR	Fleet Forces
FORSCOM	United States Army Forces Command
G/FO	general and flag officer
GAO	United States Government Accountability Office (United States General Accounting Office prior to July 7, 2004)
HQDA	Headquarters of the Department of the Army
HQMC	Headquarters, United States Marine Corps
I&L	Installations and Logistics
IMA	individual mobilization augmentee
INSCOM	U.S. Army Intelligence and Security Command
ISAF	International Security Assistance Force
ISR	intelligence, surveillance, and reconnaissance
JAG	Judge Advocate General
JDAL	Joint Duty Assignment List
JECC	Joint Enabling Capabilities Command

JFCC	Joint Functional Component Command
JFCC-ISR	Joint Functional Component Command for Intelligence, Surveillance and Reconnaissance
JFCCC	Joint Force Cyberspace Component Commander
JFHQ-DODIN	Joint Force Headquarters Department of Defense Information Networks
JIATF	Joint Interagency Task Force
JIDA	Joint Improvised-Threat Defeat Agency
JPME	Joint Professional Military Education
JTF	Joint Task Force
MARDIV	Marine division
MARFOR AFRICOM	U.S. Marine Corps Forces Africa Command
MARFOR CENTCOM	U.S. Marine Corps Forces Central Command
MARFOR CYBERCOM	U.S. Marine Corps Forces Cyberspace Command
MARFOR EUCOM	U.S. Marine Corps Forces European Command
MARFOR NORTHCOM	U.S. Marine Corps Forces Northern Command
MARFOR SOUTHCOM	U.S. Marine Corps Forces Southern Command
MARFOR STRATCOM	U.S. Marine Corps Forces Strategic Command
MARFORCOM	U.S. Marine Corps Forces Command
MARFORK	U.S. Marine Corps Forces, Korea
MARFORPAC	U.S. Marine Corps Forces Pacific
MARFORRES	U.S. Marine Corps Forces Reserve
MARFORSOC	U.S. Marine Corps Forces Special Operations Command
MAW	Marine aircraft wing
MCCDC	Marine Corps Combat Development Command
MCIA	Marine Corps Intelligence Activity
MEF	Marine Expeditionary Force
MHS	medical health system

MCM	Military Career Model
MCRC	Marine Corps Recruiting Command
MCSC	Marine Corps Systems Command
MCU	Marine Corps University
MDA	Missile Defense Agency
MEB	Marine expeditionary brigade
MEDCOM	U.S. Army Medical Command
MEF	Marine Expeditionary Force
MLG	Marine logistics group
MTF	military treatment facility
NASC	Naval Air Systems Command
NATO	North Atlantic Treaty Organization
NAVAF	U.S. Naval Forces Africa
NAVEUR	U.S. Naval Forces Europe
NAVSUP	Naval Supply Systems Command
NDAA	National Defense Authorization Act
NGA	National Geospatial-Intelligence Agency
NGIC	National Ground Intelligence Center
NORAD	North American Aerospace Defense
NRO	National Reconnaissance Office
NSA	National Security Agency
NSA/CSS	National Security Agency/Central Security Service ()
O-6	officer grade of Colonel or Captain
O-7	officer grade of Brigadier General or Rear Admiral (lower half)
O-8	officer grade of Major General or Rear Admiral
O-9	officer grade of Lieutenant General or Vice Admiral
O-10	officer grade of General or Admiral

OCO	overseas contingency operations
OEA	Office of Economic Adjustment
OLA	Legislative Assistant to the Commandant of the Marine Corps
OMCC	Office of U.S. Marine Corps Communication
ONI/NMIO	Office of Naval Intelligence/National Maritime Intelligence-Integration Office
OPNAV	Office of the Chief of Naval Operations
OSD	Office of the Secretary of Defense
OUSD (P&R)	Office of the Under Secretary of Defense for Personnel and Readiness
P&R	Programs and Resources
PACAF	Pacific Air Forces
PACFLT	Pacific Fleet
PEO	program executive officer
PFPA	Pentagon Force Protection Agency
PME	professional military education
PMG	Provost Marshal General
PP&O	Plans, Policies, and Operations
SAPRO	Sexual Assault and Prevention Response
SECAF	Secretary of the Air Force
SECARMY	Secretary of the Army
SECDEF	Secretary of Defense
SECNAV	Secretary of the Navy
SES	Senior Executive Service
SMC	Space and Missile Systems Center
SOCCENT	United States Special Operations Command Central
SOCPAC	United States Special Operations Command Pacific

SOCSOUTH	Special Operations Command South
SOJTF-A	Special Operations Joint Task Force-Afghanistan
SYSCOMs	Systems Command
TJAG	The Judge Advocate General
TRADOC	United States Army Training and Doctrine Command
TRMC	DoD Test Resource Management Center
TSOC	theater special operations commands
UIC	Unit Identification Code
UNC	United Nations Command
USAF	United States Air Force
USAFCENT	United States Air Forces Central Command
USAFE-AFAFRICA	U.S. Air Forces Europe and Africa
USAFRICOM	U.S. Africa Command
USAICoE	U.S. Army Intelligence Center of Excellence
USARPAC	United States Army Pacific
USCENTCOM	U. S. Central Command
USCYBERCOM	U.S. Cyber Command
USD (AT&L)	Under Secretary of Defense for Acquisition, Technology, and Logistics
USD (I)	Under Secretary of Defense for Intelligence
USD (P)	Under Secretary of Defense for Policy
USD (P&R)	Under Secretary of Defense for Personnel and Readiness
USEUCOM	U.S. European Command
USFJ	U.S. Forces Japan
USFK	U.S. Forces Korea
USFOR-A	U.S. Forces Afghanistan

USMC	United States Marine Corps
USNORTHCOM	U.S. Northern Command
USPACOM	U.S. Pacific Command
USSOCOM	U.S. Special Operations Command
USSOUTHCOM	U.S. Southern Command
USSPACECOM	U.S. Space Command
USSTRATCOM	U.S. Strategic Command
USTRANSCOM	U.S. Transportation Command
WHS	Washington Headquarters Services

Bibliography

Acting Undersecretary of Defense (Personnel and Readiness), "Proposing an Alternative to SASC/HASC Proposed Reductions in Federal [General] and Flag Officers (G/FO)," memorandum to the Secretary of Defense, 2016.

Anderson, Lorin W., and David R. Krathwohl, eds., *A Taxonomy for Learning, Teaching, and Assessing: A Revision of Bloom's Taxonomy of Educational Objectives*, Boston, Mass.: Allyn and Bacon, 2001.

Bandiera, Oriana, Andrea Prat, Raffaella Sadun, and Julie Wulf, *Span of Control or Span of Activity?* London: Centre for Economic Performance, CEP Decision Paper No. 1139, London School of Economics and Political Science, 2012. As of January 6, 2018: http://cep.lse.ac.uk/pubs/download/dp1139.pdf

Baum, J. Robert, and Stefan Wally, "Strategic Decision Speed and Firm Performance," *Strategic Management Journal*, Vol. 24, No. 11, 2003, pp. 1107–1129.

Brown, Reginald J., "Military Personnel Human Resources Strategic Plan–Study Service Programs Designed to Prepare Officers to Serve in General/Flag Officer Positions," memorandum to the Assistant Secretary of the Army for Manpower and Reserve Affairs, October 1, 2002.

Cancian, Mark, "Reducing Number of Four-Star General/Flag Officers," Center for Strategic and International Studies, Assessing Defense Reform Series, July 1, 2016. As of February 4, 2018: https://defense360.csis.org/restructuring-national-security-generals/

Cascio, Wayne F., "Strategies for Responsible Restructuring," *The Academy of Management Executive*, Vol. 19, No. 4, 2005, pp. 39–50.

Chairman of the Joint Chiefs of Staff Instruction 1331.01D, "Manpower and Personnel Actions Involving General and Flag Officers," Washington, D.C., August 1, 2010.

Cheney, George, Lars Thogar Christensen, Theodore E. Zorn Jr., and Shiv Ganesh, *Organizational Communication in an Age of Globalization: Issues, Reflections, Practices*, Long Grove, Ill.: Waveland Press, 2010.

Commission on Army Acquisition and Program Management in Expeditionary Operations, "Urgent Reform Required: Army Expeditionary Contracting," Washington, D.C., October 31, 2007. As of January 8, 2018: https://www.acq.osd.mil/dpap/pacc/cc/gansler_commission.html

Conley, Raymond E., Ralph Masi, Bernard D. Rostker, Herbert J. Shukiar, and Steve Drezner, *Enhancing the Performance of Senior Department of Defense Civilian Executive Reserve Component General/Flag Officers, and Senior Noncommissioned Officers in Joint Matters*, Santa Monica, Calif.: RAND Corporation, MG-621-OSD, 2008. As of February 6, 2018: https://www.rand.org/pubs/monographs/MG621.html

Defense Manpower Data Center, "Counts of Active Duty and Reserve Service Members and APF Civilians," Excel file, September 30, 2008. As of February 6, 2018:
https://www.dmdc.osd.mil/appj/dwp/dwp_reports.jsp

———, "Counts of Active Duty and Reserve Service Members and APF Civilians," Excel file, September 30, 2010. As of February 6, 2018:
https://www.dmdc.osd.mil/appj/dwp/dwp_reports.jsp

———, "Counts of Active Duty and Reserve Service Members and APF Civilians," Excel file, March 31, 2017. As of December 16, 2017:
https://www.dmdc.osd.mil/appj/dwp/dwp_reports.jsp

Defense Manpower Data Center reports. As of March 27, 2018:
https://www.dmdc.osd.mil/appj/dwp/dwp_reports.jsp

Denning, Steve, "The Management Revolution That's Already Happening," webpage, May 30, 2013. As of January 16, 2018:
https://www.forbes.com/sites/stevedenning/2013/05/30/the-management-revolution-thats-already-happening/#74f0dfe70911

Dent, Eric B., and Pamela Bozeman, "Discovering the Foundational Philosophies, Practices, and Influences of Modern Management Theory," *Journal of Management History*, Vol. 20, No. 2, 2014, pp. 145–163.

Department of Defense Deputy Chief Management Officer, webpage. As of October 18, 2017:
http://dcmo.defense.gov/Portals/47/Documents/OSD%20DAFA%20Organization.pdf

Department of Defense Directive 1100.4, "Guidance for Manpower Management," Washington, D.C., February 12, 2005.

Department of Defense Directive 1100.22, "Policy and Procedures for Determining Workforce Mix," Washington, D.C., April 12, 2010.

Department of Defense Directive 1404.10, "DoD Civilian Expeditionary Workforce," Washington, D.C., January 23, 2009.

Department of Defense Directive 3000.06, "Combat Support Agencies (CSAs)," Washington, D.C., July 8, 2016.

Department of Defense Directive 5100.01, "Functions of the Department of Defense and Its Major Components," Washington, D.C., December 21, 2010.

Department of Defense Directive 5100.03, "Support of the Headquarters of Combatant and Subordinate Unified Commands," Washington, D.C., February 9, 2011.

Department of Defense Directive 5101.1, "DoD Executive Agent," Washington, D.C., May 9, 2003.

Department of Defense Instruction 1320.04, "Military Officer Actions Requiring Presidential, Secretary of Defense, or Under Secretary of Defense for Personnel and Readiness Approval or Senate Confirmation," Washington, D.C., January 3, 2014.

Department of Defense Instruction 1320.13, "Commissioned Officer Promotion Reports," Washington, D.C., July 22, 2009.

Department of the Navy, *Military Personnel Human Resources Strategic Plan: U.S. Navy Flag Officer Management and Career Development Philosophy, Policies and Practices*, Washington, D.C., September 2002.

Dhar, Ravi, and Itamar Simonson, "The Effect of Forced Choice on Choice," *Journal of Marketing Research*, Vol. 40, No. 2, May 2003.

Dijksterhuis, Marjolijn S., Frans A. J. Van den Bosch, and Henk W. Volberda, "Where Do New Organizational Forms Come From? Management Logics as a Source of Coevolution," *Organization Science*, Vol. 10, No. 5, 1999, pp. 569–582.

Directorate for Organizational Policy and Decision Support, Office of the Deputy Chief Management Officer, Office of the Secretary of Defense, U.S. Department of Defense, "Organization and Management of the Department of Defense," briefing, February 2017.

Ducharme, Douglas, *Survey Response Categories: Guide for Using Neutral or N/A Options*, Newport, R.I.: U.S. Naval War College Wargaming Department, undated.

Eisenhardt, Kathleen M., "Making Fast Strategic Decisions in High-Velocity Environments," *Academy of Management Journal*, Vol. 32, No. 3, 1989, pp. 543–576.

Expeditionary Warfare School Distance Education Program, "Marine Corps Organization," briefing, U.S. Marine Corps, June 1, 2011.

Freeman, Ben, "General and Flag Officer Requirements," testimony before the Senate Armed Services Committee Subcommittee on Personnel, Senate Hearing 112-258, Washington, D.C., September 14, 2011.

Gebicke, Mark E., "General and Flag Officers DOD's Draft Study Needs Adjustments," testimony before the U.S. House of Representatives Subcommittee on Military Personnel, Committee on National Security, U.S. General Accounting Office, GAO/T-NSIAD-97-122, April 8, 1997.

Glenn, John, "General and Flag Officer Requirements," opening statement at the hearing of the Senate Armed Services Committee Subcommittee on Manpower and Personnel, Washington, D.C., August 10, 1988.

Harrell, Margaret C., Harry J. Thie, Pete Schirmer, and Kevin Brancato, *Aligning the Stars: Improvements to General and Flag Officer Management*, Santa Monica, Calif.: RAND Corporation, MR-1712-OSD, 2004. As of February 6, 2018:
https://www.rand.org/pubs/monograph_reports/MR1712.html

Harrell, Margaret C., Harry J. Thie, Sheila Nataraj Kirby, Al Crego, Danielle M. Varda, and Thomas Sullivan, *A Strategic Approach to Joint Officer Management: Analysis and Modeling Results*, Santa Monica, Calif.: RAND Corporation, MG-886-OSD, 2009. As of February 6, 2018:
https://www.rand.org/pubs/monographs/MG886.html

Harrington, Lisa M., Igor Mikolic-Torreira, Geoffrey McGovern, Michael J. Mazarr, Peter Schirmer, Keith Gierlack, Joslyn Hemler, and Jonathan Welch, *Reserve Component General and Flag Officers: A Review of Requirements and Authorizations*, Santa Monica, Calif.: RAND Corporation, RR-1156-OSD, 2016. As of February 6, 2018:
https://www.rand.org/pubs/research_reports/RR1156.html

Harris, Patricia, and Ken Lucas, *Executive Leadership: Requisite Skills and Developmental Processes for Three- and Four-Star Assignments*, Alexandria, Va.: U.S. Army Research Institute for the Behavioral and Social Sciences, March 1991.

Hay Group, *Study of General/Flag Officer Requirements and Distributions in the Department of Defense*, Washington, D.C., 1988.

———, *Report on the Study of Joint General and Flag Officer Requirements, Distribution, and the Assignment Process*, Washington, D.C., February 1994.

Hindle, Tim, *Guide to Management Ideas and Gurus*, Vol. 42, Hoboken, N.J.: John Wiley & Sons, Economist series, 2008.

Horton, Scott, "Jim Haynes's Long Twilight Struggle," *Harper's Magazine: Browsings, The Harper's Blog*, February 8, 2008.

Jacobson, Don, "Making the Most of Developmental Assignments: Q&A with Author Cynthia McCauley," GovLeaders.org, 2007. As of February 4, 2018:
http://govleaders.org/development.htm

Jaques, Elliot, "In Praise of Hierarchy," *Harvard Business Review*, January–February 1990, pp. 245–253.

Johnson, Kurt A., "Military Department General Counsel as Chief Legal Officers: Impact on Delivery of Impartial Legal Advice at Headquarters and in the Field," *Military Legal Review*, Vol. 82, 1993, pp. 1–81, 41.

Joint Chiefs of Staff, webpage, undated-a. As of January 16, 2018:
www.jcs.mil

———, "About the Joint Chiefs of Staff," webpage, undated-b. As of January 16, 2018:
http://www.jcs.mil/About/

———, "Joint Staff Structure," webpage, undated-c. As of January 16, 2018:
http://www.jcs.mil/Leadership/

———, Directorate of Management, "Directorates of Management," webpage, undated-d. As of January 16, 2018:
http://www.jcs.mil/Directorates/Directorates-of-Management/

———, Joint History Office, "About," webpage, undated-e. As of January 16, 2018:
http://www.jcs.mil/About/Joint-Staff-History/

———, "Organizational Development of the Joint Chiefs of Staff," April 2013. As of January 16, 2018:
http://www.jcs.mil/Portals/36/Documents/History/Institutional/Organizational_Development_of_the_JCS.pdf

Joint Enabling Capabilities Command, U.S. Transportation Command, webpage, undated-a. As of January 16, 2018:
http://www.jecc.mil/

———, "Leadership," webpage, undated-b. As of January 16, 2018:
http://www.jecc.mil/Leadership

———, "Subordinates," webpage, undated-c. As of January 16, 2018:
http://www.jecc.mil/Subordinates

Joint Publication 1, "Doctrine for the Armed Forces of the United States," Washington, D.C., Joint Chiefs of Staff, March 25, 2013.

Joint Publication 1-04, "Legal Support for Military Operations," Washington, D.C., Joint Chiefs of Staff, August 2, 2016.

Joint Publication 2-0, "Joint Intelligence," Washington, D.C., Joint Chiefs of Staff, October 22, 2013.

Joint Publication 2-01, "Joint and National Intelligence Support to Military Operations," Washington, D.C., Joint Chiefs of Staff, July 5, 2017.

Joint Publication 3-05, *Special Operations*, Washington, D.C., Joint Chiefs of Staff, July 16, 2014.

Joint Publication 3-33, "Joint Task Force Headquarters," Washington, D.C., Joint Chiefs of Staff, July 30, 2012.

Joint Staff J7 Deployable Training Division (DTD), "Joint Headquarters Organization, Staff Integration, and Battle Rhythm Insights and Best Practices Focus Paper," July 2013. As of February 5, 2018:
http://www.jcs.mil/Portals/36/Documents/Doctrine/fp/fp_jthq_org.pdf

Judson, Jen, "The Army's Cyber Ops Has a Data Problem," *Federal Times*, November 16, 2016. As of February 5, 2018:
https://www.federaltimes.com/smr/cybercon/2016/11/16/the-army-s-cyber-ops-has-a-data-problem/

Kapos Associates, *Zero-Based Analysis of General Officer Billet Requirements*, Arlington, Va., 1988.

———, *Analysis of U.S. Marine Corps General Officer Billet Requirements*, Final Report–Basic Phase, Arlington, Va., KAI 152.96F, July 31, 1996a.

———, *Analysis of U.S. Marine Corps Reserve General Officer Billet Requirements*, Arlington, Va., August 31, 1996b.

———, *Executive Summary: Preliminary Report of Navy Flag Officer Requirements and Related Issues*, January 29, 1997.

Kapp, Lawrence, *General and Flag Officers in the U.S. Armed Forces: Background and Considerations for Congress*, Washington, D.C.: Congressional Research Service, February 18, 2016.

Krulak, Charles C., "The Strategic Corporal: Leadership in the Three Block War," *Marines Magazine*, Air University, 1999.

Lang, Kurt, "Military Organizations," in James G. March, ed., *Handbook of Organizations*, New York: Routledge, 1965, pp. 838–856.

Mahler, Michael E., David E. Bertrand, Preston, T. Brown, Philip H. Crowell, Cheryl L. Daly, Elizabeth B. Dial, Terence J. Schmitt, and Keira E. Smith, *Review of Active Duty and Reserve General and Flag Officer Authorizations*, Tysons, Va.: Logistics Management Institute, predecisional working paper, PR206L1, March 2003.

Mahler, Michael E., Cheryl L. Daly, Shawn D. Mank, Kathleen L. Newbold, Keira E. Smith, Delores A. Street, and Amy T. Windisch, *General/Flag Officer Review*, Tysons, Va.: Logistics Management Institute, Report PR304T1, June 2005.

McGuire, Mark A., "Senior Officers and Strategic Leader Development," *Joint Force Quarterly*, Autumn/Winter 2001–02, pp. 91–96.

McInnis, Kathleen J., *Goldwater-Nichols at 30: Defense Reform and Issues for Congress*, Congressional Research Service, June 2, 2016. As of March 6, 2018:
http://www.dtic.mil/dtic/tr/fulltext/u2/1013813.pdf

Meier, Kenneth J., and John Bohte, "Span of Control and Public Organizations: Implementing Luther Gulick's Research Design," *Public Administration Review*, Vol. 63, No. 1, 2003, pp. 61–70.

Meyer, Igor S., "The Gaming of Policy and the Politics of Gaming: A Review," *Simulation & Gaming*, Vol. 40, No. 6, 2009.

Military Leadership Diversity Commission, "Issue Paper #45: Recent Officer Promotion Rates by Race, Ethnicity, and Gender," June 2010, p. 4. As of December 18, 2017:
http://diversity.defense.gov/Portals/51/Documents/Resources/Commission/docs/
Issue%20Papers/Paper%2045%20-%20Officer%20Promotion%20by%20Race%20
Ethnicity%20and%20Gender.pdf

Miller, Katherine, "Classical Approaches," in Katherine Miller, ed., *Organizational Communication: Approaches and Processes*, 7th ed., Stamford, Conn.: Cengage Learning, 2015, pp. 17–35.

Misangyi, Vilmos F., and Abhijith G. Acharya, "Substitutes or Complements? A Configurational Examination of Corporate Governance Mechanisms," *Academy of Management Journal*, Vol. 57, No. 6, 2014, pp. 1681–1705.

Nataraj, Shanthi, Christopher Guo, Philip Hall-Partyka, Susan M. Gates, and Douglas Yeung, *Options for Department of Defense Total Workforce Supply and Demand Analysis: Potential Approaches and Available Data Sources*, Santa Monica, Calif.: RAND Corporation, RR-543-OSD, 2014. As of December 29, 2017:
http://www.rand.org/pubs/research_reports/RR543.html

National Defense Authorization Act for Fiscal Year 2017, Section 501, Reduction in Number of General and Flag Officers on Active Duty and Authorized Strength after December 31, 2022, of Such General and Flag Officers, December 23, 2016.

North Atlantic Treaty Organization, "NATO Organization," webpage, January 4, 2017a. As of January 16, 2018:
http://www.nato.int/cps/en/natohq/structure.htm

———, "Organization," webpage, May 17, 2017b. As of February 4, 2018:
http://www.nato.int/cps/en/natolive/69463.htm

NATO, Resolute Support Afghanistan, "Mission," webpage, undated-a. As of January 16, 2018:
https://rs.nato.int/about-us/mission.aspx

———, "History," webpage, undated-b. As of January 16, 2018:
https://rs.nato.int/about-us/history.aspx

———, "Leadership," webpage, undated-c. As of January 16, 2018:
https://www.rs.nato.int/about-us/leadership.aspx

———, "RS Commands," webpage, undated-d. As of January 16, 2018:
https://www.rs.nato.int/rs-commands.aspx

NATO Supreme Headquarters Allied Powers Europe, webpage, undated-a. As of January 16, 2018:
https://www.shape.nato.int

———, "Leadership Staff," webpage, undated-b. As of January 16, 2018:
https://shape.nato.int/page1165579

———, "Organisation," webpage, undated-c. As of January 16, 2018:
https://shape.nato.int/structure

———, "What Is SHAPE?" webpage, undated-d. As of January 16, 2018:
https://shape.nato.int/page1167311

Neilson, Gary L., and Julie Wulf, "How Many Direct Reports?" *Harvard Business Review*, Vol. 90, No. 4., 2012.

North American Aerospace Defense Command, "NORAD Leaders," webpage, undated. As of January 16, 2018:
http://www.norad.mil/Leadership/

Offenhauer, Priscilla, "General and Flag Officer Authorizations for the Active and Reserve Components: A Comparative and Historical Analysis," Washington, D.C.: Federal Research Division, Library of Congress, December 2007.

Office of the Deputy Assistant Secretary of Defense for Military Community and Family Policy (ODASD [MC&FP]), *2015 Demographics: Profile of the Military Community*, Washington, D.C.: U.S. Department of Defense, undated. As of January 8, 2018:
http://download.militaryonesource.mil/12038/MOS/Reports/2015-Demographics-Report.pdf

Office of the Secretary of Defense, General and Flag Officer Management Office, *Terms of Reference*, Washington, D.C., November 21, 2016.

O'Neill, Kevin, *Sustaining the U.S. Air Force's Force Support Career Field Through Officer Workforce Planning*, Santa Monica, Calif.: RAND Corporation, RGSD-302, 2012. As of January 8, 2017: http://www.rand.org/pubs/rgs_dissertations/RGSD302.html

Operation Inherent Resolve, "CJTF-OIR Leaders," webpage, undated-a. As of January 16, 2018: http://www.inherentresolve.mil/About-Us/Biographies/

———, "Organization," webpage, undated-b. As of January 16, 2018: http://www.inherentresolve.mil/About-Us/Organization/

Pardee RAND Graduate School Center for Gaming, "Context," webpage, undated. As of November 15, 2017: https://www.prgs.edu/research/methods-centers/gaming.html

Patacconi, Andrea, "Coordination and Delay in Hierarchies," *RAND Journal of Economics*, Vol. 40, No. 1, 2009, pp. 190–208.

Perla, Peter, and ED McGrady, "Why Wargaming Works," *Naval War College Review*, Vol. 64, No. 3, Summer 2011.

Pillai, Chad, "Reorganizing the Joint Force for a Trans-Regional Threat Environment," The Strategy Bridge, January 4, 2017. As of January 16, 2018: https://thestrategybridge.org/the-bridge/2017/1/4/reorganizing-the-joint-force-for-a-transregional-threat-environment

Pryor, Mildred Golden, and Sonia Taneja, "Henri Fayol, Practitioner and Theoretician–Revered and Reviled," *Journal of Management History*, Vol. 16, No. 4, 2010, pp. 489–503.

Public Law 102-484, National Defense Authorization Act for Fiscal Year 1993, Section 403, Limited Exclusion of Joint Service Requirements from a Limitation on the Strengths for General and Flag Officers on Active Duty, October 23, 1992.

Public Law 110-417, Duncan Hunter National Defense Authorization Act for Fiscal Year 2009, Section 506, Delayed Authority to Alter Distribution Requirements for Commissioned Officers on Active Duty in General Officer and Flag Officer Grades and Limitations on Authorized Strengths of General and Flag Officers on Active Duty, October 14, 2008.

Public Law 112-81, "National Defense Authorization Act for Fiscal Year 2012, Section 502, General Officer and Flag Officer Reform, December 31, 2011.

Public Law 114-328, National Defense Authorization Act for Fiscal Year 2017, December 23, 2016.

Rajan, Raghuram G., and Julie Wulf, "The Flattening Firm: Evidence from Panel Data on the Changing Nature of Corporate Hierarchies," *The Review of Economics and Statistics*, Vol. 88, No. 4, 2006, pp. 759–773.

Rearden, Steven L., *Council of War: A History of the Joint Chiefs of Staff*, Washington, D.C.: NDU Press, July 2012. As of January 16, 2018: http://www.jcs.mil/Portals/36/Documents/History/Institutional/Council_of_War.pdf

Reed, LTC Heather, "Advantages of Assigning Forces," *Military Review*, May–June 2016, pp. 119–125.

Resolute Support Mission/U.S. Forces Afghanistan, "RSM/USFOR-A G/FO Structure," briefing slide, June 8, 2017.

Rothenberg, Alexander D., Lisa M. Harrington, Paul Emslie, and Tara L. Terry, *Using RAND's Military Career Model to Evaluate the Impact of Institutional Requirements on the Air Force Space Officer Career Field*, Santa Monica, Calif.: RAND Corporation, RR-1302-AF, 2017. As of December 29, 2017: https://www.rand.org/pubs/research_reports/RR1302.html

Schmidt, Lara, Caolionn O'Connell, Hirokazu Miyake, Akhil R. Shah, Joshua Baron, Geof Nieboer, Rose Jourdan, David Senty, Zev Winkelman, Louise Taggart, Susanne Sondergaard, and Neil Robinson, *Cyber Practices: What Can the U.S. Air Force Learn from the Commercial Sector?* Santa Monica, Calif.: RAND Corporation, RR-847-AF, 2015. As of February 15, 2018: https://www.rand.org/pubs/research_reports/RR847.html

Schirmer, Peter, *Computer Simulation of General and Flag Officer Management: Model Description and Results*, Santa Monica, Calif.: RAND Corporation, TR-702-OSD, 2009. As of December 29, 2017: http://www.rand.org/pubs/technical_reports/TR702.html

Schirmer, Peter, Harry J. Thie, Margaret C. Harrell, and Michael S. Tseng, *Challenging Time in DOPMA: Flexible and Contemporary Military Officer Management*, Santa Monica, Calif.: RAND Corporation, MG-451-OSD, 2006. As of December 29, 2017: http://www.rand.org/pubs/monographs/MG451.html

Schraw, Gregory, "Knowledge: Structures and Processes," in Patricia A. Alexander and Philip H. Winne, eds., *Handbook of Educational Psychology*, 2nd ed., Washington, D.C.: American Psychological Association, 2006.

Siggelkow, Nicolaj, and Jan W. Rivkin, "Speed and Search: Designing Organizations for Turbulence and Complexity," *Organization Science*, Vol. 16, No. 2, 2005, pp. 101–122.

Simons, Robert, "Designing High-Performance Jobs," *Harvard Business Review*, Vol. 83, No. 7, 2005, p. 54.

Simonson, Itamar, and Stephen M. Nowlis, "The Role of Explanations and Need for Uniqueness in Consumer Decision Making: Unconventional Choices Based on Reasons," *Journal of Consumer Research*, Vol. 27, No. 1, June 1, 2000.

Spoehr, Thomas, David Komar, Terrence Alvarez, and Raymond Shetzline, "Reducing the Size of Headquarters, Department of the Army—An After-Action Review," *Military Review*, January–February 2017. As of January 11, 2017: http://www.armyupress.army.mil/Journals/Military-Review/English-Edition-Archives/January-February-2017/ART-005/

Stanley, Clifford L., and William Gortney, *General and Flag Officer Efficiencies Study Group*, Washington, D.C.: U.S. Department of Defense, 2010.

———, "General and Flag Officer Requirements," testimony at hearing before the Subcommittee on Personnel of the U.S. Senate Armed Services Committee, Washington, D.C., September 14, 2011.

Starbuck, W. H., "Organizational Growth and Development," in W. H. Starbuck, ed., *Organizational Growth and Development*, Harmondsworth, U.K.: Penguin Books, 1971.

Thie, Harry J., "Planning the Future Military Workforce," in Stuart Johnson, Martin C. Libicki, and Gregory F. Treverton, eds., *New Challenges, New Tools for Defense Decisionmaking*, Santa Monica, Calif.: RAND Corporation, MR-1576-RC, 2003. As of February 15, 2018: https://www.rand.org/pubs/monograph_reports/MR1576.html

———, "Developing and Using General and Flag Officers," testimony presented to the Subcommittee on Total Force of the U.S. House Armed Services Committee, Washington, D.C., March 24, 2004.

Turner, Lisa L., "The Detainee Interrogation Debate and the Legal-Policy Process," *Joint Force Quarterly*, Vol. 53, 2009, pp. 40–47.

Turner, Roger, "U.S. Marine Corps, Expeditionary Force 21," briefing slides, undated.

Under Secretary of Defense for Personnel and Readiness, "Expanded General/Flag Officer Working Group," memorandum to Secretaries of the Military Departments, Chairman of the Joint Chiefs of Staff, Chief of Staff, U.S. Army, Chief of Naval Operations, Chief of Staff, U.S. Air Force and Commandant of the Marine Corps, Washington, D.C., January 6, 2016.

———, "General/Flag Officer Requirements Study," memorandum to Secretaries of the Military Departments, Chairman of the Joint Chiefs of Staff, Chief of Staff of the Army, Commandant of the Marine Corps, Chief of Naval Operations and Chief of Staff of the Air Force, Washington, D.C., December 6, 2016.

U.S. Africa Command, "About the Command," webpage, undated-a. As of January 16, 2018: http://www.africom.mil/about-the-command

———, "What We Do," webpage, undated-b. As of January 16, 2018: https://www.africom.mil/what-we-do

———, "U.S. Africa Command," briefing slide, September 15, 2015.

U.S. Air Force, *Air Force General Officer Authorization Study*, Washington, D.C., January 1997.

———, CONR-1AF (AFNORTH), "Biographies," webpage, undated-a. As of January 8, 2018: http://www.1af.acc.af.mil/Library/Biographies/

———, Joint Base Elmendorf-Richardson, homepage, undated-b. As of January 8, 2018: http://www.jber.jb.mil

———, Vandenberg Air Force Base, "14th Air Force (Air Forces Strategic)," webpage, undated-c. As of January 16, 2018: http://www.vandenberg.af.mil/Units/14th-Air-Force-Air-Forces-Strategic/

U.S. Army, "Who We Are," webpage, undated. As of January 8, 2018: https://www.army.mil/info/organization/

———, *1997 Army General Officer Requirements Study*, Washington, D.C., 1997.

U.S. Army Combined Arms Center, webpage, undated. As of January 8, 2018: http://usacac.army.mil

U.S. Army Forces Command, "Leadership," webpage, undated. As of January 8, 2018: https://www.forscom.army.mil/(S(tyrcxahmudbeslu4ebumvr2v))/Leadership

U.S. Army General Officer Management Office, "Army GO Organizational Structure," briefing slides, July 28, 2017.

U.S. Army Materiel Command, "AMC Leadership," webpage, undated-a. As of January 8, 2018: http://www.amc.army.mil/Organization/Leadership/

———, "AMC Major Subordinate Commands," webpage, undated-b. As of January 8, 2018: http://www.amc.army.mil/Organization/Major-Subordinate-Commands/

U.S. Army Military District of Washington, "Joint Force Headquarters—National Capital Region Organizational Structure," webpage, undated. As of January 8, 2018: http://mdwhome.mdw.army.mil/about-jfhq-ncr-main/jfhq-ncr-organization-chart

U.S. Army Pacific, "Subordinate Commands," webpage, undated-a. As of January 8, 2018: http://www.usarpac.army.mil/subordinate_commands.asp

———, "USARPAC Leaders," webpage, undated-b. As of January 8, 2018: http://www.usarpac.army.mil/biographies.asp

U.S. Army Special Operations Command, "USAJFKSWCS Organization," webpage, undated. As of January 8, 2018:
http://www.soc.mil/SWCS/_pdf/USAJFKSWCS%20Organization%2011%20AUG%2014.pdf

U.S. Army Training and Doctrine Command, "Leaders," webpage, undated-a. As of January 8, 2018:
http://www.tradoc.army.mil/Leaders.asp

———, "Organization," webpage, undated-b. As of January 8, 2018:
http://www.tradoc.army.mil/Organization.asp

———, "TRADOC Organization," webpage, undated-c. As of January 8, 2018:
http://www.tradoc.army.mil/FrontPageContent/Docs/TRADOC%20ORGANIZATION%20CHART.pdf

U.S. Central Command, "Unified Commands, CENTCOM & Components," webpage, undated-a. As of January 16, 2018:
http://www.centcom.mil/ABOUT-US/COMPONENT-COMMANDS/

———, "U.S. Central Command Leadership," webpage, undated-b. As of January 16, 2018:
http://www.centcom.mil/ABOUT-US/LEADERSHIP/

———, "Major Headquarters Activity Org Chart," briefing slide, Sept. 18, 2015.

U.S. Code, Title 10, Armed Forces, Subtitle A, General Military Law, Part I, Organization and General Military Powers, Chapter 6, Combatant Commands, Section 167b, Unified Combatant Command for Cyber Operations.

———, Part II, Personnel, Chapter 32, Officer Strength and Distribution in Grade, Section 526(a), Authorized Strength After December 31, 2022: General Officers and Flag Officers on Active Duty.

U.S. Department of Defense, *Review of Active Duty General and Flag Officer Authorizations*, Washington, D.C., March 2003.

———, *Military Health System Review, Final Report to the Secretary of Defense*, Washington, D.C., August 2014.

———, *Plan to Implement Section 1073c of Title 10, United States Code, Report to the Armed Services Committees of the Senate and House of Representatives*, Second Interim Report, Washington, D.C., June 30, 2017.

U.S. Department of Defense, Under Secretary of Defense of Acquisition, Technology and Logistics, Defense Procurement and Acquisition Policy, "Commission on Army Acquisition and Program Management in Expeditionary Operations," webpage, November 5, 2015. As of January 8, 2018:
https://www.acq.osd.mil/dpap/pacc/cc/gansler_commission.html

U.S. European Command, "Command Structure," webpage, undated-a. As of January 8, 2018:
http://www.eucom.mil/about/organization/command-structure

———, "Lt. Gen. Timothy M. Ray," webpage, undated-b. As of January 8, 2018:
http://www.eucom.mil/about/organization/senior-leadership/deputy-commander

———, "Our Forces," webpage, undated-c. As of January 8, 2018:
http://www.eucom.mil/about/organization/our-forces

———, "Rear Adm. John W. Smith," webpage, undated-d. As of January 8, 2018:
http://www.eucom.mil/about/organization/senior-leadership/chief-of-staff

———, "U.S. European Command Headquarters Commandant's Office," webpage, undated-e. As of January 26, 2018:
http://www.eucom.mil/about/organization/command-structure/u-s-european-command-headquarters-commandants-office

———, "USEUCOM Organization Chart—Shape/Deter Russia—Critical 41 and RSI," briefing slide, Dec. 28, 2015.

———, "Organization Chart—EUCOM," briefing slide, 2016.

U.S. Forces Japan, "About USFJ," webpage, undated-a. As of January 16, 2018:
http://www.usfj.mil/About-USFJ/

———, "Leadership," webpage, undated-b. As of January 16, 2018:
http://www.usfj.mil/Leadership/

U.S. Forces Korea, "Combined Forces Command," webpage, undated-a. As of January 16, 2018:
http://www.usfk.mil/About/Combined-Forces-Command/

———, "Organization United States Forces Korea," webpage, undated-b. As of January 16, 2018:
http://www.usfk.mil/Organization/

———, "United Nations Command," webpage, undated-c. As of January 16, 2018:
http://www.usfk.mil/About/United-Nations-Command/

U.S. General Accounting Office, *Military Officers: Assessment of the 1988 Defense Officer Requirements Study*, Washington, D.C., GAO/NSIAD-88-146, April 1988.

———, *Military Personnel: General and Flag Officer Requirements Are Unclear Based on DOD's 2003 Report to Congress*, Washington, D.C., GAO-04-488, April 2004.

———, *Military Personnel: DOD Needs to Update General and Flag Officer Requirements and Improve Availability of Associated Costs*, Washington, D.C., September 2014.

U.S. Marine Corps, "Commanding General, Marine Corps Combat Development Command and Deputy Commandant, Combat Development & Integration," webpage, undated-a. As of February 2, 2018:
http://www.mccdc.marines.mil/Resources/Briefs-and-Documents/

———, "Concepts & Programs," webpage, undated-b. As of February 2, 2018:
https://marinecorpsconceptsandprograms.com

———, "Marine Corps Combat Development and Integration & Marine Corps Combat Development Command," briefing, undated-c.

———, "Marine Corps Unit Directory," webpage, undated-d. As of February 2, 2018:
http://www.marines.mil/Units/

———, "Marine Corps Unit Directory: Intelligence," webpage, undated-e. As of February 2, 2018:
http://www.marines.mil/Units/srterms/intelligence/

———, "Naval Amphibious Force, TF 51, 5th Marine Expeditionary Brigade History," webpage, undated-f. As of February 5, 2018:
http://www.tf515.marines.mil/About/History/

———, "Naval Amphibious Force, TF 51, 5th Marine Expeditionary Brigade Unit Leaders," webpage, undated-g. As of February 5, 2018:
http://www.tf515.marines.mil/About/Leaders/

———, "Organization," webpage, undated-h. As of February 2, 2018:
https://marinecorpsconceptsandprograms.com/organization

———, "TECOM Training & Education Command," webpage, undated-i. As of February 2, 2018:
http://www.tecom.marines.mil/

———, "U.S. Marine Corps 36th Commandant's Planning Guidance 2015," undated-j. As of February 2, 2018:
http://www.hqmc.marines.mil/Portals/142/Docs/2015CPG_Color.pdf

———, *USMC Concepts & Programs 2013*, Washington, D.C., 2013, pp. 10–35. As of February 2, 2018:
http://www.hqmc.marines.mil/Portals/136/Docs/Concepts%20and%20Programs/2013/CP13%20CH2_WEBFA_5FEB13.pdf

———, "Marine Corps 101," web briefing, Washington, D.C., February 18, 2016. As of February 2, 2018:
http://www.marines.mil/Portals/59/Docs/MarineCorps101_2.pdf

U.S. Marine Corps, Expeditionary Force 21, "Marine Expeditionary Brigade Informational Overview," Washington, D.C., undated.

U.S. Marine Corps, MCRP 1-10.1 (formerly MCRP 5-12D), "Organization of the United States Marine Corps," Washington, D.C., February 15, 2016.

U.S. Navy, "Navy Chief of Information," webpage, undated-a. As of February 5, 2018:
http://www.navy.mil/local/chinfo/

———, "U.S. Fleet Forces Command," webpage, undated-b. As of January 8, 2018:
http://www.public.navy.mil/usff/Pages/leaders.aspx

———, "Organizational Chart for Headquarters, U.S. Pacific Fleet," webpage, March 9, 2016. As of January 16, 2018:
http://www.cpf.navy.mil/about/organization/chart.pdf

U.S. Navy, Naval Air Systems Command, "NAVAIR Leadership," webpage, undated-a. As of February 5, 2018:
http://www.navair.navy.mil/index.cfm?fuseaction=home.leadership

———, "Organizational Structure," webpage, undated-b. As of February 5, 2018:
http://www.navair.navy.mil/index.cfm?fuseaction=home.display&key=OrganizationalStructure

U.S. Northern Command, "About NORTHCOM," webpage, undated-a. As of January 8, 2018:
http://www.northcom.mil/About-USNORTHCOM/

———, "USNORTHCOM Leaders," webpage, undated-b. As of January 8, 2018:
http://www.northcom.mil/Leadership/

———, "USNORTHCOM Subordinate Commands," briefing slide, undated-c.

U.S. Pacific Command, "Leadership United States Pacific Command," webpage, undated-a. As of January 16, 2018:
http://www.pacom.mil/Leadership/

———, "Organization Chart," webpage, undated-b. As of January 16, 2018:
http://www.pacom.mil/Organization/Organization-Chart/

———, "USPACOM FY16 Activities—Headquarters Elements and Non-Headquarters Elements," briefing slide, undated-c.

U.S. Secretary of Defense, *Report of General and Flag Officer Requirements*, Washington, D.C., April 1978.

———, "Track Four Efficiency Initiatives Decisions," memorandum, March 14, 2011. As of January 11, 2017:
http://www.defensetravel.dod.mil/Docs/OSD_02974-11.pdf

U.S. Senate, "General and Flag Officer Requirements," hearing before the Subcommittee on Personnel of the Committee on Armed Services, Hearing No. 112-258, September 14, 2011.

U.S. Southern Command, "HQ USSOUTHCOM," briefing slide, undated-a.

———, "Joint Interagency Task Force South," webpage, undated-b. As of January 8, 2018:
http://www.jiatfs.southcom.mil

———, "SOUTHCOM Component Commands and Units," webpage, undated-c. As of January 5, 2018:
http://www.southcom.mil/About/SOUTHCOM-Components-and-Units/

———, "SOUTHCOM Leadership," webpage, undated-d. As of January 8, 2018:
http://www.southcom.mil/About/Leadership/

U.S. Special Operations Command, "Air Force Special Operations Command," webpage, undated-a. As of January 8, 2018:
http://www.socom.mil/ussocom-enterprise/components/air-force-special-operations-command

———, "Joint Special Operations Command," webpage, undated-b. As of January 8, 2018:
http://www.socom.mil/ussocom-enterprise/components/joint-special-operations-command

———, "Marine Corps Forces Special Operations Command," webpage, undated-c. As of January 8, 2018:
http://www.socom.mil/ussocom-enterprise/components/
marine-corps-forces-special-operations-command

———, "Naval Special Warfare Command," webpage, undated-d. As of January 8, 2018:
http://www.socom.mil/ussocom-enterprise/components/naval-special-warfare-command

———, "Theater Special Operations Command—Africa," webpage, undated-e. As of January 8, 2018:
http://www.socom.mil/Pages/socafrica.aspx

———, "Theater Special Operations Command—Central," webpage, undated-f. As of January 8, 2018:
http://www.socom.mil/Pages/soccent.aspx

———, "Theater Special Operations Command—Europe," webpage, undated-g. As of January 8, 2018:
http://www.socom.mil/soceur

———, "Theater Special Operations Command—Korea," webpage, undated-h. As of January 8, 2018:
http://www.socom.mil/sockor

———, "Theater Special Operations Command—North," webpage, undated-i. As of January 8, 2018:
http://www.socom.mil/Pages/socnorth.aspx

———, "Theater Special Operations Command—Pacific," webpage, undated-j. As of January 8, 2018:
http://www.socom.mil/socpac

———, "Theater Special Operations Command—South," webpage, undated-k. As of January 8, 2018:
http://www.socom.mil/socsouth

———, "United States Army Special Operations Command," webpage, undated-l. As of January 8, 2018:
http://www.socom.mil/ussocom-enterprise/components/army-special-operations-command

———, "United States Special Operations Command Fact Book," webpage, 2017. As of January 5, 2018:
http://www.socom.mil/FactBook/2017%20Fact%20Book.pdf

U.S. Strategic Command, "Leadership," webpage, undated. As of January 16, 2018:
http://www.stratcom.mil/About/Leadership/

————, "USSTRATCOM Organization Chart," briefing slide, September 14, 2015.

U.S. Transportation Command, "Component & Subordinate Commands," webpage, undated-a. As of January 16, 2018:
https://www.ustranscom.mil/cmd/component.cfm

————, "Organizational Structure," webpage, undated-b. As of January 16, 2018:
http://www.ustranscom.mil/cmd/organization/

Washington Headquarters Services, Directorate for Information Operations and Reports, *Department of Defense General/Flag Officer Worldwide Roster*, Washington, D.C., June 1998.

Williams, Brett T., "The Joint Force Commander's Guide to Cyberspace Operations," *Joint Forces Quarterly*, No. 73, 2nd Quarter, 2014.

Winter, Matthew E., "Finding the Law—The Values, Identity, and Function of the International Law Adviser," *Military Law Review*, Vol. 128, 1990, pp. 1–13, 14.

Wong, Yuna, "How Can Gaming Help Test Your Theory?" RAND blog, RAND Corporation, May 18, 2016. As of November 15, 2017:
https://www.rand.org/blog/2016/05/how-can-gaming-help-test-your-theory.html

Wren, Daniel A., and Arthur G. Bedeian, *The Evolution of Management Thought*, 6th ed., Hoboken, N.J.: John Wiley & Sons, 2009.